Touching Space

The Story of Project *Manhigh*

Gregory P. Kennedy

Schiffer Military History
Atglen, PA

Dedication
for Marta

Book Design by Ian Robertson.

Copyright © 2007 by Gregory P. Kennedy.
Library of Congress Control Number: 2007928740

Printed in China.
ISBN: 978-0-7643-2788-9

We are interested in hearing from authors with book ideas on related topics.

Published by Schiffer Publishing Ltd.
4880 Lower Valley Road
Atglen, PA 19310
Phone: (610) 593-1777
FAX: (610) 593-2002
E-mail: Info@schifferbooks.com.
Visit our web site at: www.schifferbooks.com
Please write for a free catalog.
This book may be purchased from the publisher.
Please include $3.95 postage.
Try your bookstore first.

In Europe, Schiffer books are distributed by:
Bushwood Books
6 Marksbury Avenue
Kew Gardens
Surrey TW9 4JF
England
Phone: 44 (0) 20 8392-8585
FAX: 44 (0) 20 8392-9876
E-mail: Info@bushwoodbooks.co.uk.
Free postage in the UK. Europe: air mail at cost.
Try your bookstore first.

Contents

Acknowledgments

This book represents a long-time interest in *Project Manhigh* and piloted stratospheric ballooning. Although my primary interest started as the history of space flight, *Manhigh* piqued my curiosity because it seemed to be an important chapter in the history of astronautics; an important chapter that was missing from most popular historical accounts. In the 1950s, the personnel of the Aeromedical Field Laboratory at Holloman Air Force Base in New Mexico were on the cutting edge of space flight. They conducted research, often at great personal risk, on the limits of human tolerance to deceleration, effects of cosmic radiation on living organisms, and sealed capsule design. These were important study areas before anyone ventured beyond the atmosphere. The contributions of rocket development and high-speed flight to space exploration have been well documented, but somehow the contributions of the Aeromedical Field Laboratory seemed largely overlooked. Hopefully, this book will help more people become aware of the contributions made by these individuals.

Mark Santiago, George House, and Michael Smith of the New Mexico Museum of Space History provided copies of photographs. Dr. David Simons, chief scientist for *Manhigh*, and pilot of the second flight, graciously answered my questions, and pointed out some details I overlooked in the chapter describing his flight. Mike Smith of Aerostar (successor to Winzen International) provided copies of reports, and reviewed the manuscript for technical errors. I am also indebted to the late Dr. John Paul Stapp, who provided copies of photographic slides he took during the first two *Manhigh* flights, and was always willing to discuss *Manhigh* whenever I brought it up. Tom D. Crouch of the Smithsonian's National Air and Space Museum provided advice early on.

While working on this book, I made several new friends who share my passion for the history of high altitude ballooning. Luis Eduardo Pacheco, who runs the internet site http://stratocat.com.ar, would head the list, for he provided help obtaining copies of original technical reports and reviewed my manuscript. Luis offered many helpful suggestions as this book came together. Anyone interested in modern stratospheric balloons should definitely check his web site, which for him is a labor of love. Doris (Susie) Morris, Library Technician, Information International/Zimmerman Associates, was also particularly helpful with research.

My fiancée Marta, my muse, helped and encouraged me as this project developed. Her family (Anna, Ali, and Mom Trudi) also tolerated my sometimes (perhaps "constant" would be a better description) obsession with this topic. Mom Trudi patiently proofread the completed manuscript. My kids—Pam, James, and Dan—provided inspiration to follow through with this project. Coworkers at the American Helicopter Museum and Education Center—Sherron Trio, Denise Afssa, Nancy Phelan, and Janice Plekan—were also very supportive and understanding during this project. A special thanks needs to go to my good friend and fellow author Alan Heller, who introduced me to Schiffer Publishing. Others who offered moral support, advice, and encouragement include my fellow authors at the Wordwrights group from the Barnes and Noble in Exton, PA, especially Walt Trizna, who reviewed portions of the manuscript, and provided information on cosmic radiation research.

Finally, I would like to acknowledge the help, advice, and patience of Bob Biondi and Ian Robertson at Schiffer Publishing.

Thank you, one and all.

1

Science Takes Flight

Science gained a new perspective in 1783 when French brothers Jacques Étienne and Joseph Michel Montgolfier launched the world's first hot air balloon. Suddenly, scientists had a new realm to explore—a vertical realm above the Earth's surface. At first, the brothers proceeded cautiously and conducted several tests in private. Finally, on June 4, 1783, the Montgolfiers performed the first public demonstration of their invention near Annonay, France. This balloon, like the ones they had launched so far, carried no passengers.

When word of the brothers' accomplishment reached Paris, a 37-year old physicist, Professor Jacques Charles, resolved to match their feat. Charles, however, decided to fill his balloon with hydrogen instead of hot air. British chemist James Cavendish discovered hydrogen, which he called *flammable air*, in 1766, and described its properties, including its low density. (French chemist Antoine Lavoisier named the gas hydrogen.) For his balloon, Charles used a 13-foot diameter envelope made from rubber-coated silk developed by another pair of brothers, Jean and Noël Robert.

Charles' balloon, which was named *The Globe*, took to the skies on August 27, 1783. It took four days to make enough hydrogen to fill *The Globe*. Like the Montgolfier's first hot air balloons, *The Globe* carried no passengers. Benjamin Franklin, who at the age of 77 was on a diplomatic mission to France, witnessed *The Globe's* takeoff. When asked what practical use there could be for such an invention, Franklin reportedly replied "What good is a newborn baby?"

Charles' balloon landed 45 minutes later, near the village of Gonesse, where fearful peasants decided it had to be some sort

When the first hydrogen-filled balloon landed near a French village, fearful peasants attacked what they were sure was a demon, tearing it to shreds.

of demon that had descended from the sky. They attacked it with rocks, clubs, pitchforks, and anything else they had on hand. Gas escaping from the holes and tears inflicted by the attacks propelled the balloon along the ground with a series of hisses and other sounds, adding to the villagers' terror. Once they subdued the "monster," the villagers tied it to a horse and dragged it through the fields until it was completely shredded.

Hearing about the hot air balloon, King Louis XVI summoned the Montgolfiers to Versailles for a demonstration. Étienne went to Paris in early September, and conducted a tethered test flight for the Academy of Sciences in preparation for his royal demonstration. The tethered flight went well for the assembled academicians. Then, on 14 September, a sudden and particularly violent rainstorm destroyed the balloon. With only five days before he and his brother were scheduled to appear before the King, Étienne rushed to build another balloon. It was ready in time, and the brothers launched a balloon on September 19, 1783, for the King and his court.

Following the first flights from Paris, people began to wonder if it was possible to fly in a balloon, but they had no idea what effect leaving the ground would have on a person. To find out if flying posed any unknown dangers, the Montgolfiers' balloon launched for the Royal Court carried the first living passengers into the air. To see if flight was safe for people, the Montgolfiers attached a cage containing a lamb, a duck, and a rooster to the base of the balloon. Astronomers on the ground used triangulation to calculate the balloon's altitude, and determined it reached 1,700 feet before it settled gently back to the ground. Only the rooster was injured—the lamb had kicked it before take off. The next step would be a manned flight, but who should be the pilot?

Although the animals seemed unharmed from their voyage, there was still some question as to what effects a flight would have on a person. Because of the uncertainty, the King suggested that the risks be borne by a condemned prisoner who would be pardoned if he survived. However, an adventurous aristocrat, Francois Pilatre de Rozier, argued that the honor of being the first human to fly should not belong to a criminal. De Rozier had a scientific bent, and had founded the natural history museum in Paris. He prevailed upon the Marquis d'Arlandes to carry his arguments to the French court. The King relented, and agreed that an honorable Frenchman should have the privilege of being the first aeronaut. Of course, the honor went to de Rozier. D'Arlandes, who championed de Rozier's cause to the King, insisted that he should also make the flight as payment for his efforts.

De Rozier began with a series of tethered ascents, working his way to an altitude of 320 feet! D'Arlandes accompanied him

Liftoff of the first manned balloon flight.

on his last two ascensions. Finally, everything was ready for a free flight. The site of mankind's first flight was the Crown Prince's palace at the Bois de Boulogne. On November 21, 1783, Pilatre de Rozier and Francois Laurent, the Marquis d'Arlandes, made history's first flight in a hot air balloon built by the Montgolfier brothers. They reached an altitude of 3,000 feet, and traveled some 5 miles across Paris in a flight that lasted 25 minutes.

On December 2, 1783, Professor Charles and one of the Robert brothers made the first piloted flight in a hydrogen-filled balloon. As with Charles' first unmanned flight, Benjamin Franklin witnessed the takeoff. "All Paris was out" he recorded, as he delighted in the size of the crowd. Professor Charles and Noël Robert flew for two hours. Robert had devised a valve at the top of the balloon. By pulling on a rope that ran through the envelope, he could open the valve and release hydrogen to descend.

Throughout the flight, Charles and Robert monitored a barometer they carried, and vented gas or tossed ballast overboard to maintain a constant altitude. They touched down in a field 27 miles from their departure point, but when Robert stepped out of the gondola, the balloon shot skyward with Charles still on board. While climbing, he noticed the temperature dropped with increasing altitude. Using his barometer, Charles concluded that he reached 10,000 feet. Suddenly, he felt a sharp pain in his right ear and jaw from the pressure change, so he decided to end the flight. Professor Charles released some of the hydrogen through the valve in the top of the balloon and landed in a plowed field. Charles found the experience so unsettling that he vowed to never fly again.

Following these early successes, a few intrepid adventurers became full-time aeronauts. Chief among them was Jean Pierre Blanchard, who conducted a number of public ascents in 1784. All too frequently the demonstrations went awry, and the French audiences became increasingly jaded with Blanchard's exploits (and his personality, which was reportedly humorless and egocentric). Eventually, he set out for England and fresh patrons. Although the British were first skeptical of this new French invention, Blanchard managed to eke out a living, and eventually found a sponsor, Dr. John Jeffries.

Dr. Jeffries was a physician who had been born in Boston. During the American Revolution he moved to England due to his British sympathies. On November 30, 1784, Blanchard and Jeffries performed a flight for the Prince of Wales and other dignitaries. Jeffries carried a thermometer, barometer, hygrometer, chronometer, and bottles to collect air samples for the Royal Society. During the flight Jeffries noted changes in temperature, humidity, and barometric pressure at various altitudes. After their landing, Blanchard and Jeffries began planning what was then a very ambitious project—the first crossing of the English Channel by balloon.

Jeffries covered the 700-pound expense of the flight in exchange for his being allowed to accompany Blanchard. Not wanting to share in the glory of the voyage, Blanchard reportedly tried to find ways to exclude Jeffries from the flight. A few days before the flight, Blanchard even resorted to having a tailor sew weights into his vest. While wearing the vest, he planned to declare that the balloon would be overweight and, therefore, Jeffries would have to remain behind for the flight to have any chance of success. Jeffries discovered the ruse and demanded his rightful place on the flight.

Blanchard and Jeffries took off from Dover on January 7, 1785, bound for France. They occupied a boat-shaped gondola adorned with banners, oars (that Blanchard theorized could be used to steer the balloon), and other unnecessary equipment. Jeffries took a barometer and thermometer along. Blanchard carried a bundle of leaflets promoting his aeronautical prowess that he planned to scatter over the countryside. At first their sojourn went well, as the wind carried them eastward. Once over the Channel, however, the balloon lost altitude, and the pair began tossing ballast overboard to remain aloft. By the time they were two-thirds of the way across all their ballast was gone, so they began tossing everything in the gondola they possibly could.

The flags that adorned the gondola went overboard, along with the oars. Their jackets and trousers even went overboard. About two hours after take off they crossed the French coast clad only in their underwear and the cork life jackets they brought in case they

Dr. John Jeffries, an American-born physician, made the first aerial crossing of the English Channel with Jean Pierre Blanchard in 1785. Jeffries carried meteorological instruments with him.

landed in the water. Blanchard and Jeffries continued inland for another half-hour. Fearing a crash landing in a forest, they dumped the life jackets, and even urinated in bottles that they tossed from the gondola to lighten the aerostat as much as possible. Blanchard cleared the trees and brought the balloon to a landing in a small clearing. Jeffries' barometer and thermometer were among the few things left in the gondola.

Jeffries and Charles began a tradition of using balloons to explore the atmosphere. Throughout the late 18th and early 19th centuries, improvements in balloon designs meant scientists could reach higher and higher altitudes. However, as balloon pilots climbed to greater altitudes, they faced greater risks. Balloonists soon ascended high enough to encounter the effects of hypoxia, or oxygen deficiency, and extreme cold.

Italian aeronauts Andreoli, Brasette, and Count Francesco Zambeccari took off from Bologna on October 7, 1803. They reached an altitude where their hands and feet froze, and they lost consciousness from hypoxia. Fortunately the balloon cooled and descended on its own. They landed alive in the Adriatic Sea, where passing sailors retrieved them. Count Zambeccari lost all his fingers from the experience, but at least he survived.

British scientists James Glaisher and Henry Coxwell reached 30,000 feet in 1862. They barely survived the flight due to the effects of hypoxia, or lack of oxygen. His hands frozen from the extreme cold, Coxwell resorted to opening the gas valve on the balloon with his teeth.

On September 5, 1862, two English scientists, Henry Coxwell and James Glaisher, had a similarly harrowing experience. They had planned an ascent to measure high altitude winds, temperatures, and solar affects using a balloon they named *Mammoth*. Glaisher was a meteorologist who headed the department of meteorology and magnetism at the Greenwich Observatory. Prior to his appointment at Greenwich, he helped form the British Meteorological Society and served as its secretary. His credentials also included work at the Cambridge Observatory, and several years with the Ordnance Survey of Ireland. The British Association sponsored the scientific flight of the *Mammoth*.

Coxwell and Glaisher filled their balloon with *coal gas*, a mixture of hydrogen and methane that came from the processing of coal. During the 19th century coal gas was widely used in England for illumination and heating, and numerous plants existed for its production. The gas for the *Mammoth* came from the Stafford Road works in the Borough of Wolverhampton. Although it did not provide as much lift as hydrogen alone, coal gas had the advantages of being cheap to produce and widely available.

At 26,400 feet, with the temperatures well below freezing, Glaisher found he could no longer read his instruments, and soon passed out. Realizing how perilous their situation had become, Coxwell tried to open the gas valve so the *Mammoth* could descend. His hands frozen, Coxwell had to turn the valve with his teeth. As gas vented from the balloon, he noticed the altimeter read 30,000 feet, but this reading is suspect, because he was on the brink of losing consciousness himself. Coxwell passed out, and the balloon began its return to the ground. As they descended, Glaisher and Coxwell recovered and landed near Ludlow without any further problems.

In France, scientists Joseph Crocé-Spinelli and Theodore Sivel were not as fortunate as Glaisher and Coxwell. Accompanied by Gaston Tissandier, they attempted a high altitude flight on April 15, 1875, using a balloon they named *Le Zénith*. Tissandier was an experienced balloonist, and served as pilot for the two scientists. Crocé-Spinelli and Sivel carried barometers, temperature gauges, spectroscopes, compasses, and test tubes to collect samples of the rarefied air aloft. They also carried crude oxygen systems provided by Dr. Paul Bert in Paris.

Bert studied the effects of reduced air pressure in an altitude chamber he constructed in 1874, and is generally credited with being the first physician to investigate the physiological problems of flight. Bert's apparatus comprised two cylindrical chambers and a vacuum pump driven by a steam engine. He could create a vacuum equivalent to an altitude of 36,000 feet in the chambers. Using the chamber, Dr. Bert devised the first oxygen breathing system for aeronautical use. Crude by today's standards, it was little more than a bladder filled with oxygen-enriched air, and a pipestem that the aeronaut held in his teeth. Crocé-Spinelli and Sivel tested the oxygen systems in Bert's altitude chamber, and were confident they would be able to reach 30,000 feet without difficulty.

The flight started out fine. At 14,000 feet they tried the oxygen systems and they worked perfectly, just as they had in the test chamber. Tragically, the trio wrongly assumed they only needed to use the oxygen system intermittently, when they began to feel physical symptoms. As the balloon climbed past 23,000 feet, Sivel began feeling sick and drowsy. He took a breath of oxygen and immediately felt better. Tissandier and Crocé-Spinelli did likewise with the same effect. Since they were all feeling better, they determined to drop some more ballast and press on to 30,000 feet.

Their intermittent use of their oxygen systems soon proved insufficient to sustain them. Tissandier felt himself growing weaker as the balloon climbed. Unable to lift his arms or speak, Tissandier passed out as they passed through 25,000 feet. Thirty-eight minutes late, he regained consciousness. *Le Zénith* was dropping rapidly, propelled by a strong downdraft. His companions were lying on the floor of the basket. He tried to wake them but couldn't before passing out again.

Once the balloon reached a lower altitude, Crocé-Spinelli woke up and then shook Tissandier awake. His judgment impaired by the effects of hypoxia, Crocé-Spinelli decided the balloon could reach their goal of 30,000 feet, and they were in good enough shape to continue the ascent. The balloon shot upward when he dropped ballast and tossed some instruments overboard. Tissandier passed out again as *Le Zénith* reached an estimated altitude of 28,000 feet.

More than an hour later, Tissandier woke up and discovered the balloon was dropping rapidly. His companions were huddled in the floor of the basket, covered by their cloaks. Neither was breathing, and their mouths were full of what appeared to be blood. Despite feeling extremely weak, Tissandier shook them to no avail. Still trying to revive Sivel and Crocé-Spinelli by yelling at them, Tissandier turned his attention to the falling balloon. He dropped the remaining ballast, and managed to safely land *Le Zénith*. Crocé-Spinelli and Sivel were dead, the first aviation related deaths from hypoxia.

Tissandier apparently survived because he was in better physical condition than his companions. It is also likely that, as an experienced balloonist, he was more acclimated to the higher altitudes than either Crocé-Spinelli or Sivel.

Following the deaths of Crocé-Spinelli and Sivel, manned high altitude flights declined for a number of years. German meteorologist Arthur Berson reached 30,000 feet in a hydrogen balloon in 1894 using the same type of oxygen breathing system as Tissandier, Crocé-Spinelli, and Sivel. Berson reached an even greater height (35,433 feet) on June 30, 1901, with fellow German Reinhard Süring. Other than these two flights, there were not any piloted high altitude flights for the next quarter century.

High altitude research continued, but it was performed with unmanned sounding balloons that carried recording instruments. In 1902 French scientist Leon Teisserene de Bort "discovered" the stratosphere. Interested in studying atmospheric conditions, he launched instrumented balloons that measured air pressure and temperature. On the other side of the Atlantic, Professor A. Lawrence Rotch of Harvard University became an early collaborator of Bort's.

After launching 238 balloons between them, they noticed the temperature dropped as expected until reaching a height of about 8 miles, after which it remained constant at around −67 degrees Fahr-

French scientists Joseph Crocé-Spinelli and Théodore Sivel attempted to reach 30,000 feet in 1875. They had crude oxygen systems that they used intermittently during the flight. Unfortunately intermittent use did not protect them from the effects of hypoxia, and they were the first aeronauts to die from lack of oxygen.

enheit. They first thought their instruments had malfunctioned, but soon realized this was a distinct layer of the atmosphere, which Bort named the "stratosphere." Years later, atmospheric scientists found the temperature remained stable to an altitude of 20 miles, when there is a sharp increase to about 200 degrees at 40 miles.

On August 20, 1905, the Spanish Army sponsored one of the most complex scientific balloon expeditions to date when they launched three balloons with pilots and observers to study a total solar eclipse. Colonel Pedro Vives commanded the effort, which took off from Burgos, along the path where the period of totality was longest. Two of the balloons came from the Spanish Army. Civilian aeronaut Jesús Fernándo Duro volunteered his balloon, *El Cierzo* (The North Wind), to complete the expedition. The plan was to compare observations of the eclipse made by the balloonists to those obtained on the ground.

Colonel Vives piloted the first balloon; German aeronaut Arthur Berson was co-pilot and observer. In the second balloon, Professor Augusto Arcimis, Director of the Spanish Meteorological Observatory, accompanied Captain Alfredo Kindelán. Emilio Herrera, an engineering officer who had recently received his balloonist's license, and Duro piloted the third balloon. Herrera was assigned to sketch the solar corona and make detailed observations of a phenomenon known as "flying shadows" as the sun emerged from behind the Moon.

A solid layer of clouds lay over Burgos on the day of the eclipse, but preparations for the ascensions continued. As the time approached for totality, the first two balloons took off with no problems. Then, with only a few minutes remaining, Duro and Herrera noticed their balloon was not climbing. The ground crew held them down. A large board that had been painted white was suspended beneath the basket of their balloon to let Herrera observe the "flying shadow" effect.

The ground crew was arrayed in full military regalia, including sabers. One of the sabers worn by a member of the launch crew caught on the board during launch and was pulled from its scabbard. It dangled from the board, threatening to fall and seriously injure someone on the ground. In their efforts to retrieve the sword, several members of the launch crew held on to the board. Finally the sword fell harmlessly to the ground, and the balloon was allowed to ascend.

With the eclipse already underway, Herrera and Duro climbed through the clouds. They finally broke through the layer, only to discover another solid layer above them. They quickly decided to cast off all their ballast to climb above the second layer. By this time they were in total darkness—the eclipse was nearing totality, and they began to despair that they would miss the event when they broke through the clouds at an altitude of 16,000 feet. They were awed by the spectacle of the star-filled sky and the glittering solar corona.

Duro was so excited by the view that he began jumping up and down in the basket, making it difficult for Herrera to complete his drawing. As soon as the totality was over, Herrera started watching the surface of the board for the "flying shadows." He didn't see any, and was about to give up when Duro directed his attention to their hands and other objects in the basket. There were alternating light and dark bands, about a centimeter wide. These were the elusive "flying shadows," but with one significant difference.

The bands Herrera observed were considerably narrower than those typically seen on the ground during an eclipse. At 16,000 feet, they were above nearly half the atmosphere, so Herrera reasoned the air density had to affect the width of the bands. Because the bands were narrower than those seen on the ground, Herrera concluded they were seeing interference patterns produced as light from the sun passed through the atmosphere.

Since they had dumped all their ballast to get above the clouds, the pair had no way to control their landing. After the eclipse was over, Herrera and Duro continued flying for several hours, waiting for the combined effects of gas leakage and cooling to bring them back to earth. They finally landed near the village of Villasar de Herreros, north of Burgos. The aeronauts regaled the townspeople with tales of their flight before being treated to supper and overnight accommodations in the Town Hall. The next day they arranged for transportation for themselves and their balloon back to Burgos.

Scientists also began flying radiation detectors on balloons in the early years of the 20th Century. Antoine Henri Becquerel accidentally discovered radiation in 1896 when he left a piece of uranium on a photographic plate. When the plate was developed, Becquerel noted that the plate was fogged where the uranium had been. Two years later, Marie and Pierre Curie deduced that radiation was a phenomenon associated with atoms. Physicists soon observed that radiation was all around us, but its source remained a mystery.

Austrian physicist Victor Franz Hess began a series of experiments in 1911 to probe the nature of this mysterious radiation. At first, most scientists believed the source of the radiation was the earth itself. Then, researchers carried detectors to glaciers and found that the radiation was still present, but was lower than they observed near rocks. These were followed by experiments in caves, where there was no reduction of the radiation levels. These experiments led to the conclusion that the radiation was in the air. The logical extension of this line of thinking was that as one ascended, with less air around you, there should be less radiation. Hess wondered how far one had to move away from the surface of the Earth to escape this radiation.

At first, he made measurements at the top of the Eiffel Tower in Paris, which was 1,000 feet above the ground. Hess found the radiation did not decrease as quickly as expected. He next turned to balloons, and made flights to 0.6 miles (1 kilometer) and 3.1 miles (5 kilometers) in altitude. His results astounded the scientific community, because he discovered that above one kilometer radiation *increased* as he ascended. At five kilometers, the radiation level was several times what was measured on the Earth's surface.

Hess' results forced scientists to alter their theories as to the source of this radiation, and most agreed it likely came from the sun. Then Hess performed another experiment, measuring radiation levels during a partial solar eclipse on April 12, 1912. When the radiation levels did not change, Hess ruled out the sun as the source. Hess postulated the radiation came from outer space.

American physicist Robert Millikan initially disputed Hess' results. Millikan launched instruments on unmanned balloons to altitudes as high as 50,000 feet in 1922, and measured different radiation levels than Hess had reported, but wide temperature variations affected his results. The next year he journeyed to the top of Pike's Peak in Colorado, and found that a two-inch lead shield screened out the increased radiation. He erroneously believed the lead offered the same screening effects as the remaining atmosphere above him, which ruled out an extraterrestrial source for the radiation. Lead, as it was subsequently learned, is a much better radiation shield than air. Finally, he conducted a series of experiments in mountain lakes, and found the radiation decreased as one went deeper into the water. This last experiment convinced Millikan that Hess had been correct, and the radiation came from beyond the earth's atmosphere. Millikan coined the term "cosmic rays" to describe the phenomenon.

At the time these experiments were being conducted there were no nuclear reactors, no particle accelerators, and atomic physics was in its infancy. Many scientists came to believe that "cosmic rays" (also called cosmic radiation) held the key to unlocking the secrets of the atom. If these secrets could be coaxed out of streams of energy that bombarded our planet from space, atomic energy could be harnessed to provide a limitless potential as a new source of power for a variety of applications.

Balloons, the oldest form of aircraft, offered the best platform for the study of "cosmic rays." At the time, balloons could fly higher and remain aloft longer than airplanes. They could also carry entire laboratories into the sky. During the 1920s and '30s, teams of scientists and adventurers mounted a number of expeditions into the stratosphere. A few were for the sheer sport of establishing a new altitude record; a few were honest attempts at scientific research. Some were a little of both.

2

Probing the Stratosphere

U. S. Army Captain Hawthorne C. Gray wanted to reach the stratosphere, not for scientific research, but to set a world altitude record. Captain Gray was a skilled balloon pilot, and he wanted to surpass the existing altitude record of 35,424 feet set by German balloonists Reinhard Süring and Arthur Berson in 1901. On his first attempt, which took place on March 9, 1927, he did not break the world record, but at least managed to set an American altitude record of 28,510 feet.

Gray rode in an open wicker basket, wore a fur-lined flying suit over woolen undergarments, took blankets along for extra warmth, and breathed oxygen carried in steel tanks. As was typical of oxygen systems of the time, Gray breathed through a pipestem that was only slightly better than the one designed by Dr. Paul Bert. He carried 2 tons of sand as ballast, in 50-pound bags suspended around the sides of the basket. To release ballast, Gray had to haul individual bags into the gondola, slit them with a knife, and

German cigarette card depicting Auguste Piccard boarding the *FNRS* gondola.

then dump the sand overboard. On the ground, he could easily lift the bags. Gray took off from Scott Field, Illinois, confident in his ability to reach the stratosphere.

By the time he reached 20,000 feet, the sand had dulled all three knives he carried with him, and he felt short of breath. His knives useless, Gray resorted to tearing at the canvas bags with his bare hands. The oxygen system finally proved inadequate, and Gray passed out at 27,000 feet. Fortunately, he regained consciousness as the balloon descended. Dropping at more than 1,200 feet per minute, Gray began rapidly dumping ballast in a desperate attempt to bring the balloon under control. He crash landed, and suffered a sprained ankle.

Captain Gray tried again on May 4, 1927, more determined than before to set a world record. Gray made several improvements to his oxygen system that he felt would enable him to better endure the harsh environment. This time he reached 42,470 feet, well into the stratosphere. To reach such an extreme altitude Gray dropped most of his ballast. Feeling the effects of hypoxia, he quickly vented hydrogen from the balloon and began his descent. Gray released too much gas, and with no ballast left the balloon was soon falling out of control. (High altitude aeronauts have since learned that the rate of descent established in the stratosphere will double as the balloon passes through the tropopause.) He had seriously overballasted to reach his goal, and had nothing left to control the descent.

Seeing he was headed for a swamp, Gray jumped from the basket and landed with a parachute near Grayville, Illinois, about 300 miles from Scott Field. The Fédération Aéronautique Internationale (FAI) in Paris is the governing body for world flight records, and has strict rules and guidelines. The FAI did not recognize Gray's flight, because to establish an official record the pilot has to land in the aircraft. He tried again on 4 November. After reaching 40,000 feet, he dropped the last of his ballast. Gray climbed another 2,470 feet before he exhausted his oxygen supply and quickly lost consciousness.

The next morning a young boy found Gray and his balloon on a farm near Sparta, Tennessee. Captain Gray was dead. Again, the FAI denied an official record, since he was not in control of the aerostat when it landed.

In Belgium, Professor Auguste Piccard wanted to reach the stratosphere in a balloon, not just for setting altitude records, but to study cosmic radiation. Hawthorne Gray's flights showed, with tragic results, the limitations of venturing into the stratosphere in an open basket with the equipment then available. Piccard, who wanted to loft a suite of scientific instruments, reasoned that a sealed capsule with a life support system would be the best approach.

Auguste Piccard and his identical twin brother Jean were born in Basel, Switzerland, on January 28, 1884. Their father, Dr. Jules Piccard, was a chemistry professor at the University of Basel. Their uncle, Paul Piccard, helped design and build the turbines at Niagara Falls. Growing up in such a family, Auguste and Jean both developed interests in science, and attended the Swiss Institute of Technology. Auguste studied physics and mechanical engineering. Jean took his degree in organic chemistry.

Their interest in balloons started at an early age. At the age of ten they made hot air balloons from paper. Auguste and Jean eventually became avid balloonists, and served with the Swiss Army's balloon corps. In 1913 the brothers conducted a thirteen-hour flight across Europe. Jean handled the balloon while Auguste collected measurements of wind speed, air density, and temperature.

Jean accepted a position as an Associate Professor at the University of Chicago in 1916, where he taught for three years. While in Chicago, he met and married Jeanette Ridlon. Jeanette had recently received her Masters' degree in organic chemistry from the University of Chicago. Shortly after his marriage in 1919 Jean returned to Europe with his new bride, and became a lecturer at the University of Lausanne in Switzerland. Auguste received an invitation to become a professor at the Polytechnic Institute of Technology at Brussels University in Belgium in 1922. There, he conducted research on cosmic rays, radioactivity, and magnetism.

During the 1920s a controversy existed over the nature of cosmic rays, and there were two opposing theories to describe them. One camp believed them to be photons or electromagnetic radiation; the other theorized they were charged particles. Two of the greatest names in American science, Nobel laureates Arthur Compton and Robert Millikan, fueled the debate. Compton subscribed to the charged particle theory, while Millikan believed in the photon model.

At a family reunion in 1926, Auguste told Jean of a plan he devised to study cosmic radiation. Auguste wanted to loft a fully equipped laboratory into the stratosphere to conduct direct observations of this mysterious radiation. His plan had one serious drawback—such an expedition was beyond the means of Piccard and the University. Fortunately, King Albert I of Belgium had established the "Fonds National de la Recherche Scientifique" (National Scientific Research Fund) to promote research in his country. King Albert and his wife Queen Elizabeth were both proponents of aviation; the King had even traveled by air to the Belgian Congo. In the 1920s such a trip was considered a remarkable feat. Auguste submitted a grant request, and received $14,000 for his project.

Piccard designed a spherical gondola, or capsule, suspended from an immense hydrogen-filled balloon made from rubberized cotton for his flying laboratory. Looking at various materials, Piccard selected aluminum for the capsule, and contracted the firm of Société Belge d'Aluminum G. L'Hoir in Liége. Techniques for welding aluminum were well advanced in Belgium thanks to the production of vats for beer brewing. Engineers at L'Hoir could form sheets of pure aluminum into rounded containers with welded seams that retained most of the strength of the original metal. At the time this was not the case with alloys like Duralumin, which weakened when welded.

L'Hoir fabricated the gondola in two hemispheres. Each half was made from three pieces of aluminum sheet that were 3.5 millimeters thick. A band around the gondola's equator joined the halves. Piccard designed it with two hatches so that no matter how it landed, at least one hatch would be clear. It also had 8 small windows (3.15 inches in diameter) made from double panes of quartz glass.

Piccard very clearly specified the hatches were to be circular, rather than the oval shaped openings generally used in aluminum vats. He designed the hatches so they were slightly larger than the openings, and would fit against the interior capsule wall. This way, air pressure inside the gondola would help seal them against the capsule shell. Because the hatches were larger than the openings and circular, the hatches had to be placed inside the shell before the last segment was welded into place.

The worker responsible for fabricating the capsule ignored the Professor's instructions, and when Piccard came to inspect the finished piece, he noted the hatches were not inside. The workman told him it would be no problem—he'd put them inside right away. Being used to oval shaped hatches and openings, the workman was stymied when he tried to put them in the shell. When Piccard returned to the L'Hoir plant a few days later, the hatches were inside the gondola. He never figured out if the workmen cut open the shell, or cut the hatches and rewelded them after they were inside, because the repairs were invisible. The finished gondola shell was 7 feet in diameter and weighed 300 pounds. With its full complement of instruments and a two-man crew, the gondola weighed 850 pounds.

For his balloon, Piccard turned to Riedinger in Augsburg, Bavaria. The balloon was 94.8 feet in diameter, had a volume of 500,000 cubic feet, and weighed about 1,600 pounds. Prior to this, standard practice had been to place a net over the balloon envelope to provide attachment points for the basket. Professor Piccard realized this would be too heavy for such a large balloon, so he designed a reinforcing band, or girdle, that circled the lower third of the bag. This band had the attachment points for the cabin. A second band about a third of the way down from the top provided attachments for ground handling ropes before launch. There was a rope-operated valve in the top of the balloon to vent hydrogen for the descent. The valve could be operated by means of a pulley on a shaft that passed through the wall of the gondola.

Piccard wanted to take off from the Riedinger plant in Augsburg, so he needed German approval. One of his concerns was that the aerostat might drift over water, and Augsburg was far enough inland that it offered a good probability for a successful landing. He also liked the idea of having technical help on site if there were any problems with the balloon prior to takeoff. However, the German authorities would not approve such a radical balloon for flight from their country. It seemed everything about Piccard's balloon, which he named *FNRS* in honor of his sponsor, was beyond anything that had ever flown, and much of what he devised was outside the existing regulations.

Even something as mundane as Piccard's choice of ballast material became a problem. For ballast, Piccard planned to use fine lead shot that would be released in a stream from inside the gondola through a special valve. At the time, the only ballast materials approved for ballooning in Europe were sand or water. Because he was flying in a pressurized gondola, he had to carry all his ballast inside the cabin. Sand and water were not dense enough, and the cabin wasn't large enough to carry the volume of either material that he would need for the flight. Piccard went so far as to stand beneath a stream of his intended ballast dropped from a roof to

demonstrate its safety, but the rule remained a potential stumbling block. He resorted to calling his ballast material "lead sand" to remove official objections. The subterfuge worked, and nothing more was said about the ballast.

Although his ballast material was approved, he still did not have the government-issued airworthiness certificate needed to fly from Augsburg. The use of a girdle to secure the gondola rather than a net was another area of concern, and the certificate was withheld. Professor Piccard turned to the Swiss government, which issued a permit for the *FNRS* after reviewing his design. Since European governments were obligated to honor licenses and certificates for aircraft issued by each other, Piccard at last had clearance to launch the *FNRS* from Augsburg. He planned to make the flight in September 1930. Piccard chose Paul Kipfer, one of his university assistants, to accompany him on the ascent.

Word of Piccard's plans spread, and soon scores of reporters from around the world gathered in Augsburg to witness the flight. The weather looked favorable on September 13, 1930, for a flight the next day. That afternoon, Piccard's ground crew unpacked the balloon and prepared it for flight. During the night they began inflating it with hydrogen. Soon, the balloon towered nearly 200 feet above the ground. Piccard only partially inflated the balloon for launch; it was about 20% full, and resembled a large inverted teardrop. As it ascended, the hydrogen would expand and fully inflate the envelope. Although the balloon was ready for launch, Piccard and Kipfer still had a number of tasks to perform before they could take off. They had plenty of time to finish their preparations, for it was still dark, and they wanted to wait until dawn to begin their flight. Suddenly, there was a drop in barometric pressure as an unanticipated weather front moved in. Clouds formed, and soon no stars could be seen.

So far the winds remained calm, and the balloon stood straight up. This situation did not last, and a light breeze began buffeting the balloon. Piccard and Kipfer quickened the pace of their preparations, but the wind began to increase. Soon the balloon leaned heavily to one side. If they tried to take off under such conditions, the gondola would be dragged along the ground, possibly damaging it. Professor Piccard reluctantly gave the order to empty the balloon.

The reporters who were on hand to cover the flight had a field day, describing Piccard as an "absentminded professor" who forgot to account for the weather in his calculations. They took great delight in reporting that instead of rising ten miles, the *FNRS* only rose ten feet. Piccard did not try to refute the reports. He feared trying to contradict the stories would only give them credibility. Instead, he decided to remain silent and wait until spring, when the weather would allow another flight attempt.

Piccard was ready to try again on May 27, 1931. Again, weather threatened to derail the flight when a gust of wind caught the balloon and pulled the capsule off its cradle just before Piccard and Kipfer boarded it. A quick inspection showed no obvious damage, so the scientists climbed in the gondola and sealed the hatches. They discovered that most of the instruments had been jarred loose and were scattered on the floor. Fortunately, the most sensitive instruments were in padded baskets. (These baskets doubled as "crash helmets" during takeoff and landing.) While Piccard and Kipfer were busy putting everything back, the ground crew eased the tension in the handling ropes, and the balloon rose a few yards. Unknown to Piccard, the ground crew attached an extra rope to the balloon to help handle it in the wind.

Inside the cabin, Piccard and Kipfer waited for word from the ground crew that the *FNRS* was being released. While they waited, Kipfer happened to look through one of the small windows and noticed chimneys and roofs beneath them. The ground crew apparently neglected to notify the aeronauts that they were releasing the balloon. (How the command of "Let go everything!" was to be communicated between the aeronauts in their sealed gondola and the ground crew is not clear. The *FNRS* did not carry a radio.) They took off at 3:57 in the morning.

Once they were airborne, Piccard soon discovered the gondola had in fact been damaged when it was pulled from the cradle. There was a one-inch diameter hole for an electrostatic probe in the base of the cabin. After take off, Piccard was supposed to put the probe through the hole. When he tried to do this, the Professor found the bump had dented and deformed the capsule so that the probe would not fit in the opening.

Kipfer reported they were at 15,000 feet, and the interior pressure was the same as that outside. Clearly, they could not go much higher with the open hole in the gondola. Kipfer took over from Piccard and finally worked the probe into place, but broke the quartz tube that comprised an insulator for the sensor. Air still leaked through the opening. Granted, it was leaking at a slower rate than before, but it was still leaking. A high-pitched whistle could be heard as air flowed out of the cabin.

Professor Piccard thought to carry a supply of oakum (a material normally used to caulk boats) smeared with petroleum jelly to plug any leaks in the gondola that might develop during the flight. Piccard sprinkled liquid oxygen on the cabin floor to build up the air pressure, but this was only a temporary solution. He began packing the oakum/petroleum jelly mixture around the broken probe, but had trouble sealing the leak. The opening was under the floor and difficult to reach.

Just 28 minutes after launch, the *FNRS* reached its peak altitude of 51,775 feet. Final Piccard sealed the leak, and the whistling stopped. "Never was silence more blessed," wrote Piccard in a later account of the flight. Due to the activities during the ascent, Piccard and Kipfer had not been able to make any scientific measurements. Floating nearly ten miles above the ground, they collected one set of data.

Kipfer dropped a thermometer, which broke and spilled mercury inside the capsule. Mercury reacts with aluminum, so Piccard had to quickly clean up the liquid metal before it ate holes through the capsule. After chasing small globules of mercury around the bottom of the capsule, Piccard hit upon an easy way to clean up the spill. He attached a piece of rubber tubing to an outside vent and used it as a vacuum cleaner to collect the mercury.

Peering out the windows, Piccard noted the sky above him was a deep purplish blue, "ten times darker than on earth, but still not quite dark enough to see the stars." He marveled at the appearance of the ground, particularly the Alps. From his vantagepoint nearly ten miles above the earth, he could see 280 miles in any direction.

The pair decided to descend, but discovered the rope that controlled the valve on the balloon to release the lifting gas had become tangled with the rope that had been added without Piccard's knowledge just before launch. With no way to vent hydrogen, they had to wait until night, when the gas in the balloon would cool and let it descend.

This gave rise to another problem. The leak and Piccard's release of liquid oxygen to restore cabin pressure had depleted their supply. Running out of oxygen before they descended low enough

British cigarette card of Auguste Piccard and the *FNRS* balloon.

German collector's card showing Professor Auguste Piccard (inset) and the *FNRS* balloon.

to open the capsule hatch was a very real threat. The aeronauts sat perfectly still on the floor of the gondola, trying to conserve their precious oxygen supply.

Piccard's sealed capsule was, in many ways, an ancestor of modern spacecraft. It was pressurized to maintain a sea-level atmosphere. He studied the oxygen systems used on submarines and incorporated a modified "Draeger" system built for German U-boats. Soda lime absorbed carbon dioxide in the cabin atmosphere. Fans circulated 20 gallons of air through the alkali every minute. Piccard carried two packets of soda lime; he estimated each would last eight hours. This was more than enough, Piccard reasoned, because the flight was only supposed to last ten hours. The Draeger apparatus added two quarts of oxygen to the atmosphere every minute to replenish what the aeronauts consumed. Again, the amount of oxygen carried was predicated on a ten-hour flight, plus a reserve.

Piccard tried a black and white paint scheme to achieve thermal control. Thinking the balloon would rotate, he painted one side of the sphere black, the other white. If it didn't rotate on its own, he mounted a small fan outside the capsule that would act like a propeller to rotate the balloon. Unfortunately, once they were at their ceiling altitude, Piccard discovered there was a short circuit in the motor's wiring, and it would not work. Temperatures inside the cabin soared to 104° Fahrenheit because it remained stable, with the black side facing the sun.

They drank all the water in the capsule, and soon had nothing to relieve their thirst. Prior to the flight, Piccard requested that two large containers of water be placed in the cabin. He only found one small bottle on board once they were airborne. Piccard asked Kipfer: "Now that you're up in the stratosphere, what do you think of it?" Kipfer replied "I'd trade it all for a glass of water."

Although temperatures inside the cabin were over 100 degrees, ice formed on the cabin wall on the side away from the sun. From time to time, they scraped some of the frost off of the wall to slake their thirst. Moisture ran down the wall of the gondola and pooled beneath the floor. Unfortunately, this water contained an unappetizing (and unhealthy) mixture of mercury and oil, so it was undrinkable.

Piccard hit upon another way to gather moisture. He poured some liquid oxygen in a metal cup and waited for moisture from the capsule atmosphere to condense on its outer surface. The first time he and Kipfer tried to lick some of the ice off the cup, it was so cold it hurt their tongues. They had to wait until the oxygen evaporated completely and the cup warmed to a more tolerable temperature.

The most serious problem they faced, however, was that the heat softened the gaskets around the hatches, and the capsule began leaking air again. Piccard also had to pack more oakum around the hole in the bottom of the capsule, because the heat melted the petroleum jelly and let it flow out of the gondola. Their ears popped several times, indicating the pressure inside the capsule was leaking out. Piccard and Kipfer could do little except sit in silence and wonder if they would survive the flight.

As the day progressed and the sun rose higher in the sky, the capsule was finally in the shadow of the balloon, and the temperatures abated. However, their oxygen supply remained a concern. They began to descend around 2:00 PM, but the rate was so slow—about 100 feet per hour—that Piccard calculated it would take three weeks to reach the ground. To preserve their precious oxygen supply they decreased the amount of the life-sustaining gas being released into the cabin. An hour later, the descent rate increased slightly, but it still wasn't fast enough.

Their scheduled landing time passed. With no word of the explorers many reporters presumed the worst, and newspapers around the world carried stories of their presumed demise. Eager for a story, reporters in America called Jean (who returned to the United States in 1926) and asked for a statement. He expressed his confidence that his brother was still alive. Despite Jean's optimism, headlines proclaimed that his brother and Paul Kipfer were lost and probably dead.

As sunset finally came, the *FNRS* was passing over the Bavarian Alps. At last the balloon cooled, and it began to descend at a faster rate. Now they faced the very real possibility that the tangled rope would open the vent, because as the balloon descended, it shrank around its girth and became longer. This would have resulted in an out of control descent and crash landing. Fortunately the rope broke, which eliminated this hazard. The descent continued at a steady rate. Piccard conserved his ballast so they could land safely, provided they did not drift over the Adriatic Sea.

At 8:00 PM they were still seven and a half miles up, but they had heard stories of earlier aeronauts that survived at such an altitude, which brought them some small measure of comfort. By 8:50 they were down to 15,000 feet. Piccard opened the hatch and let the cool, refreshing air in. The capsule had been sealed for seventeen hours.

Now Piccard faced another quandary—he didn't know where they were. He could not discern any landmarks in the dark, but did see mountains looming below. At least they weren't over water, but were they going to crash into a mountain? Or, would they land on the edge of a cliff and fall off once they pulled the cord to the rip panel and released all the hydrogen? All Piccard and Kipfer could do was hope for a safe landing, since they were at the mercy of

The *FNRS* gondola landed on a glacier, as illustrated on this German cigarette card from the 1930s.

the winds. They still had ballast remaining, but if Piccard dropped too much, they ran the risk of rising again. Piccard saw a village beneath them. As the village passed from view, he noted they were heading towards a glacier. At first, Piccard saw nothing but a maze of crevasses.

Piccard held the strap that controlled the rip panel to deflate the balloon. They bounced across some snow, and finally flew over a large, flat glacier. Piccard pulled the strap. The capsule rolled to a stop as the balloon spilled its load of hydrogen. Looking across the cabin, Piccard saw Kipfer under a heap of instruments and ballast bags. Fortunately, the *FNRS* landed on a relatively smooth glacier near Ober-Gürgl, in the Austrian Tyrol. After landing, Piccard and Kipfer wrapped themselves in the balloon's fabric to remain warm through the rest of the night. Piccard slept fitfully. Several times he dreamed the sound of a nearby waterfall was air leaking from the cabin, and he woke with a start. The next morning they hiked to the nearest village using ropes from the balloon and a bamboo pole from its rigging.

While on their way down the glacier, they encountered a small band of climbers on their way to the capsule. The *FNRS* had been spotted as it flew over the village, and a group set out at first light to find the balloon. The group guided Piccard and Kipfer to the village of Gurgl.

Upon reaching the village, the first thing Piccard did was telegram his wife to let her know he was safe. Then, he organized a team to recover the balloon from the glacier. Forty men—twenty civilians and twenty soldiers—carried the balloon on their shoulders to the village, being careful not to damage it. The gondola was left on the glacier until the following spring, when it was retrieved. Piccard declared he would not attempt another stratospheric flight out of consideration for his wife and family. However, within a few weeks of his flight, critics emerged who attributed Piccard's success to luck, and derided the venture as reckless. If Professor Piccard wanted to establish the manned stratospheric balloon as a valuable research tool, he needed to demonstrate its reliability and safety. This meant he had to make another flight.

Belgium honored Piccard's flight with a set of three postage stamps.

The Belgian FNRS again sponsored the effort, but Piccard also received a great deal of help and support from the Swiss Aero Club. Piccard repaired the original balloon, but he needed a new gondola. He incorporated several lessons from the first flight in the second gondola's design. The new gondola was painted all white, to avoid the overheating problem. Piccard eliminated the external pulley control for the vent valve. The control ropes passed through the gondola wall through sealed ports. He also added a radio. Kipfer's parents prevailed on him not to make such a dangerous flight again, so Piccard selected Max Cosyns to accompany him.

While Piccard prepared the second *FNRS* gondola, King Albert and Queen Elizabeth visited him. The royal couple spent several hours with the Professor, who eagerly showed them the gondola and described his upcoming flight.

For his second flight, Piccard opted to take off from Dubendorf Airport at Zurich because of the help he received from the local Aero Club. His flight would take him across the Alps and into Italy. By early August 1932 everything was ready. Piccard began preparing for the flight, then received a telephone call from the Belgian Meteorological Institute. A storm was heading their way. As had happened during his first flight attempt, there were complaints from the gathered reporters, particularly because the sky was completely clear. A few hours later, however, a terrific storm broke over Zurich.

For two weeks, everyone waited for suitable weather. Finally, on 18 August, Piccard had the conditions he needed for the flight. Piccard and Cosyns boarded the gondola at 5:06 AM. Leaning out of the hatch, Piccard gave the signal to release the restraining ropes. He waved to the cheering crowd as the balloon lifted off. At first the ascent was sluggish, so they released some ballast and began to climb. Piccard closed the hatch at an altitude of 1,700 feet.

Twenty minutes into the flight, Piccard and Cosyns could hear an airplane circling them as the variometer (an instrument that showed rate of ascent or descent) indicated they were rising at five feet per second. Cosyns began the cosmic radiation observations. Peering through one of the portholes, they saw ice particles falling from the balloon as they passed through 28,000 feet, the same height as Mount Everest. A little more than an hour after launch frost formed inside the gondola. In his diary, Piccard described the inside of the cabin as looking like a "crystal grotto." Piccard dropped more ballast to coax the *FNRS* higher. It continued to get colder inside the gondola, but the pair pushed on.

Cosyns sent the first radio message from the stratosphere during the ascent. "All is going well. Observation is good. Our altitude is approximately 47,000 feet."

At 10:12 AM, Piccard emptied six more bags of ballast. They had 24 left. He soon passed the altitude he reached on the first flight. "The sky is no longer blue, but is dark violet and grey," noted Piccard. According to the log, they were down to 20 bags of ballast at 11:50 AM, and decided to begin their descent. Piccard opened the vent valve for the first time at noon.

He and Cosyns were so cold they took a break from their research for hot milk and chocolate. In the background, the cosmic ray counters sounded like "rain falling on the roof of a hut." Despite the fact that they had vented some of the hydrogen, the balloon continued to rise, and finally reached an altitude of 54,120 feet. Piccard made a second radio broadcast, and mentioned the intense cold, but he assured everyone on the ground that everything was all right aboard the *FNRS*.

When they began to descend, the *FNRS* was drifting north of Lake Garda, in Italy. As the balloon lost altitude the sun heated the remaining hydrogen, and they began to ascend again. Piccard released more hydrogen and established a descent rate of ten feet per second. They were still above the north shore of Lake Garda.

By carefully venting hydrogen and dropping ballast Piccard maintained control over the descent. Their rate of descent varied between five and ten feet per second as they drifted over the lake. Once they were below 20,000 feet Piccard opened the hatches. He and Cosyns continued collecting cosmic ray data. They touched down a little past 5:00 PM near the southern end of Lake Garda. After landing, Professor Piccard asked to use a telephone to call his wife.

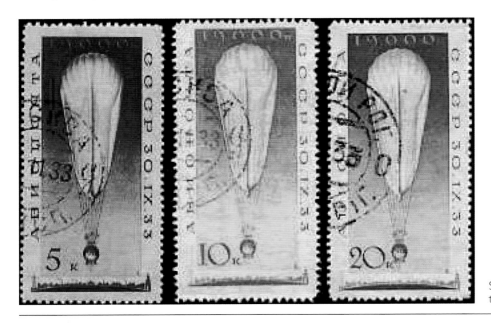

Soviet stamps issued to celebrate the 1933 flight of the *Stratostat USSR*.

Not to be outdone, aeronauts in the Soviet Union mounted a stratospheric balloon program. A little over a year after Piccard's second flight, Soviet aeronauts Georgi Prokivief, Ernest Birnbaum, and Konstantine Godrenow reached 60,695 feet in the balloon *Stratostat USSR*. Their balloon had a volume of 880,000 cubic feet, making it the largest that had ever been built. They rode in an aluminum gondola that comprised 16 segments that were riveted together.

Auguste Piccard's flights catapulted him to fame as the conqueror of the stratosphere. (King Albert knighted Piccard and Kipfer after the first flight.) Belgium issued a set of three postage stamps that depicted the *FNRS* balloon. He published an article titled "Ballooning in the Stratosphere" in the March 1933 issue of *The National Geographic Magazine*. During the 1920s and '30s, many European cigarette and chocolate companies included collectors' cards in packages of their products. They soon had cards highlighting Piccard's exploits. His brother Jean helped organize a speaking tour for him in the United States. At the time Auguste Piccard rose to prominence, planning for the 1933 Chicago World's Fair Exposition, "A Century of Progress," was well along.

Around the world scientists studied cosmic radiation. One of the foremost researchers was Robert Millikan. The main difference between the approaches taken by Millikan and Piccard was over the use of manned versus unmanned balloons. Millikan conducted much of his research with unmanned balloonsondes that collected data without the expense, complexity, or risk of a piloted gondola. While such an approach certainly had many advantages, it did not capture the public imagination, nor did it generate the level of interest (and support) that manned balloons did. Recognizing the publicity value of such a flight, organizers of the Chicago Exposition invited Auguste Piccard to mount a stratospheric expedition from the fairgrounds. The idea came from a Chicago reporter, who proposed that Piccard make the flight in the *FNRS* gondola.

The fair was timed to celebrate Chicago's centennial, and it highlighted technological innovation and scientific progress. The motto for "A Century of Progress" was "science finds, industry applies, man conforms." An expedition to the stratosphere, particularly one to settle the debate between Drs. Millikan and Compton over the nature of cosmic rays, could be a highlight of the fair.

Although the second *FNRS* gondola was exhibited at the fair, it was in no shape for the flight. A new one would have to be built for the Chicago flight. Jean Piccard directed the construction of the gondola, according to his brother's specifications. The fair even ordered a Draeger air regeneration system from Germany like the ones used in the *FNRS* gondola. The new gondola was named *A Century of Progress*, after the fair.

One significant deviation from the *FNRS* design was in the choice of material for the shell. The gondola was a seven-foot diameter sphere made from a lightweight magnesium alloy called "Dowmetal." Dow Metal Company in Midland, Michigan, built the capsule's shell, which weighed just 196 pounds. This was one-third less than a comparable size aluminum shell would have weighed. They fabricated the shell from eight segments of 1/8-inch thick metal welded together. Dow donated the capsule because they felt the project would showcase their new alloy.

The Goodyear Zeppelin Company in Akron, Ohio, fabricated the balloon. It had a volume of 600,000 cubic feet. Goodyear made the balloon from rubberized single-ply cotton fabric. Karl Arnstein led the Goodyear team that produced the balloon.

Jean became the middleman between his brother and the Exposition's organizers. When negotiations began, Jean was with the Bartol Research Foundation of the Franklin Institute, after having worked as a chemist at Hercules Powder Company. At Bartol, William F. G. Swann was developing a center for the study of cosmic radiation. Auguste first agreed to the Chicago flight, but had to withdraw because he wanted to return to Belgium and help Max Cosyns prepare for another flight. This disappointed the fair organizers because of Auguste's fame after the *FNRS* flights, and they believed his participation would ensure a large number of admission paying spectators. Auguste suggested that Jean make the flight instead. This would at least give the flight an association with the Piccard name. Jean had wanted to make the flight all along, either with his brother or with an American scientist. Auguste believed the notoriety associated with the flight would help Jean find a more suitable university position and further enhance the family name.

Many of the fair's backers felt the flight would showcase American science and determination to be preeminent in this new frontier. However, they recognized the publicity value of the Piccard name, so the flight was frequently called the "Piccard Balloon Flight." Arthur Compton provided instruments for the flight, so it also became known as the "Piccard-Compton Flight." This played particularly well with local audiences, since Compton was with the University of Chicago. The flight of *A Century of Progress* promised to be one of the highlights of the exposition. Jean eagerly anticipated reaching the stratosphere like his brother and looked forward to the flight, but it turned out exposition organizers had other ideas.

While negotiating the contract for the flight, friction developed between Jean Piccard and the organizers. Their relationship deteriorated. Piccard was unhappy over such issues as ownership of the balloon and gondola once the fair was over, and how proceeds from admissions to witness the launch would be divided. The exposition committee wanted to ensure that Auguste was at least present for the flight, but Jean could not make such a guarantee due to his brother's other commitments. With the gondola being made by Dow, and the balloon coming from Goodyear in Ohio, there were those who felt the flight should be an "all American" effort, with Piccard excluded. Similar nationalistic feelings had helped generate support for the flight after word reached the United States about Soviet plans for setting a new record.

Another complication was that Jean did not hold a valid American balloonist's license. The Goodyear Zeppelin Company proposed Navy balloonist Lt. Commander Thomas G. W. "Tex" Settle pilot the balloon. Further strengthening the case for Settle as far as Goodyear was concerned, he was the Navy's chief inspector for balloons, and was well known to company executives. Piccard tried to claim that piloting a balloon to the stratosphere required a different set of flying skills, so the fact that Settle held a balloonist's license was not necessarily an advantage, but this argument was not given much weight.

Sensing he was fighting a losing battle, Piccard offered to accompany Settle as the scientist who would make cosmic radiation observations during the flight. Partly because of the friction that developed during pre-flight negotiations, and partly because he was a chemist, not a physicist, the fair organizers finally decided that Piccard would not make the flight. The official reason given was that by flying with only one person, the balloon would be lighter and could reach a greater altitude.

Settle attempted a solo flight from the fair grounds on August 5, 1933. *A Century of Progress* took off around 3:00 AM. The hydrogen vent valve in the top of the balloon stuck open, and Settle did not reach more than a few thousand feet before beginning to descend. He skillfully controlled the balloon as best he could to avoid the nearby Sky Ride towers and the Goodyear Zeppelin dock before managing to land in a railroad yard a few blocks away. Settle knew there was a problem with the valve before attempting the flight, but he launched anyway. He felt pressured to launch because the spectators in the grandstands at Soldier Field were growing increasingly impatient and restless during the long night of preparations.

The Marine launch crew under the command of Major Chester L. Fordney quickly secured the landing area, and protected the balloon. Eager souvenir hunters tried to tear off pieces of the fabric, so it needed protection. There was also the fear that someone would casually drop a cigarette and ignite the hydrogen that remained in the balloon. The balloon and gondola were recovered and shipped to the Chicago Museum of Science and Industry while the question of their ownership was sorted out.

Piccard felt *A Century of Progress* was his because the contract said he was to receive the balloon after it flew. To Piccard, this meant the *entire* aerostat, including the gondola. For a while, fair organizers claimed a strict interpretation of the contract, which meant he did not get the gondola. Adding to the confusion, Piccard sold his title to the balloon to a Chicago newspaper. Goodyear Zeppelin imposed this as a condition before they would repair the balloon. Willard Dow, of Dow Chemical, insisted that his company kept title to the gondola. Eventually everything was sorted out, and the fair committee kept *A Century of Progress* for another

flight attempt. Settle would make the second flight, but again without Piccard.

Determined to succeed this time, Settle decided he needed a copilot because he found there was simply too much for one person to do during the launch. Settle chose Major Fordney to accompany him into the stratosphere as "aide and scientific observer." By the time everything could be readied for another attempt the Chicago Exposition was about to close. However, it was decided to proceed with the flight anyway. Settle moved the launch site to the Goodyear Zeppelin Company plant in Akron. Launching at the Goodyear Zeppelin plant removed the pressure of having to fly before a crowd. It also meant the balloon could be inflated in Goodyear's blimp hangar and moved outside when it had been thoroughly checked. All they needed was favorable weather.

The gondola carried a variety of instruments to "observe and record various data and phenomena, mainly in the stratosphere." Scientific equipment included the following:

> Geiger counter;
> ionization chamber;
> film plates to capture cosmic radiation particles;
> spectroscopic camera for sun and sky spectra;
> Fairchild aeronautical camera;
> Eastman Kodak camera with infrared filters;
> light polarization indicator;
> air sample bottles;
> standard color charts for comparing color of the sky; and plant disease spores. (Fruit flies were supposed to have been taken, but they did not arrive in time.)

The film plates were passive experiments that had to be recovered to return any results. When a cosmic radiation particle struck one of these plates, it left a microscopic track of its path. The length and size of a particular track indicated the energy level of the "hit."

Inflation and final rigging of the balloon began November 17, 1933, inside the mammoth airship hangar. At dawn on the morning of 20 November, the ground crew moved the inflated balloon

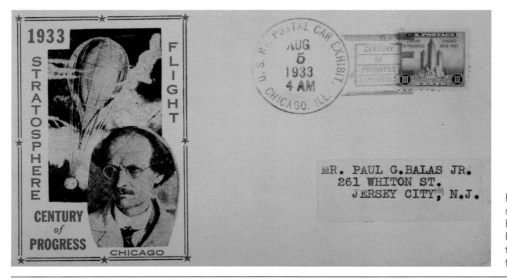

Postal cover canceled on August 5, 1933, to commemorate the launch of the "Piccard-Compton Flight" at the Chicago World's Fair "A Century of Progress." Neither Piccard nor Compton piloted the balloon, which only reached a few thousand feet before it landed in a nearby rail yard.

outdoors. The aerostat had a gross weight of 7,700 pounds. Settle and Fordney boarded *A Century of Progress* and prepared for take-off. The actual takeoff was delayed while they waited for the right winds. Finally, at 9:30 AM, the ground crew released the balloon.

In just 15 minutes Settle and Fordney were 4,200 feet above the ground; at 10:20 they reached 4,900 feet. Then they lost altitude, eventually descending to 1,900 feet at 11:00. Dropping ballast, Settle and Fordney resumed their ascent. They closed the hatches on the gondola when they reached 13,500 feet at 12:45 PM.

Once they sealed the cabin, the aeronauts established a rate of climb between two and four meters per second. They set an official world altitude record of 61,237 feet while floating across Pennsylvania. While at their ceiling altitude the pair had excellent radio communications with Akron, New York, Chicago, and Washington, D.C. The sky above them was a very dark blue. A thick layer of haze in the troposphere obscured the ground beneath them.

Throughout the flight the temperature inside the gondola varied between 40° and 50° F. Learning from Auguste Piccard's experience with the pair of *FNRS* gondolas, engineers at Dow Metal Company painted the top half of the capsule white and the lower half black. That way, the upper portion of the gondola would reflect the worst of the sun's heat, while the lower portion absorbed warmth from the Earth. The life support system worked well, too.

Carbon dioxide concentration inside the capsule remained at or below 2%.

They began their descent at 4:20 PM. Their maximum rate of descent was five meters per second. At about 30,000 feet they began equalizing the pressure inside the capsule with the outside air, and at 26,500 feet they opened the hatches.

Settle and Fordney landed seven miles southwest of Bridgeton, New Jersey, at 5:50 PM. They were in an area of marshes, water holes, ditches, and bayous. They decided it was best to stick together in such terrain after dark, and the balloon should be protected during the night. Therefore, the aeronauts opted to camp out in *A Century of Progress* for the night. The next morning they hiked about three miles to the nearest farm and asked to use a telephone. Studying the data collected, scientists concluded that 99% of high altitude radiation comprises charged particles from outer space.

The following 30 January, a Soviet team attempted to recapture the altitude record with an ascent from Mazilovo, near Moscow. Paul F. Fedoseyenko, Andrey B. Wasienko, and Ilya Usyskin reached 73,000 feet. Tragically, during their descent the gondola tore free of the balloon. Unable to open the hatch in time to parachute away from the plummeting gondola, the crew died on impact. All three received hero's funerals, and their ashes were interred in the Kremlin.

3

Explorers Aloft

During 1933 Army Air Corps Captain Albert W. Stevens began pressing his superiors to mount a stratosphere expedition using a balloon. While the Army eventually endorsed the notion, the service could not provide any funding. Army support would be limited to the use of personnel and facilities. He turned to the one organization he felt would have both the willingness and means to support such an undertaking—the National Geographic Society. Stevens presented the flight as an opportunity to loft a fully equipped scientific laboratory for the study of high altitude photography techniques, properties of the upper atmosphere, and cosmic radiation. It would also establish a new altitude record, perhaps as high as 75,000 feet.

Society officials already knew Stevens. As the Army's top aerial photographer, he sometimes provided photographs for articles in *The National Geographic Magazine*, including what was until then the highest altitude photograph ever taken—32,220 feet over Dayton, Ohio, in 1924. Society President Gilbert Grosvenor embraced the expedition, and provided most of the financial support. Other supporters for the flight included United Aircraft and Transport Corporation, Eastman Kodak Research Laboratory, Fairchild Aviation Corporation, and the Sperry Gyroscope Company. Stevens even donated several thousand dollars of his own money to support the flight. The list of individual contributors included William A. Burden, Colonel Edward A. Deeds, Sherman M. Fairchild, Phillip G. Johnson, Charles F. Kettering, Dr. A. Hamilton Rice, Cornelius V. Whitney, and George D. Widener.

Grosvenor appointed a committee to oversee the scientific agenda for the flight. The Scientific Committee comprised the following people:

- Dr. Lyman J. Briggs, Director, U.S. National Bureau
    of Standards;
- Dr. Frederick V. Coville, Chairman of the Research Committee,
    National Geographic Society;
- General Oscar Westover, Assistant Chief, U.S. Army Air Corps;
- Captain R. S. Patton, Director, U.S. Coast and Geodetic Survey;
- Dr. W. F. G. Swann, Bartol Research Foundation,
    Franklin Institute;

- Dr. Floyd K. Richtmyer, Director, Department of Physics,
    Cornell University, and member, National Research Council;
- Dr. Charles K. Mees, Director, Research Laboratory,
    Eastman Kodak Company;
- Dr. Charles F. Marvin, former Director, U. S.
    Weather Bureau; and
- Dr. John Oliver La Gorce, Vice President, National
    Geographic Society.

The Army Air Corps appointed a three-man crew: Major William E. Kepner, pilot; First Lieutenant Orvil A. Anderson, alternate pilot; and Captain Stevens as scientific observer. Kepner and Anderson were seasoned balloon pilots. Both served during the World War—Kepner in the infantry in France, and Anderson in an aviation unit. Following the war Anderson became a balloon instructor. In 1922 Anderson was a crewmember of the transcontinental airship *C-2*. Kepner transferred to the Air Service and became a balloon observer and dirigible pilot. Major Kepner commanded several airship school detachments, and flew in four national and international balloon races between 1927 and 1929. Besides his work with high altitude photography from aircraft, Stevens had also performed a parachute jump from 26,500 feet in 1924.

When the expedition was first announced to Society members in the April 1934 issue of *The National Geographic Magazine*, the crew comprised Kepner and Stevens. Anderson subsequently became a full fledged member of the flight crew, going from alternate to co-pilot. (He was also promoted to the rank of Captain.) The initial announcement indicated the flight would occur in June, with a follow-up flight in September to "check observations under similar conditions." Officially named The National Geographic - Army Air Corps Stratosphere Expedition, it is generally known by the name *Explorer*.

Explorer carried full size laboratory instruments to ensure the greatest attainable accuracy. With a crew of three, this meant *Explorer* would be somewhat crowded despite its eight-foot, four-inch diameter. Dow Chemical Company in Midland, Michigan, built the capsule from Dowmetal, the same magnesium alloy used for *A Century of Progress*. Drawing upon experience of previous gondolas, the upper half of the sphere was painted white to reflect the sun's heat; the lower half was black to absorb heat from the earth. Several three-inch diameter windows made from double-pane Pyrex glass let the crew see outside. One of these was in the top of the capsule so they could look at the balloon during their flight.

To reach the desired altitude *Explorer* would need a truly gigantic balloon; one with a volume of 3 million cubic feet. This was five times larger than *A Century of Progress*. The Goodyear-Zeppelin Company assembled the balloon in Akron, Ohio. The balloon required 2 1/2 acres of cotton fabric, which arrived on 130 rolls that were 42 1/2 inches wide and 300 feet long. Warwick Mills in New Hampshire provided the fabric. Transforming rolls of flat fabric into a 178-foot diameter inflatable sphere was no small task. The material had to be cut into 3,320 major pieces, each of which had to be passed through a rubberizing machine 30 times. To ensure the airtightness of the finished envelope, it was fabricated without stitches—all the pieces were glued together. This consumed more than 300 gallons of cement made from pure rubber dissolved in gasoline and benzol. To reinforce the seams, each one had to be covered on both sides with fabric-backed rubber tape.

Even the building where the balloon was built took special preparation. The seams around the windows were sealed, and the air in the building was pumped through flannel filters to remove dust. Workers wore special cloth slippers to protect the fabric. The finished balloon weighed an incredible 5,000 pounds.

A reinforced section called the *catenary band* girded the balloon about a third of the way from the base. This was similar to the girdle that Piccard used on the *FNRS*. When the balloon was fully inflated to its 178-foot diameter, the band became a belt around the lower third of the envelope. The catenary band had attachment points for 160 ropes, which extended to the load ring. The gondola hung from the load ring via ten ropes. *Explorer* used two different weights of fabric. The fabric above the catenary band weighed three ounces per square yard; the envelope below the band did not support the weight of the gondola, so it used a fabric weighing two ounces per square yard.

While the balloon and gondola were being built, Kepner and Anderson searched for a launch site. They eventually found a spot in the Black Hills of South Dakota, about 12 miles southwest of Rapid City. The launch site was a grassy meadow 600 feet square in a natural depression surrounded by steep cliffs. It subsequently became known as the *Stratobowl*. Launching a balloon the size of the *Explorer* required a sheltered site, because such a balloon could easily whip around like a sail if caught by the wind. Several hundred feet deep, the *Stratobowl* offered the needed protection from surface winds. Prevailing winds would carry the balloon over the midwestern plains for a landing in relatively flat, clear terrain. Historical data indicated they would likely have three or four opportunities for ideal weather from mid-June to mid-July.

Early in June personnel began arriving in the area, and established the *Stratosphere Flight Camp*, which came to be known simply as the *Stratocamp*. Anderson directed the growth of the *Stratocamp* from its creation to a community of more than a hundred people with its own drainage system, sawdust covered streets,

parking areas, sewage disposal plant, electric lighting systems, waterworks, and a hospital with an ambulance. Log cabins, utility buildings, and tents popped up as the camp grew. The *Stratocamp* even had its own fire department with two professional fire fighters, a pump truck, a dozen fire extinguishers, and a crew of volunteers. Having a fire department on site was particularly important since the *Explorer* balloon used highly flammable hydrogen gas for lift. The Rapid City Chamber of Commerce supported most of the development at the encampment, including railings around the rim of the *Stratobowl* for the anticipated crowds of spectators.

The *Stratocamp* attracted numerous visitors. These included the wife of the Governor of South Dakota and residents from the nearby Sioux reservation, who toured the site while wearing traditional Native American garb. Mrs. Berry, the governor's wife, "christened" the gondola by pouring liquid oxygen over it.

A detail of 120 soldiers from the Fourth Cavalry at Fort Meade, in Sturgis, South Dakota, assisted at the *Stratocamp*. Although they had no previous balloon experience, they comprised the ground crew for *Explorer*, and learned the art of handling large aerostats by launching a 35,000 cubic foot test balloon. Because they were only needed for the actual launch, the soldiers did not stay in the *Stratocamp*; rather, they were bussed to the launch site when needed.

The South Dakota National Guard also supported *Explorer*. Filling the mammoth balloon took 1,500 cylinders of hydrogen gas that were delivered via railroad to Rapid City. The South Dakota National Guard provided a convoy of 42 trucks and drivers to transport the cylinders from Rapid City to the *Stratocamp*. Each cylinder held 190 cubic feet of gas and weighed 131 pounds. The cylinders were stacked along one side of the launch site. The soldiers erected a canopy of pine boughs over the cylinders to shade and protect them from the heat of the sun.

The actual launch site was a 200-foot diameter circle in the center of the *Stratobowl*. It was covered with a 4-inch thick layer of sawdust to protect the balloon during inflation. Since a great deal of work would take place during the night before the launch, a ring of searchlights circled the launch site.

One of the high points of the preparations came on the day the gondola arrived on a truck from Midland, Michigan. It was immediately installed in the Gondola House, which served as storage shed and workshop for the sphere. Several days later another truck arrived from Akron, Ohio, carrying the balloon. It was packed in a waterproof box, and was deposited in the center of the sawdust circle. A canvas tent erected over the box provided further protection from the elements. Equipment continued to pour in, including an Army Air Corps liquid oxygen generator. Other items delivered to the *Stratocamp* ranged from mundane equipment like machine tools, to delicate instruments and electronic apparatus needed to outfit the gondola.

By 9 July everything was ready for the flight, and Kepner, Anderson, and Stevens could have taken off at any time. All they had to do was wait for favorable weather. Because aerial photography was one of the primary goals of the flight, they needed particularly clear skies, not only over the *Stratobowl*, but also along the projected track of the flight. Each morning and night, Major Kepner checked the latest weather maps and forecasts with the team of meteorologists. Mr. V. E. Jakl of the Weather Bureau office in Kansas City headed the meteorological team. The *Stratocamp* boasted one of the best-equipped weather stations in the country, and received reports from stations as far away as Alaska, Iceland, and Cuba. The station was set up with the cooperation of the U.S. Weather Bureau, the Army Signal Corps, and the Army Air Corps.

Kepner watched and waited for the ideal conditions for more than two weeks. He and his crewmates spent their days in the Gondola House testing and fine tuning the equipment aboard *Explorer*. Drs. Lyman Briggs and W. F. G. Swann occupied their time during the weather hold by constructing a dehumidifier that removed excess moisture from the atmosphere inside the gondola.

Finally, on the morning of 27 July, Kepner determined the weather conditions would be right for a flight the next day. A large high-pressure area drifting in from the west promised clear skies along the flight path. At noon Kepner announced his decision. The *Stratocamp* became a beehive of activity as everyone made the final preparations for the flight. From that time on only essential personnel were allowed in the launch area.

The troops from the Fourth Cavalry carefully removed the balloon from its packing crate and laid it out within the sawdust covered launch bed. To make the balloon easier to handle prior to inflation, the fabric below the catenary band had been inverted and folded back into the main body of the envelope. While the troopers laid out the balloon, scientists inside the Gondola House checked their instruments one last time, installed batteries in *Explorer*, and filled its liquid oxygen bottles.

A little past dusk the ground crew began inflating the balloon, a process that took six hours. As with much of the preliminary work, Anderson directed the crew while they piped hydrogen to the balloon through a series of canvas tubes. By two o'clock in the morning the inflation was complete. The balloon held 210,000 cubic feet of highly flammable hydrogen gas. As the *Explorer* ascended, the hydrogen would expand and fully inflate the 3,000,000 cubic foot envelope at 65,000 feet.

The gondola was wheeled out of its shed and brought into position beneath the balloon. Attaching the capsule to the gasbag took nearly three hours. A little past five o'clock everything was nearly ready. After loading warm flying clothing, a small sack of mail, and their personal parachutes, Anderson and Stevens climbed into the gondola. Kepner clambered to the top of the gondola, among its rigging, where he could direct the final ground preparations. At 5:45 AM Kepner gave the command "Cast off!," and *Explorer* took off.

Climbing quickly, the crew surveyed the ground beneath them. For miles around they saw hundreds of cars and thousands of people who had come to the *Stratobowl* to witness the ascent. Anderson joined Kepner on top of the gondola. *Explorer* was climbing too rapidly, and they had to slow it down. They needed to release some of the hydrogen through the vent at the top of the balloon.

There were two means of venting hydrogen. Unlike previous high-altitude balloons that used rope-controlled vent valves, *Explorer* had a *pneumatic valve* that could be controlled from inside the cabin. A simple tube that carried compressed air to activate the valve extended up through the inside of the balloon from the gondola. As a backup to the pneumatic valve, *Explorer* still had a rope-controlled valve, but it was relegated to emergency purposes, and could only be actuated from outside the cabin.

Unsure of how the immense balloon would respond, Kepner and Anderson took the rope that controlled the emergency vent valve in their hands. They called to Stevens inside the gondola to open the pneumatic valve. They found the pneumatic valve worked properly, and soon had the ascent under control. Anderson rejoined Stevens inside *Explorer*, and they halted the ascension at 15,000 feet.

Stevens climbed out of the hatch and joined Kepner on top of the gondola. Working together, they lowered the 125-pound spectrograph on a 500-foot long quarter-inch rope. This task took nearly half an hour. This instrument recorded the spectrum of the sun as *Explorer* climbed into the atmosphere. These recordings provided information on the nature of the ozone layer of the atmosphere. With the spectrograph suspended 500 feet below the capsule, Kepner and Stevens climbed back inside and secured the hatch.

The National Broadcasting Company (NBC) provided a lightweight radio set for *Explorer*. While the balloon floated at 15,000 feet, the crew established contact with Washington, D.C. They talked with General Westover and Dr. La Gorce. NBC carried their broadcasts live across its network of stations, giving radio audiences a sense of connection with the flight.

Anderson dropped 400 pounds of lead shot ballast and *Explorer* began climbing again. They halted at 40,000 feet to conduct instrument readings. *Explorer* carried an array of Geiger counters arranged to determine the direction of cosmic rays. On the ground, the counters registered one or two "hits" per minute. At 40,000 feet, the rhythm was much faster. After an hour and a half they began climbing to 60,000 feet. It was nearly noon—*Explorer* had been aloft for six hours.

An hour later the balloon reached the 60,000-foot level. So far, everything was going according to plan. Kepner and Anderson controlled the balloon while Stevens transmitted instrument readings to the ground. The Geiger counters sounded like "many typewriters in a newspaper office," or "like a flock of chickens pecking grain from a metal pan." Inside the gondola, it was 42° Fahrenheit despite an outside temperature of 80 degrees below zero. Just like Settle and Fordney found with *A Century of Progress*, the *Explorer* crew discovered painting the *Explorer* gondola white on top and black on the bottom provided much better temperature control than either of the *FNRS* capsules.

Suddenly there was a clattering on top of the gondola.

Looking through the three-inch diameter window above the hatch, the aeronauts saw part of the rope connected to the balloon appendix had fallen. The appendix was an open sleeve at the base of the balloon. Once they were at 63,000 feet and the balloon fully inflated, excess hydrogen vented through the appendix. Further examination soon showed why the rope fell—there was a large rip in the base of the balloon!

The rubber compound used to coat the balloon fabric left it slightly sticky. To keep the fabric from sticking together, it was dusted with a layer of powder. Unfortunately, this did not prevent adhesions, particularly when the lower portion of the balloon was folded inside the upper portion prior to launch. This put a lot of stress on the two-ounce fabric, and it tore as the balloon approached full inflation.

Kepner, Anderson, and Stevens quickly decided against trying to go any higher. They opened the pneumatic valve to vent hydrogen. However, the sun was heating the balloon and made the gas expand. They continued to rise for another twenty minutes, eventually reaching 60,613 feet. This was within 624 feet of the mark set by Settle and Fordney. Despite their situation, Anderson and Stevens took time to collect samples of the air at 60,000 feet. Kepner stood by with his hand on the lever that would release the 80-foot diameter emergency parachute. Finally, *Explorer* began to descend.

Within 45 minutes they were down to 40,000 feet. Inside the gondola, Kepner, Anderson, and Stevens could hear the fabric tearing. Another 30 minutes passed, and their altitude was just 20,000 feet. Throughout the flight they wore parachute harnesses. Now they clipped their emergency parachutes to the harnesses. Working quickly, they opened the hatch and climbed on top of the gondola to inspect the balloon. Large tears appeared in the lower part. Suddenly the entire bottom of the bag dropped out.

What had been a balloon became a parachute filled with a mixture of hydrogen and air. They dropped rapidly. Stevens dumped ballast overboard as Anderson and Kepner released the heavy spectrograph, which was on a parachute. By 10,000 feet the descent rate still had not slowed. Throughout the descent, the crew kept up their radio transmissions, sharing the drama with audiences around the world.

Barely half a mile above the ground they abandoned the craft, relying on their personal parachutes for landing. Anderson tried to jump first, but his parachute container caught on the rigging, spilling his canopy. He gathered the fabric under one arm and prepared to jump. While gathering the fabric, he slipped and had both feet inside the open hatch. "Hey, get your big feet out of the way! I want to jump!" yelled Stevens, who was still inside the gondola. Just as Anderson cleared the hatch the hydrogen that remained in the balloon exploded and the capsule plummeted like a stone.

Pieces of the disintegrating balloon landed on top of Anderson's parachute, and at first it looked like they would collapse the canopy. Fortunately, the pieces slid off, and his descent continued safely. Stevens tried twice to get out of the gondola, but the wind-blast forced him back. On the third try Kepner pushed him with his boot as he lunged through the hatch. Stevens found the capsule fell at the same rate of speed as he did, so he was not falling away from it. He turned over in freefall and pulled the ripcord. His parachute opened immediately and checked his fall. Major Kepner was last to jump, opening his parachute only seconds before the capsule hit the earth with a terrific thud in a cornfield owned by Mr. Reuben Johnson near Holdrege, Nebraska.

All three pilots landed nearby, shaken but safe. Hundreds of people streamed toward the impact point after chasing the balloon in their cars across the Nebraska prairie. The chase plane, piloted by Lieutenant J. F. Phillips, landed in an adjacent field.

Everyone—aeronauts, airplane crew, and spectators—pitched in and helped gather wreckage, although many spectators collected pieces of balloon fabric as souvenirs. Kepner and Stevens walked to the Johnson farmhouse and asked to use the telephone.

At first, it looked as though the flight was a total loss from a scientific standpoint. Most instruments, particularly the electroscopes used to gauge cosmic rays, were smashed. The film magazines from the aerial cameras appeared to be likewise destroyed. However, the barographs that provided official recordings of the altitude survived with barely a scratch. Of course, the spectrograph that had been jettisoned during the descent was recovered intact. Although everyone expected the film records to be ruined, photographic technicians developed them anyway. When they did this, they discovered that most of the film recordings of the instruments and ground miraculously survived. Of 200 exposures made during the flight, 163 yielded usable prints.

Kepner, Anderson, and Stevens each received the Distinguished Flying Cross from the Secretary of War for the flight. Despite the loss of the capsule and the near loss of the crew, enough experimental data was recovered so that, from a scientific standpoint, the flight was considered a success. Fortunately, Society President Grosvenor insured the flight through Lloyd's of London. Lloyd's paid $30,170 on the policies that covered the balloon, gondola, and instruments. The Army and the National Geographic Society began planning another flight.

Meanwhile, Max Cosyns made another stratospheric ascent on August 18, 1934. Neree van der Elst accompanied him. They took off from Hour-Havenne, Belgium, reached 52,952 feet, and flew over Germany and Austria before landing near Senaulje, Yugoslavia. They used the original *FNRS* balloon, which by now was showing some signs of wear. This was the last high altitude flight for the envelope, but not the last time it was used. Auguste converted it for use as a hot air balloon. Sadly, it caught fire during one of its flights.

Jean Piccard finally got a chance to reach the stratosphere using *A Century of Progress*. His wife Jeanette accompanied him as pilot so he could operate the instruments. This required her to get a balloon pilot's license. Finding backers for the flight proved to be quite a challenge. Most of the organizations that might be willing to support such a venture were already committed to the National Geographic Society flight. In addition, some potential sponsors did not want to be associated with a flight that included a wife and mother because of the potential for adverse publicity if something went wrong. Even Dow Chemical withdrew their official support, and asked that their name be removed from the gondola. The Piccards eventually found support among civic leaders in Detroit, Michigan. Corporate patrons included the Grunow Radio Company and the People's Outfitting Company. The gondola carried the names of these firms. Jean and Jeanette also replaced *A Century of Progress* on the gondola with *Piccard Stratosphere Expedition*.

Drawing on his experience working with explosives, Jean devised a new way to drop ballast. He placed a blasting cap inside each bag of ballast, which he hung on the outside of the gondola. Detonating the caps from inside the gondola burst the bags and released the ballast. He also used small explosive charges to sever the ropes that held the balloon prior to launch. This way he could control the launch, and avoid the sort of problem his brother encountered on the first *FNRS* flight. This added a certain element of risk, however, because the balloon was filled with hydrogen.

Henry Ford developed an interest in the flight, and let the Piccards use the hangars at the Ford Airport at Dearborn, Michigan. Ford's generosity, other in-kind donations, and volunteer labor let them stretch their meager budget and made their flight possible. On the morning of October 23, 1934, Jean and Jeanette Piccard set out for the stratosphere. Jean climbed into the gondola to tend the instruments; Jeanette leaned out of the hatch to monitor the launch. A cheer rose from the crowd of spectators when the explosives severed the restraining ropes. The cheers quickly turned to gasps when the balloon did not rise, but stayed within a few feet of the ground, headed towards the trees that bordered the airport. Mrs. Piccard dropped some ballast and the balloon started to climb. It cleared the trees and continued gaining altitude.

The weather proved to be a problem. Pre-launch predictions called for clear skies, so the Piccards took off as planned. Once aloft, they discovered a solid overcast. As they passed through a layer of clouds, the balloon began swaying from side to side. Still standing in the open hatch, Mrs. Piccard nearly fell out of the gondola as she reached for the rope that controlled the vent valve. Fortunately she regained her footing, secured the rope, and closed the gondola hatch. Although she wore a parachute, had she fallen, it would have had disastrous consequences, because they were above Lake Erie at the time. The balloon soon cleared the clouds and broke into bright sunshine.

People on the ground spotted the balloon briefly over Akron and again above Sandusky, Ohio, but the Piccards could not see through the clouds, and could not tell where they were. Depending on how high they reached and how long they remained aloft, there was a risk they could land in the Atlantic Ocean. Settle and Fordney landed less than 50 miles from the ocean. What Jean and Jeanette couldn't tell was that they were still over Ohio when they reached their maximum altitude of 57,979 feet. For all they knew, they could be over Pennsylvania or New York. They could have

dropped more ballast in an attempt to set an altitude record, but decided it would be better to try to land rather than risk an ocean landing. Mrs. Piccard opened the hydrogen vent valve, and they began their descent.

As the balloon entered the clouds it cooled and contracted, increasing their rate of descent. Suddenly they were dropping out of control. Jeanette dropped all their ballast in an attempt to regain control over the balloon. They were still falling too fast as she emptied the last bag. She opened the hatch and tossed a battery (that was attached to a parachute) overboard. They carried cosmic ray instruments provided by Swann and Millikan. The latter instrument was shielded with 550 pounds of lead shot. Jean began dropping the lead shot through a special chute in a desperate attempt to slow their fall.

A heavy layer of fog blocked their view of the ground, so they still couldn't tell what was beneath them. Suddenly there was a break in the clouds, and they saw they were headed straight towards the roof of a farmhouse. They threw some more weight overboard and barely managed to clear the structure, bouncing between the house and the nearby barn. They continued to drift along the ground until the gondola finally settled into the limbs of a large elm tree. The Piccards landed on a farm near Cadiz, Ohio.

When told where they were, Mrs. Piccard laughed. "Oh dear, and I had wanted to land on the lawn of the White House," she told the gathering crowd. Reporters quickly descended on the small town. Jeanette Piccard was, after all, the first woman to reach the stratosphere. Someone asked if she would be willing to make such a risky trip again. "Oh, just give me a chance," was her reply. The bottom of the capsule was crushed up to the floor level from the hard landing, but the Piccards were safe.

In the February 1935 issue of *The National Geographic Magazine*, Society President Gilbert Grosvenor announced there would be another *Explorer* flight. Like the first flight, this one would be jointly sponsored with the Army Air Corps. The Air Corps appointed three officers as the flight crew. Captain Anderson was the mission commander, Captain Stevens was pilot and scientific observer, and Captain Randolph P. Williams was appointed alter-

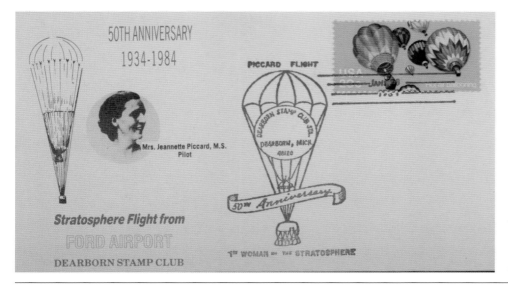

Jean Piccard finally reached the stratosphere on October 23, 1934. His wife Jeanette piloted the balloon. Fifty years later, the Dearborn Stamp Club celebrated the flight with a special anniversary cancellation.

nate pilot. Major Kepner was unavailable because he had been appointed to the Air Corps Tactical School. (Kepner eventually reached the rank of Lieutenant General. During World War II, he commanded the 8th Fighter Command in the European Theater at the time of the D-Day invasion. In the closing months of the war he commanded the 9th Air Force.)

The June issue of *The National Geographic Magazine* carried further details about the upcoming expedition to the stratosphere, and announced the flight would be named *Explorer II*. To avoid the chance of an explosion like the one that occurred during the first *Explorer* flight, this balloon would use helium. While this enhanced the overall safety of the flight, it meant that *Explorer II* needed a larger balloon than its predecessor, because helium only has 92% of the lifting capacity of hydrogen.

The *Explorer II* balloon was bigger than any previously built, with a volume of 3.7 million cubic feet. It weighed 6,500 pounds. Goodyear-Zeppelin built the balloon in Akron, Ohio. Karl Arnstein led the team that designed and built the balloon. Fully inflated, the balloon had a diameter of 192 feet. The Wellington Sears Company provided the balloon fabric—cotton cloth weighing 4 ounces per square yard for the upper portion of the envelope, and 3-ounce fabric for the lower portion. When coated with rubber, the upper fabric weighed 7.2 ounces per square yard; the lower portions increased to 5.3 ounces. Otherwise, the construction techniques were similar for the larger bag as they were for the first *Explorer*. Prior to launch, the aerostat would tower 315 feet above the ground.

Dow Chemical built the *Explorer II* gondola from Dowmetal. The *Explorer II* capsule was much roomier than its predecessor; it was nine feet in diameter. Like *A Century of Progress* and the first *Explorer*, the gondola was painted black on the lower half and white on top. *Explorer II* sported a 14-foot arm with a fan that would presumably rotate the aerostat as it floated at altitude so that cosmic radiation instruments could collect observations pointing in different directions. The empty sphere with its hatch covers and arm weighed 638 pounds. This was considerably lighter than the smaller *Explorer I* capsule, which weighed 700 pounds. Improvements in "secondary details," like the size and location of hatches, method of suspension to the balloon, and removal of shelving inside the capsule made the weight savings possible. Captain Stevens preferred to bolt instruments directly to the wall of the gondola, rather than place them on shelves. This not only saved weight, but it provided a more efficient use of space inside the capsule.

Explorer II used the same ballast release system Jean Piccard created for his flight with the *A Century of Progress* gondola. Forty bags of ballast, each one loaded with 75 pounds of lead shot, were attached directly to the load ring, and hung around the exterior of the gondola. Anderson and Stevens also had several bags of ballast inside the capsule that they could dump overboard when the hatch was open. Mounting the ballast sacks to the load ring meant it could be attached directly to the gondola shell. This proved to be lighter than the way it had been done on the first *Explorer*. The batteries that powered the equipment aboard *Explorer II* weighed in at nearly 1,000 pounds. They were arranged around the exterior of the gondola, and could be released (with individual parachutes, of course) as ballast during landing.

Stevens designed the life support, or "air conditioning" system (as it was called at the time). He used a mixture of 46% liquid oxygen and 54% liquid nitrogen to replenish the cabin atmosphere. The liquefied gas mixture passed through a copper expansion coil, where it vaporized. Pressurized helium gas forced the oxygen/nitrogen mixture out of its storage container into the coil. A sylphon-type regulating valve designed by Stevens and Mr. Oscar Steiner admitted gas to the cabin as needed to maintain atmospheric pressure.

The expansion coil was housed in the top of a cabinet that held cloth bags of sodium hydroxide pellets. A circulating fan forced air over the coil and through the cloth sacks. The sodium hydroxide pellets removed carbon dioxide from the atmosphere. Sodium hydroxide also readily absorbs moisture. As the air conditioning unit scrubbed both deadly carbon dioxide and unwanted excess moisture from the atmosphere, the result was a solution of sodium carbonate and water that was absorbed by a layer of sawdust in the bottom of the cabinet.

At launch, *Explorer II* carried a 53-pound supply of liquefied oxygen and nitrogen in a 25-liter insulated flask. Stevens and Anderson also had a reserve supply of 32.5 pounds of a 50/50 oxygen/nitrogen mixture in case a leak occurred in the gondola.

By spring 1935 the second Army Air Corps/National Geographic Society *Explorer* flight was ready. Anderson and Williams conducted two test flights with an 80,000-cubic foot balloon on 21 and 28 April. Flying in an open basket, they reached 25,000 feet and 24,500 feet, respectively. During these flights they tested the air-conductivity apparatus that would be carried on *Explorer II*, and observed the effects of dropping ballast on the instrument.

In May camp was again established at the *Stratobowl*. Meteorological personnel were among the first to arrive; they reported to the site between 6 and 10 May. For the next two months, activities proceeded much as they had for the first *Explorer* flight. Troops from Fort Meade were again called upon to be the ground crew.

Throughout June everyone waited for suitable weather for the flight. Because of his background and training, Captain Williams was in charge of the meteorological station. Criteria for the flight were very strict. Surface winds at the *Stratobowl* could not exceed 4 miles per hour, skies over the flight path had to be clear, and winds at the landing site had to be less than 14 miles per hour. The weather station opened each morning at 5:45 AM, and the radio operators received coded messages from Arlington and San Francisco. The morning radio reception was usually finished by 9:30. The meteorologists used the data to prepare weather maps of the North American continent and adjoining Pacific Ocean, winds aloft maps, and a pressure change map. They also used reports from aircraft flying from Cheyenne, Billings, Omaha, and Oklahoma City to create charts of upper air humidity and stability. Throughout the day, the weather personnel made hourly measurements of pressure, temperature, and humidity. In addition, they frequently released and tracked small balloons to gauge how *Explorer II* would behave under various weather conditions.

June passed without the right conditions for a flight. Finally, on 10 July, Williams observed the formation of a large, dry Polar air mass that created the needed high-pressure area. He tracked the mass as it headed for Rapid City. At noon on 11 July conditions were ideal for a flight the next day. Skies were clear, and winds were calm in the *Stratobowl*.

Balloon inflation went smoothly in the early morning hours of 12 July, and the crew looked forward to a record-breaking flight. With the balloon inflated, all that remained was to wheel the gondola into position underneath the bag and attach it. The ground crew finished attaching the gondola to the balloon, and began final checks before the crew boarded. Suddenly the balloon tore near its top, spilling its load of helium. In "six or seven seconds," the three-ton bag was laying on the ground. Some of the personnel were not fast enough to get out of the way and were trapped beneath nearly three acres of fabric. Fortunately, others helped them crawl out unharmed. The balloon was gathered up and shipped back to Goodyear Zeppelin.

Balloons of that time had a "rip panel" near the apex of the bag as a safety feature. When landing, the pilots pulled a rope that tore the balloon along the edges of the panel, releasing the gas, and preventing the gondola from being dragged or bounced along by the wind. *Explorer II*'s failure showed there was more stress on the rip panel in large balloons than previously thought. Unable to bear the stress, the V-shaped panel tore. Goodyear engineers designed a new system to open the bag after landing. It used a steel cable which, when pulled, would tear the fabric and release the helium in a few seconds. Goodyear repaired the balloon at no cost, installed the new rip cable, and shipped it to the *Stratobowl* for another flight attempt.

A week after the *Explorer II* attempt the Soviets tried to set a stratospheric record. On July 26, 1935, a balloon named *USSR* took off, but only reached 52,000 feet, far short of the record.

On the afternoon of November 10, 1935, ground crews spread out a huge canvas ground cloth in the middle of the *Stratobowl*. It was bitterly cold, only a few degrees above zero. Finally, it was time to lay out the balloon. It had been kept in a tent heated to 50° F, so the rubberized fabric was pliable and easy to manipulate at first. It soon became stiff and difficult to unfold as it lay on the cold ground.

Working by the illumination of 36 floodlights ringing the launch area, ground crews inflated the balloon using 1,685 cylinders of helium. Near midnight, one of the technicians noticed a "pocket" of gas forming beneath the folds of fabric near one of the inflation tubes. The unequal stress was too much. There was a gentle pop as the fabric tore. The ground crew gradually let the balloon rise as they searched for the rupture. When they found it, it was 17 feet long! Despite the bitter temperatures, they decided to patch the tear. Working quickly, the Goodyear Zeppelin Company and Army men glued a piece of balloon fabric over the hole. They used a 1,500-watt light bulb and a reflector to warm the repair and cure the glue. With the repair finished, they resumed inflating the balloon. Amazingly, finding and repairing the tear only put them a little more than an hour and a half behind schedule.

Lift off occurred at 7:01 AM, Mountain Standard Time, on 11 November. Hundreds of people gathered around the top of the *Stratobowl* to watch the ascent. The capsule had just cleared the walls of the bowl when the balloon began dropping. Anderson was outside the gondola; Stevens was inside. Anderson climbed through the open porthole and announced "I believe the balloon is leaking!" Fearing a crash, they dropped 750 pounds of lead shot ballast.

To observers on the ground, it looked like streams of water pouring out of the capsule. Most of the people beneath the lead shower scattered. One unfortunate gentleman got caught in the middle of the stream and was covered with fine lead shot. Lighter, *Explorer II* again ascended over the South Dakota Badlands. There was no leak; the balloon simply encountered a strong down draft as it cleared the rim. The pilots clambered outside the capsule, amongst the rigging throughout much of the early ascent. When they reached 16,000 feet, they climbed into the sphere and sealed the hatch. Testing the capsule for leaks, they pressurized the cabin to the equivalent of 13,000 feet. They maintained this pressure throughout the flight.

During the climb, temperatures inside *Explorer* dropped to 21° F. Anderson tried to eat a sandwich, but he discovered it had frozen. Actually, both he and Stevens were so busy that they weren't

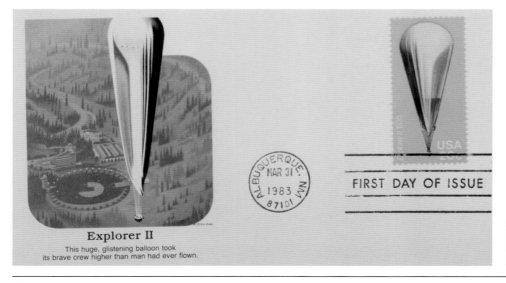

Explorer II
This huge, glistening balloon took
its brave crew higher than man had ever flown.

On March 31, 1983, the United States Postal Service issued a set of commemorative stamps honoring ballooning. One of them depicted the *Explorer II*.

particularly hungry, so Anderson placed the sandwich on top of one of the instrument cabinets and quickly forgot about it. They were very thirsty, however, and drank hot water from a gallon container. Anticipating cold temperatures aloft, they carried three containers of hot water with them.

At first, the winds carried them southeast, towards Pine Ridge and the border with Nebraska. Around 40,000 feet the winds shifted, and *Explorer II* began following a more easterly track. Three hours and 29 minutes after launch, Anderson and Stevens reached 65,000 feet. The balloon was inflated to its full 192-foot diameter. Anderson dropped ballast, gently coaxing the balloon higher. At 11:40 AM, *Explorer II* settled out at 72,395 feet. They were above 96% of the atmosphere, higher than anyone had ever ventured. The temperature inside the gondola climbed to 43°.

From such a great height, Stevens reported they saw mostly patches of green or brown on the ground. Railroads were the only recognizable features, and then only by an occasional cut or fill. Larger farms could be picked out by their rectangular patterns. A new American flag hung from the rigging. The sky above them was a darker blue than that on the flag. They recorded the first photographs that showed the curved top of the troposphere and the curvature of the Earth. Anderson and Stevens calculated they could drop another ton of ballast and gain another 2,000 feet, but decided not to. They had to conserve their remaining ballast to guard against a crash landing.

Around noon they began their descent. Once Stevens was sure they were on the way down, he dropped a device that would collect airborne spores down to an altitude of 36,000 feet. At first the parachute did not open, but it must have, because the device was recovered intact and returned to the U.S. Department of Agriculture. Subsequent analysis revealed ten types of spores, bacteria, and fungi had been collected. This was considered important, because this was the first time that living spores had been found above 36,000 feet in the atmosphere. When they began their descent, the pilots collected samples of the rarefied air for later analysis.

Explorer II carried a cosmic ray telescope that comprised a series of Geiger Müller tubes arranged to record incoming radiation in the horizontal plane; 10° elevation; 30° elevation; 60° elevation; and vertically. The pilots were supposed to use the arm-mounted fan to turn the capsule once they were at peak altitude and obtain readings facing different azimuths.

Unfortunately, Anderson and Stevens discovered the air was too thin for the fan to turn the capsule. Despite this problem, they observed the number of cosmic rays entering the vertical telescope increased steadily up to 57,000 feet. After that, the number of recorded rays decreased. At 40,000 feet, cosmic ray intensity was 40.1 times greater than at sea level. Cosmic radiation intensity peaked at 55 times greater than sea level at an altitude of 57,000 feet. Beyond that, it fell to 42 times sea level at 72,395 feet. These changes in intensity generally agreed with data collected by *Explorer I* and Jean Piccard. Examining the data, Swann concluded that most of the observed radiation effects were due to "secondary rays" created when primary rays enter from space and collide with air molecules in the upper atmosphere.

Stevens and Anderson also had an instrument called a *stoss chamber* to record "bursts of energy" from cosmic rays striking atoms of metallic materials. The chamber comprised a 20-inch diameter sphere of Dowmetal containing nitrogen pressurized to 250 pounds per square inch. A 5/8-inch thick lead plate was placed above the chamber. Most of the time, a cosmic ray particle would pass through the shield without striking any lead atoms. Occasionally, a particle would strike a lead atom and send a shower of secondary particles into the chamber that caused a sharp increase in the ionization of the nitrogen.

Dr. W. T. Wilkins of the University of Rochester provided packages of film plates similar to those carried by Settle and Fordney on *A Century of Progress*. When a cosmic radiation particle hits one of the film plates, it leaves a track in the photographic emulsion. Two packages of film plates, wrapped in lightproof black paper, were attached to the outside of the gondola. In the laboratory, Wilkins observed that an alpha particle from the element Radium with an energy level of 7.7 million electron volts left a track 33 grains long. After the *Explorer II* flight, Wilkins discovered a track that, if made by an alpha particle, had an energy level of 100 million electron volts.

Medical scientists also used *Explorer II* to see what effect cosmic radiation might have on living organisms by sending *Drosophila* fruit flies aloft. Although they were carried inside the gondola, all of the adult flies in the package died due to the cold temperatures encountered during the flight. At first, the scientists feared the experiment would be a total loss; then they found some of the larvae and eggs survived, and they ended up with 98 individuals for breeding. Subsequent results were inconclusive for any radiation-induced mutations due to the small number of flies returned.

Explorer II also carried instruments to study the sun and atmosphere. Two spectrographs obtained spectra of the sun and upper atmosphere. This latter was considered important, because it measured the quantity of ozone aloft. Another set of instruments mounted outside the gondola measured sky brightness. The pilots measured the brightness of the sun, and found it appeared 20% brighter at 72,395 feet than it did on the ground. Using a specially designed probe, Anderson and Stevens studied the electrical conductivity of the atmosphere above 30,000 feet. They also brought back a full photographic record of their flight, including the first color images of the stratosphere.

Throughout the flight, Stevens talked with engineers from the National Broadcasting System (NBC) who were on the ground at Rapid City. NBC provided an 8-watt radio for *Explorer II*. As the pilots talked, instruments could be heard in the background. Particularly audible was the rattle of an electric hammer every 90 seconds that beat on the barometer case. The case contained both mercury and aneroid barometers. Striking it with a hammer jarred the column of mercury and the aneroid needle so they would not lag, and improved the precision of Anderson's and Stevens' altitude measurements.

A little past 2 PM, the *Explorer II* aeronauts talked directly to the Pan American Airways "China Clipper," which was flying over the Pacific Ocean enroute from San Diego to San Francisco. "Hello! Calling stratospheric balloon!" came the call from W. Burke Miller of NBC and Captain Edwin C. Musick, Pan American's chief pilot, who were aboard the airliner. Then they talked with a radio announcer in London. These transmissions were broadcast live over the NBC system. The banter continued until the balloon reached 16,000 feet, where Anderson and Stevens had to open the capsule's hatches. They dumped the remaining liquid oxygen and liquid nitrogen they carried to replenish the cabin atmosphere, then dropped batteries and ballast to control the final descent. In preparation for landing the pilots donned leather football helmets loaned to them by the Rapid City High School team.

Anderson and Stevens saw a large open field coming up, and agreed it would be a good landing area. They also spotted clouds of dust raised by hundreds of cars that followed them towards the landing spot. The pilots dropped a drag rope and hollered for some of the growing crowd of spectators to grab it. No one did, so they prepared to use the rip cord as soon as they touched solid ground. Anderson called to Stevens "Make ready for landing!" Stevens scrambled across the cabin just in time to help him with the rip cord. Glancing through the porthole in the bottom of the capsule, Stevens saw they were only a foot or two off the ground. They pulled the cord, and felt the steel cable rip a hole in the top of the balloon. The pair grabbed a linen strap strung across the gondola just as the capsule touched down and rolled over on its side. They were showered with lead ballast that had been spilled in the capsule during the ascent. Stevens and Anderson climbed out to the cheers and congratulations of the crowd. Their flight had lasted 8 hours, 13 minutes, and they landed near White Lake, South Dakota, about 225 miles east of the *Stratobowl*.

Following the flight of *Explorer II*, the National Geographic Society made bookmarks from the balloon that they distributed to all members.

Officials at the National Geographic Society realized the balloon was best retired, so they had it cut into souvenir bookmarks that were distributed to their approximately one million members. One side of the bookmark had an image of *Explorer II* aloft; the reverse side contained statistics on the flight. Dow Chemical Company also produced souvenirs of the flight—they created medallions made from Dowmetal. The obverse side had a representation of the balloon. The reverse bore the inscription: "Sample of Dowmetal from which stratospheric gondola was fabricated."

Explorer II Flight Log

Time	Altitude	Air Temp	Remarks
7:01 AM			Take-off
7:30	16,500	0° F	Brought to equilibrium
8:00	16,500	-1° F	Inspection and check
8:30	16,500	-1° F	Gondola being sealed
8:40	17,000	0° F	Rising at 200 feet per minute
9:00	19,000	-8° F	Rising at 300 feet per minute
9:30	30,000	-27° F	Rising at 400 feet per minute
10:00	45,000	-71° F	Rising at 600 feet per minute
10:30	63,000	-76° F	Rising at 600 feet per minute
10:35	65,000	-72° F	Pressure height reached
10:50	73,000	-76° F	At rest at ceiling
12:20 PM	73,000	-76° F	Starting down
12:30	72,000	-76° F	Valving freely; descent slow
1:00	60,000	-76° F	Valving frequently; descending at 300 feet per minute
1:30	50,000	-74° F	Valving frequently; descending at 300 feet per minute
2:00	37,000	-71° F	Valved last at 40,000 feet; descending at 500 feet per minute
2:30	18,000	-4° F	Descending at 700 feet per minute; released ballast and equipment to check fall
3:00	3,000		Falling slowly; drag rope out
3:14	1,600		Landed

Emilio Herrera, the Spanish aeronaut who observed the 1905 solar eclipse from a balloon, decided to mount a stratospheric expedition. He hoped to reach an altitude of 80,000 feet. Unlike the most recent European and American expeditions, he opted to use a full pressure suit instead of a sealed capsule. Herrera received widespread support for his flight. The rubberized silk for the balloon was donated, as were a variety of instruments and other equipment.

His pressure suit was very innovative for its day, and comprised three distinct layers. The first was a wool undergarment he wore for warmth. Next came an impermeable rubberized fabric that formed the actual pressure garment. Herrera covered the pressure garment with an outer protective layer. This outermost layer was made of cloth reinforced with steel cables. An aluminum helmet with a round visor topped the suit. He also carried a silver lamé cape to reflect the intense rays of the sun at high altitudes.

Herrera devoted a great deal of attention to the joints—he realized that the suit would be difficult to move around in when pressurized. This has always plagued pressure suit designers. Colonel Herrera solved the problem by designing joints with accordion-style pleats that maintained a constant internal volume when flexed. When he flexed one of his joints (take the elbow for example), the portion of the suit inside the joint contracted, while the other side of the joint expanded. This kept the volume, and therefore the pressure, inside the suit constant. Without such an arrangement, trying to bend a joint like the elbow would be like trying to fold an over-inflated balloon. Steel cables secured the joints and kept them from over-inflating. (Decades later, the suits worn by Apollo astronauts on the Moon incorporated constant-volume joints.)

Herrera tested the suit in a metal tunnel surrounded by dry ice. Although the temperature around him was –79° C, the temperature inside the suit was a comfortable 33° C. The Spanish Aerostatic Service in Guadalajara fabricated the balloon to his specifications. Everything was proceeding smoothly for the flight, which Herrera planned for October 1936.

During the summer of 1936, he presented a course on aerodynamics at the University of Santander. While there, he met Auguste Piccard and the Soviet balloonist Georgi Prokivief. Piccard was very enthusiastic about Herrera's upcoming flight, and offered him a lot of advice. Prokivief was very pessimistic about the Spaniard's chances for success. It did not matter who felt what about the flight, because the ascent was canceled due to the Spanish Civil War. Herrera, a Republican loyalist, found himself out of favor with the Fascist forces under General Francisco Franco. The balloon was cut up, and the rubberized fabric used for rain ponchos.

Polish balloonist Captain Zbigniew Burzynski, who twice won the annual Gordon Bennett balloon race, also wanted to reach the stratosphere. Burzynski based his quest on a desire to set an altitude record, but he found he could not gain the needed support without a scientific rationale for the flight. Professor Mieczyslaw Wolfke of the Warsaw Technical University proposed that the flight be used as an opportunity to study cosmic radiation.

The Poles built an egg-shaped balloon and spherical capsule that was named *Star of Poland*. For thermal control, the gondola was painted in alternating black and white stripes. It carried a bat-

Polish postal souvenir sheet issued for the *Star of Poland* balloon.

tery of 30 Geiger-Müller tubes to measure cosmic ray intensity versus altitude. The balloon was filled with hydrogen. Captain Burzynski piloted the balloon; Dr. Konstanty Jodko-Narkiewicz, a physicist who specialized in studying cosmic radiation, accompanied him. The flight was set for September 1938 in the Chocholowska Valley area of the Tatra Mountains, near the town of Zakopane. As frequently happened with stratospheric expeditions, weather delayed the flight.

Finally, on October 14, 1938, the weather cooperated. *Explorer* veteran Albert Stevens observed the launch. At first, the flight went smoothly. Then, when the *Star of Poland* was less than a hundred feet above the ground, the hydrogen ignited. Fortunately there were no casualties, but the balloon was destroyed. Polish authorities resolved to try again the following year, and began work on a replacement balloon. Stevens even arranged for a shipment of helium from Texas.

Germany attacked Poland on September 1, 1939, starting World War II. As the German Army poured across the border, Polish authorities released the helium into the air to prevent it from being captured. With the start of the Second World War manned stratospheric ballooning ended, at least for the time being.

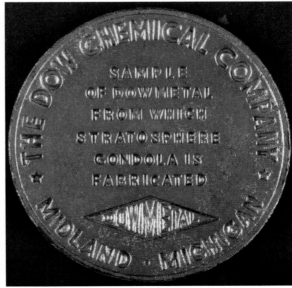

Dow Chemical Company issued medals made from the same type of metal used for the *Explorer II* gondola.

4

Blossom, *Aerobee*, and *Skyhook*

Explorer II represented the practical limit for a balloon made from rubberized fabric. Larger balloons were possible, but their increased weight would have negated any gains in performance. To venture higher, new materials were needed. In 1935 Jean Piccard, working with Dr. Thomas Johnson of the Bartol Research Foundation, constructed and flew a cellophane balloon at Swarthmore, Pennsylvania. The following year Piccard received an appointment as a special lecturer at the University of Minnesota, where he continued his work with cellophane balloons.

Piccard's cellophane aerostats were the first *constant level* balloons. Constant level balloons are so called because of the manner they fly. High altitude balloons are only partially inflated at launch. For example *Explorer II*, which had a volume of 3,700,000 cubic feet, was only filled with 125,000 cubic feet of helium at launch. As the balloon ascended, the gas expanded to fully inflate the envelope. Rubber balloons, which are sealed, will keep expanding until they burst. Constant level balloons are open at the bottom, so once the lifting gas fully inflates the container, any excess simply vents overboard. The balloon will then fly along at a more or less constant altitude. Because the gas pressure inside the balloon cell equals the surrounding air pressure as they float, *constant level* balloons are also called *zero pressure* balloons. Cellophane has two major disadvantages for high altitude balloon use: it becomes brittle at low temperatures, and it tears easily.

Despite these disadvantages, Piccard promoted the use of cellophane. In the late 1930s, it was the lightest material available. At the University of Minnesota one of his graduate students, Jean Barnhill, and two undergraduate aeronautical engineering students, Harold Larson and Lloyd Schumacher, helped fabricate the cellophane balloons. They cut the individual gores by hand, and then glued them together with one-inch wide cellophane tape. Each gore was 33 feet long. His first balloon launch from the University of Minnesota occurred on June 24, 1936.

While he worked on cellophane balloons, Piccard came up with another idea for reaching extreme altitudes. If one relatively small balloon could lift a few pounds, then why not cluster a large number of balloons to carry a much heavier weight? To Piccard's way of thinking, such an arrangement provided a greater margin

One of Jean Piccard's early cellophane balloons, launched from the University of Minnesota football stadium on June 24, 1936. *Source: International News Photos*

of safety, because he needn't be as concerned should an individual balloon fail—there were plenty of others that still supported the gondola. Descending would be a matter of releasing individual balloons, which eliminated the vent valve and control line that gave his brother so much trouble on the first *FNRS* flight. Piccard named the project *Pleiades*, after the seven-star constellation. Eventually he hoped to reach 100,000 feet, but he first contented himself with a small-scale demonstration of his idea using a cluster of rubber weather balloons and an open gondola.

Looking for materials that were less expensive and lighter than traditional wicker baskets, Piccard built a box-shaped gondola from aluminum and magnesium. Since his stratospheric flight he had received his balloonist's license. He taped it inside the metal basket behind a piece of celluloid. As had been the case in the 1934 stratospheric flight, Piccard had to raise money to support *Pleiades*. The Kiwanis Club of Rochester, Minnesota, supported the flight. *Pleiades* used a cluster of 98 balloons, grouped in two tiers. The top group reached about 100 feet above the ground; the lower group about 50 feet. Piccard placed a small explosive charge around the lines between the two clusters so he could release the top group when he was close to the ground. He also had the option of cutting balloon cords with a knife, or shooting individual cells with a pistol.

On July 19, 1937, he took off from Soldiers' Field in Rochester, Minnesota, with *Pleiades*. He reached 10,000 feet, then began his descent. No experiments were carried on the flight because Piccard did it solely to demonstrate the technique of using balloon clusters. When he was about to touch down, Piccard released the top group of balloons. The severed end of the rope landed in the gondola. Piccard noticed it was still smoldering from the explosives. The celluloid cover he had used to protect his balloonist's license caught fire and ignited the magnesium components in the gondola. Piccard jumped clear, and could only stand by helplessly and watch the *Pleiades* gondola burn.

Except for the Japanese FUGO program, balloon research stopped during World War II. In 1944 and 1945 the Japanese resorted to high altitude balloons, which they designated FUGO, to carry bombs to the United States. The hydrogen-filled balloons flew at 30,000 feet, riding the prevailing winds across the Pacific. FUGO balloons usually carried antipersonnel and incendiary bombs with the hope of terrorizing civilians and starting massive forest fires in the Pacific Northwest. More than a few survived the journey, although the damage they caused was minimal.

Remnants of FUGO balloons were found as far as Iowa, Nebraska, Texas, and Kansas. Fragments of an incendiary bomb were found near Farmington, Michigan, and a balloon and shroud lines were discovered near Grand Rapids. As it turned out for the Japanese, the winter of 1944-45 was particularly wet in the northwest region of North America, so the anticipated forest fires never materialized. The War Department also instituted a strict censorship policy to avoid public panic over the new weapon, so the Japanese never knew if any of their balloons reached America.

Sadly, withholding information on the FUGO balloons meant the public was not aware of the hazard they presented. On May 5, 1945, the Reverend Archie Mitchell and his wife Elsie took their Sunday school class on a picnic near Bly, Oregon. Mrs. Mitchell and a group of the children found something in the woods. Reverend Mitchell, who had heard rumors about the devices, yelled a warning just as the bomb went off, killing his wife and five children. They were the only casualties caused by the FUGO balloons.

The balloons were made from lacquered paper or rubberized silk, and had a barometric device that helped them maintain a preset altitude. When the balloon descended below the desired level, ballast was automatically released to make it rise. During the day, as the sun heated and expanded the hydrogen, excess gas was released through a vent valve. This gave them similar flight characteristics to the constant level balloons developed by Piccard, but they relied upon active flight control to maintain altitude.

World War II saw amazing advances in aircraft and rocket technology. Bombers and fighters routinely ventured into the lower reaches of the stratosphere, exposing flight crews to the sort of conditions that had proven fatal to Hawthorne Gray in the late 1920s. Rocket powered airplanes like the Bell X-1 were well along in their development, and more advanced aircraft were on the drawing board. These aircraft would be capable of brief sojourns above 100,000 feet! In the closing months of the war, German crews launched thousands of V-2 rockets against the Allies. These rockets followed ballistic trajectories that took them more than 50 miles above the earth's surface, across the threshold into outer space as they delivered their one-ton warheads to targets 200 miles away. Already, visionaries talked of the day when rockets would carry humans beyond the stratosphere and across that threshold. (For more information on the V-2, see *Germany's V-2 Rocket* by Gregory P. Kennedy, Schiffer Publishing, Ltd.)

Auguste Piccard spent World War II in Switzerland, and worked on precision instruments; Jean developed oxygen systems for the Navy at the University of Minnesota and taught United States Navy officers enrolled in the aeronautical engineering program. After the war, Auguste turned his attention to undersea exploration. When the war ended in Europe, Jean was part of the technical mission dispatched to London to evaluate captured German documents. Upon his return to the United States, Jean began work on a proposal for another piloted stratospheric balloon flight.

In late 1945 he met Otto Winzen, chief engineer for the Minnesota Tool and Manufacturing Corporation. Winzen was seeking advice from the University of Minnesota on developing instruments for Navy dive-bombers. Born in Cologne, Germany, Winzen immigrated to the United States in 1937, and studied aeronautical engineering at the University of Detroit. Because he was a German immigrant, he spent the Second World War in a series of internment camps. With the war over, he began working for a small engineering company in Minneapolis. Piccard's enthusiasm for the stratospheric balloon project caught hold with Winzen, and the two agreed to work together.

They approached the United States Navy with a proposal created by Piccard called *Pleiades II*. As originally conceived, *Pleiades II* would use a spherical capsule carried to an altitude of 100,000 feet by a cluster of cellophane balloons. Piccard based the *Pleiades* capsule on the *FNRS* gondolas built by his brother. He omitted one of the manholes and replaced it with a large Lucite window. If the capsule landed such that the hatch was blocked, Piccard intended to carry half a dozen hacksaw blades that he would use to cut his way out of the shell.

Jean Piccard proposed that he and his wife should make the stratospheric flight. The Piccards even practiced exiting from a capsule mockup to show that only one door was needed. "Tests have shown that we (Dr. Jeanette Piccard and Dr. Jean Piccard) can both escape through one door with parachutes on our backs in 24 seconds if she goes first while I push the parachute behind her. I follow by myself. I would not, in any case, jump through one door before I knew that she was out," wrote Piccard in the project proposal.

Like the *FNRS* gondolas, *Pleiades II* had shelves for instruments and equipment. The main shelf was three inches below the equator of the sphere. A smaller shelf was located below the main one. Placing the main shelf below the equator of the sphere made it less obtrusive than earlier designs. The floor of the gondola was four feet in diameter; the cylindrical area between the floor and the top of the capsule was reserved exclusively for the crew. The portion of the gondola between the lower shelf and the floor comprised storage lockers for blankets and warm clothing. Piccard specified that the area beneath the floor, which had been referred to as "the cellar" on previous gondolas, should be kept empty so that it would be free to crush in case of a hard landing.

The *Pleiades II* proposal did not specify what sort of scientific instruments would be carried on the flight. Instead, Piccard offered general guidance for size and location of instruments under the title "Suggestions to the Scientific Collaborators." His "suggestions" included practical advice like "no instruments shall protrude inside the living space. Sharp angles directed toward the center of the gondola must be avoided," and "any spilling of any liquid (except pure water) at the landing must be avoided, and it must be kept well in mind that the gondola is not ventilated, so that all pollution by fumes of organic liquids must be prevented."

He specified there would be numerous standardized "outlets" through the capsule wall that were sealed with number 6 rubber stoppers that could be removed as needed for wires or gas tubes that needed exposure to the stratosphere. "The pilot and copilot, whose lives depend on the proper functioning of every single outlet, would like to assist the scientific collaborators in the insertion of the stoppers," wrote Piccard.

Intrigued by the proposal, Commander George Hoover of the Office of Naval Research (ONR) provided limited funding to pursue the project. The Navy created a Technical Committee under the leadership of Commander Hoover to manage the effort, which became known as *Helios*.

Realizing the limitations of cellophane, Winzen and Piccard sought a better balloon material. Most of the materials tested (which included saran, nylon, and Pliofilm) had various undesirable characteristics like poor tear resistance, or brittleness at cold temperatures. They needed a material that was lightweight, inexpensive, and strong. It had to remain flexible in the frigid upper atmosphere, and be relatively unaffected by intense ultraviolet radiation. Final-

ly, a suitable material was found: polyethylene. Available in very thin sheets, it remained pliable over a wide temperature range, was unaffected by ultraviolet radiation, and cost a fraction of what rubberized fabric did. Polyethylene was developed in Great Britain in 1933. During the war, it was used as an insulating material in submarines and radar sets. In the United States, the Visking Corporation manufactured polyethylene in large sheets.

Because of its proximity to the University of Minnesota, Piccard asked General Mills to build the *Helios* capsule. Although best known as a manufacturer of flour and cereals, General Mills was a widely diversified company. In 1928 James Ford Bell created General Mills through the merger of the Washburn Crosby Company with four other mills. "Where research leads, the company follows," was one of Bell's favorite sayings, as he led General Mills on a program of expansion and diversification. In the Second World War, the Mechanical Division of General Mills produced gun sights and torpedoes for the Navy. After the war Bell continued the path he charted, and General Mills worked on a variety of engineering projects, including *Helios*.

The *Helios* gondola was a 7-foot, 2-inch diameter sphere with an interior volume of 192 cubic feet made from eight segments of 1/8-inch thick 3003-SO aluminum. Space inside the capsule was allocated as follows:

- Scientific Instruments	52 cubic feet
- Free Space	26 cubic feet
- Aeronautical Equipment	26 cubic feet
- Living Space for Crew	88 cubic feet

Shortly after work started on *Helios*, Winzen went to work for General Mills, and led the team that designed their first plastic balloon, which he launched on September 25, 1947. One of the challenges facing Winzen was how to join the balloon panels, or gores. He devised a heat sealing system that fused the gores together. The heat-sealed joints were very strong, but the thin plastic film was

Otto Winzen, who designed the first polyethylene high altitude balloons. He is shown launching one of the balloons using a special trailer that let it inflate smoothly. *Source: Winzen Research, Inc. photograph*

still very fragile. Tape placed over the joints provided a suspension system that actually carried the load, so the delicate plastic skin served only as a barrier material for the lifting gas. Improper handling at any step from manufacture to launch could seriously damage the balloon. Despite "millions of tiny pinholes in the film, leaky seams covered with adhesive tapes, and makeshift launch method," the balloon carried a 63-pound payload to 100,000 feet. Obviously, the concept was sound. He later received U.S. Patent Number 2,526,719 for the invention.

Winzen's first plastic balloon had a volume of 30,000 cubic feet, but he felt 200,000 cubic foot balloons were a realistic goal. *Helios* would, he calculated, need a cluster of balloons totaling 14 million cubic feet to reach the desired altitude. In other words, *Helios* would need to be launched by 70 balloons! (Piccard's original *Pleiades II* proposal called for 100 balloons.) Trying to launch such a cluster would have been impractical, so the Navy canceled *Helios* in late 1947. General Mills had already finished the capsule shell, which was placed in storage at the Naval Air Station at Lakehurst, New Jersey. The ONR asked Winzen to instead concentrate on building large individual balloons. This endeavor became known as *Skyhook*.

Winzen's next two attempts failed, so Hoover convened a "balloon conference" to sort out the problems. After the conference, the next flight ascended as intended, but refused to land for three days due to a failure in the radio control system. Two scientists from the Brookhaven National Laboratory, Drs. Hornbostle and Salant, placed a pair of photographic emulsion plates on the balloon's instrument package to capture cosmic radiation particles. The delayed landing proved fortunate, for it provided a much longer exposure time for the plates than originally planned. Winzen later fondly remembered the excited phone call from the scientists, who exclaimed, "It will take years to analyze the wealth of cosmic ray events in these plates!"

Independent of the Navy project, the Army Air Force was developing high altitude balloons too. Codenamed *Project Mogul*, this effort sought to monitor Soviet missile and atomic tests using acoustical instruments. Researchers had detected underwater "sound channels" that reflected pressure waves from explosions over long distances. Could such "sound channels" exist in the atmosphere? Examining recorded data, they found that the volcanic explosion at Krakatoa in 1883 produced a low-frequency pressure pulse that circled the globe 8 times. Therefore, they theorized the detonation of an atomic bomb would produce an acoustical signature that could be reflected over great distances. The acoustical signal could be measured if they had instruments at the right altitude.

On November 1, 1946, the Research Division of the New York University College of Engineering received Air Materiel Command contract W28-099-ac-241 "to design, develop, and fly constant-level balloons to carry instruments to altitudes from 10 to 20 km." *Mogul* was so highly compartmentalized that only a small group of people knew the full scope of the project. For their initial flights, the NYU group used trains of rubber weather balloons attached to a single long cable. They conducted their first flights from Bethlehem, Pennsylvania. Launches from Pennsylvania took

the balloons too close to the busy air routes in and out of New York, so they moved someplace that was sparsely populated and away from commercial air lanes.

A little more than six months after receiving the contract, on June 4, 1947, the NYU Group launched an aerostat from Alamogordo Army Air Field in southern New Mexico. Alamogordo Army Air Field was situated along the southwestern edge of the White Sands Proving Grounds (WSPG), which took its name from the nearby National Monument. The Army established the WSPG in 1945 as a testing center for captured German V-2 missiles. A significant portion of the Proving Grounds came from the bombing range that had been set up for the Air Field.

Planning for the Alamogordo Army Air Field began in 1941 as a training base for the British Overseas Training Program. The base was adjacent to the small desert community of Alamogordo, near the foothills of the Sacramento Mountains in the Tularosa Basin. With the entry of the United States into World War II, the War Department took over the project and decided to use it for American aircrew training. Construction began at the base on February 6, 1942, and units began arriving in May. During the war, the Alamogordo Army Air Field served as a training center for B-17, B-24, and B-29 bomber crews. When World War II ended the base was placed on a standby status and nearly closed. Then, in January 1948, the newly created Department of the Air Force announced Alamogordo Army Air Field would become the home for the service's pilotless aircraft and missile development programs. It was renamed Holloman Air Force Base in honor of Colonel George V. Holloman, a pioneer in guided missile research.

For their first flight from Alamogordo, the NYU team continued their practice of using a long train of rubber weather balloons attached to a single cable. The balloon train for this flight was more than 650 feet tall. To help track the aerostat, NYU scientists attached four radar reflectors. Despite the presence of the reflectors, they lost track of the balloon somewhere between Capitan and Arabela, New Mexico. It eventually landed on the Foster Ranch near Corona, where rancher Mac Brazel found it. This balloon and the payload it carried became the basis for the rumors of a crashed flying saucer near Roswell. Because of the highly classified nature of *Mogul*, Army Air Force officials claimed Brazel had found remnants of a "weather balloon."

The next day, they launched an instrument package to 58,000 feet on a six-hour flight. The payload for this flight also landed near Roswell, but was recovered. *Mogul* required its instrument packages to remain aloft for long periods of time. Recognizing the limitations of rubber balloons for long-duration flights, researchers at NYU began looking for other materials. After going through much the same process as Winzen and Piccard, the NYU team also selected polyethylene. Less than a month after their first flight in New Mexico using rubber weather balloons, the NYU group had their first plastic ones. They launched a cluster of ten 7-foot diameter polyethylene balloons from Alamogordo Army Air Field on July 3, 1947. The balloon reached an altitude of 18,500 feet, and was airborne for 195 minutes.

Harold A. Smith, Inc. of Mamaroneck, New York, manufactured the first plastic balloons used by NYU. Like those made by

WINZEN RESEARCH INC.

FLIGHT 1 O S · 3

In 1948 Otto Winzen set up his own company, Winzen Research, Inc., at Fleming Field, in South Saint Paul, Minnesota. This photograph shows an early Winzen balloon being launched from Fleming Field. *Source: Winzen Research,*

Seeing a commercial opportunity in the balloon field, Otto Winzen left General Mills and started his own company, Winzen Research, Inc. (WRI). WRI was incorporated on October 28, 1948, and set up operations at Fleming Field in South St. Paul, Minnesota. Winzen Research received its first order, dated January 5, 1949, from the NYU College of Engineering. They ordered twenty 4,300-cubic foot polyethylene balloons for $2,300.00. The teardrop-shaped balloons were 20 feet in diameter, and were made from 1.5-mil DuPont PM-1 plastic. NYU also purchased 1-mil balloons from General Mills and 4-mil balloons from Goodyear Tire and Rubber Company. Goodyear only manufactured ten polyethylene balloons for NYU, at a cost of $475.00 each. General Mills provided more than 200 balloons for NYU, ranging in size from 7 feet in diameter to 70-foot diameter giants.

On February 5, 1949, Winzen delivered the first two balloons produced under the contract. NYU researchers were quite pleased with the performance of the Winzen balloons—one of them was launched on 11 February, and spent the day floating above 40,000 feet. Winzen shipped the remaining 18 balloons later in the month.

Otto Winzen developed a new heat sealing system for welding the gores together, and he began producing 20-foot diameter balloons at an initial production rate of 2 per day. The heat sealing system was so strong that these balloons did not need any adhesive backed tape over the seams. Winzen hoped his 20-foot diameter balloons would become standard research tools. On January 18, 1949, he inflated the first balloon to come off the assembly line, and kept it filled with helium for three days to measure any loss of lift that occurred. After three days no loss of lift was noted—he had devised a leak-proof balloon. One of the interesting features of

General Mills, the NYU balloons used sheets of polyethylene heat sealed together to form a spherical envelope. However, all the joining was done by hand with the Harold A. Smith balloons, which limited the potential size of the cells. Acetate tape applied over the joints reinforced the balloon, and provided the load-bearing structure of the balloon. The thickness of the plastic is expressed in thousandths of an inch, or mils. The NYU balloons were made from 4- and 8-mil plastic. General Mills made their balloons from much lighter 1-mil polyethylene.

A German V-2 rocket at White Sands Proving Ground. Captured German missiles carried the first American space biology experiments. Passengers included corn seeds, mold spores, monkeys, and mice. *Source: U. S. Army*

this balloon was that Winzen did not use any tape over the seams because he wanted to demonstrate the strength of his manufacturing technique.

With the cooperation of the U.S. Weather Bureau, the same balloon was launched on January 23, 1949, carrying a six-pound payload. The launching took place in a snow and freezing rainstorm. Despite the adverse weather conditions, the balloon reached 57,000 feet. Adding to the severity of the test, the temperature at ceiling altitude was -95° F, a record winter low for the St. Cloud, Minnesota, weather station.

NYU continued working under the Air Materiel Command contract until March 1949, making more than 100 flights. By that time, Air Force personnel at Holloman were also launching *Skyhook* balloons purchased from Winzen and General Mills. These personnel were assigned to the Balloon Branch, which was created within the Base's Electronics and Atmospheric Projects Section.

While *Mogul*, *Helios*, and *Skyhook* were underway, the U.S. Army was busy launching V-2 missiles from White Sands Proving Ground. Captured German missiles provided the first opportunities for American scientists to launch payloads into space. If launched straight up, the V-2 could reach an altitude of more than 100 miles. American V-2 flights did not carry explosives. However, because the V-2s were designed to carry one-ton warheads, they needed ballast to compensate for the missing explosives to remain stable. The Army reasoned if the rockets had to carry weight in their nose cones, why not let that weight be scientific instruments? Scientists leapt at the chance, and the American-launched V-2s carried a variety of experiments, including the first biological payloads.

White Sands V-2 #7, launched on July 9, 1946, carried pouches of a special strain of corn seeds provided by Harvard University. Biologists hoped to see if cosmic radiation exposure caused any genetic mutations in the corn. Although the missile reached an altitude of 83.5 miles, the seeds were not recovered. The scientists had enough seeds for a second attempt, and tried again on July 19, 1946. This rocket only climbed 3 miles when it blew up 28.5 seconds after launch. Although they were out of the special strain of seeds, the researchers decided to try again. After two failures little hope was given for recovery, so a package of ordinary corn seeds was purchased at a hardware store in Las Cruces, New Mexico, and placed aboard the rocket launched on July 30, 1946. As it turned out, the rocket reached an altitude of 100.4 miles and the seeds were recovered.

Later that year, on December 17, 1946, researchers from the National Institutes of Health launched five Lucite cylinders containing fungus spores aboard White Sands V-2 #17. Scientists hoped the spores would show if cosmic radiation caused genetic mutations or other abnormalities. The missile reached an altitude of 114 miles. Unfortunately, the Lucite cylinders were not recovered.

The Air Force Cambridge Research Laboratory was assigned seven V-2s for testing and development of recovery systems. Because they tested parachutes, the series was named "Blossom." The first rocket of the series carried fruit flies, rye seeds, and cotton seeds in a cylinder that also contained a radar beacon, a device to measure parachute opening shock, and a camera. Launched

on February 20, 1947, Blossom I reached an altitude of 60 miles before it ejected the canister. The 14-foot diameter nylon ribbon parachute worked, and the payload landed intact. No radiation induced mutations or other changes appeared in the test subjects or their offspring.

The Air Force Aero Medical Laboratory at Wright Field in Ohio provided the biological payloads for Blossom I. In April 1948 the Parachute Branch at Wright Field invited the Aero Medical Laboratory to launch a monkey aboard Blossom III.

Dr. James P. Henry, who headed the Laboratory's Acceleration Section, supervised the experiment, while Captain David G. Simons assisted him. Henry was already well known within the aviation community as the developer of the partial pressure suit for high-altitude flight. Simons, a 1946 graduate of Jefferson Medical College in Philadelphia, requested an assignment in a research facility when he entered the Air Force on August 17, 1947, as a First Lieutenant. Simons was assigned to the Aero Medical Laboratory Acceleration Section. This assignment let him combine medicine with his other long-time interest, electronics. Promoted to Captain in 1948, Simons designed and built electronic devices for the laboratory centrifuge.

One day, Dr. Henry asked Simons if he thought man would ever go to the moon. In college, Simons had read articles about space travel, and answered he believed it certainly was possible. Henry continued, "Well, what would you think of having an opportunity to help us put a monkey in a captured V-2 rocket that would be exposed to about two minutes of weightlessness, and measure the physiological response to weightlessness?" After Simons' enthusiastic and unqualified yes, Henry appointed him Project Officer for the experiment. Henry and Simons had only two months to design and build the capsule. They selected a nine-pound American-born Rhesus monkey for their passenger. Someone in the Wright Field Parachute Branch nicknamed the monkey "Albert," and the name stuck.

Because it was added to the flight so close to the launch, the capsule had to fit in space left over by other experiments, and was oddly shaped. Its irregular shape made it difficult to fabricate, and led to numerous leaks when pressurized. Simons tried to patch the leaks by dabbing rubberized sealant over them, and finally had a capsule that was more or less airtight.

Another problem was that the capsule was not as large as the doctors would have liked. This was compounded when Simons discovered the capsule bulged when pressurized, and wouldn't fit in the allotted space, so he had to weld stiffening bands inside it. The bands further reduced the space for the monkey. To fit in the capsule, Albert had to be crammed into a very awkward position, with his chin against his chest. The launch was set for June 11, 1948.

The night before the flight, Simons anesthetized Albert with sodium phenobarbital, and attached biosensors that would measure his pulse and respiration. As a further protective measure, Simons injected Albert with Luminal, a muscle relaxant, to help him endure a hard landing. The respiration sensor, which was a mechanical lever sutured to Albert's chest, stopped working after Simons sealed the capsule, but the heart sensors continued to work.

When Dr. Simons climbed the launch tower to load the capsule in the nose of the missile, he noticed someone had written "Alas, poor Yorick, I knew him well" across one side of the rocket. After Simons loaded the capsule in the missile, the heart sensors showed no activity. Either the sensors failed, or Albert had suffocated in the cramped confines of the capsule. Simons and Henry surmised the latter was the more likely possibility. In any event, Albert would not have survived the 37-mile high flight, because the parachute tore away from the nose cone.

The next attempt to launch a monkey aboard a V-2 took place on June 14, 1949, on Blossom IV-B. With a year to prepare for Albert II, Henry and Simons built an improved capsule and instrumentation system. The new capsule was a 36- by 12-inch diameter cylinder, and offered plenty of room for the passenger. The breathing sensor that had proven so balky on Albert I was completely revamped. Albert II wore a miniature oxygen mask. A heated wire inside the mask registered each breath the monkey took.

Henry and Simons also refined their test procedures. They selected two monkeys for the flight, a primary and an alternate. For several weeks before the flight, blood was drawn from both to provide a baseline from which to measure any effects of cosmic radiation. On the morning of the launch, the doctors sealed Albert II in his capsule and loaded it in the rocket by X-45 minutes. (The early White Sands launches used the term "X" to denote launch time.)

Albert II reached 83 miles. There was no telemetry; heart and respiration rates were registered on an internal recorder, so recovery of the payload was critical. Unfortunately, the parachute again failed. The nose section created a crater ten feet across and five feet deep. Some pieces were buried 12 feet, and only a few fragments could be identified. Fortunately for the scientists, those fragments included the precious pulse and breathing recordings. Albert survived the launch and weightless portions of the flight with no ill effects. During powered flight, Albert's pulse rate slowed from 190 to 110 beats per minute, and his respiration went from 90 to 60 breaths per minute. Twenty seconds after motor burnout, as the rocket coasted to its apogee, the heart rate returned to 190, but the respiration rate rose only to 65 breaths per minute.

After Albert II, Simons left the Aero Medical Laboratory to attend the School of Aviation Medicine at Randolph Air Force Base, Texas. He was graduated from the Advanced Course in Aviation Medicine as a certified Flight Surgeon in 1950. His next assignment was at Yakota Air Force Base in Japan as a Flight Surgeon for the Far East Air Force.

Dr. Henry continued flying biological payloads aboard V-2s. Albert III's V-2 exploded in midair on September 16, 1949. Three months later, on 8 December, the parachute (again) failed after opening when Albert IV flew. Results were the same as Albert II; the data recordings showed the monkey tolerated acceleration and weightlessness. Acceleration during launch reached 5.5 g's, and 12 g's on parachute opening. (Acceleration is expressed by the term "g." One g is the normal acceleration of gravity. Someone experiencing a 2-g acceleration will feel as though they weigh twice their normal weight; 3-gs, three times; etc.)

With only one Blossom V-2 remaining, Dr. Henry decided to try another line of research, and placed a mouse aboard the missile.

Henry did not try to measure the rodent's heart and breathing rate. Instead, a camera recorded the mouse's reaction to weightlessness. The rocket, which was launched on August 31, 1950, reached 85 miles. As with the earlier primate flights, the parachute failed, but the film survived because the camera was heavily armored. It showed the mouse retained "normal muscular coordination" throughout the weightless portion of the flight, and it "...no longer had a preference for any particular direction, and was as much at ease when inverted as when upright relative to the control starting position."

The V-2s represented a finite resource for researchers, because the Army only had enough parts to assemble about 70 missiles. Dr. Henry switched to *Aerobee* sounding rockets. The *Aerobee* was a small liquid fuel rocket built by the Aerojet General Corporation for the Navy. The Johns Hopkins University Applied Physics Laboratory developed the *Aerobee* for the Navy Bureau of Ordnance as an inexpensive vehicle for high altitude scientific research. It could not carry nearly as much instrumentation as a large rocket like the V-2, but it was considerably less expensive. Therefore, the *Aerobee* could make up in number of flights what it lacked in payload capacity.

Recovery of the Rhesus monkey carried on Aeromedical *Aerobee* flight number two. Although the monkey was recovered alive, it died about two hours later from the effects of heat prostration. *Source: United States Air Force*

The Air Force decided to purchase *Aerobee* rockets for its own research efforts. Air Force rocket programs began at Holloman with the *North American Test Instrument Vehicle*, or *NATIV*. Prior to the *Aerobee*, the Air Force contracted North American Aviation to build an experimental rocket. There were four *NATIV* flights from Holloman in 1948, and the project was terminated the following year. Air Force *Aerobees* used a new launch pad not far from the tower and blockhouse that had been built for *NATIV*. The first *Aerobee* flight from Holloman took place in December 1949.

Aeromedical *Aerobee* #1 carried a Capuchin monkey in its nose on April 18, 1951. The *Aerobee* burned an oxidizer of Red Fuming Nitric Acid (RFNA), and a fuel mixture of furfuryl alcohol and aniline, a particularly noxious combination of propellants. Because of the hazardous nature of the propellants, technicians who fueled the rocket had to wear bulky and heavy asbestos suits. On the day of the first aeromedical flight, one of the fueling technicians adorned the helmet of his suit with electronic tubes and bits of wire in honor of the passenger despite the increased weight. His decorations included a "control panel" that bore the names of the planets.

The *Aerobee* lifted off flawlessly. Unfortunately, the results were the same as the V-2 flights; physiological data on the primate's reactions were successfully recorded, but the parachute failed. The first live recovery finally occurred on September 20, 1951, with the second aeromedical *Aerobee*. After carrying a Rhesus monkey and 11 mice to 236,000 feet, the rocket's parachute deployed properly, and all animals landed alive. Then things went wrong.

Recovery crews took several hours to find the nose cone. Rhesus monkeys do not tolerate heat very well, and the desert sun proved too intense for the monkey. It died of heat prostration about two hours after recovery. Two of the mice also succumbed to the midday sun. The final biological *Aerobee* carried two Capuchin monkeys named Pat and Mike and two mice, Mildred and Albert, on May 21, 1952. The parachute worked properly after the rocket reached 36 miles. This time the capsule was recovered quickly, and all four passengers were in good shape.

The monkeys and mice that flew aboard V-2s and *Aerobees* indicated living organisms could tolerate the rigors of acceleration, vibration, and weightlessness encountered during rocket flight. However, there was still one big unknown regarding the health effects of space flight—namely, how much of a health hazard did cosmic radiation present?

During the balloon flights of the 1920s and 30s, physicists noticed that geomagnetic latitude affected cosmic radiation intensity. They concluded that cosmic radiation comprised charged particles that were deflected by the earth's magnetic field. At first, little thought was given to potential health concerns from these particles. Then, in the years following World War II, scientists announced further findings regarding the nature of the charged particles grouped under the heading cosmic radiation.

Approximately 99% of primary cosmic radiation particles comprised protons and alpha particles; that is, they were nuclei of hydrogen and helium atoms. The remaining 1% were the most worrisome from a health standpoint, because they were nuclei of heavier elements like carbon and iron. Because of their size and tremendous velocities, they carried extremely high energy levels that meant they could potentially cause physical harm, particularly to nervous system tissue.

Most cosmic radiation particles are absorbed in the upper atmosphere through either a process known as "thinning down," or collision with the nuclei of other atoms. The film packs flown aboard balloons showed, in spectacular detail, what happens when a cosmic ray particle collides with another atom. A particle produces a straight track through the film emulsion until it hits the nucleus of another atom. When such a collision occurs, it results in a "star," where bits of the nucleus shoot out in all directions. The initial particle is referred to as a "primary particle"; the particles that result from the collision form "secondary particles." If no collision occurs, the particle often simply loses energy and slows down as it passes through material. This process is called "thinning down." Secondary particles and primary particles that are thinning down can cause serious tissue damage, too.

Cosmic radiation "star" captured in a film emulsion plate. When a cosmic radiation particle hits another atom, in this case, a silver atom in the emulsion, it sends secondary particles in all directions. *Source: United States Air Force*

The only way to gauge the health threat posed by cosmic radiation was to expose living organisms and tissue samples to it. Rockets did not remain aloft long enough to ensure adequate exposure to get measurable results. The only vehicle that could reach high enough altitudes and long enough flight times to ensure exposure was the balloon. Specifically, the large plastic constant altitude balloons developed for *Skyhook*.

Early Space Biology Rocket Flights

- June 11, 1948: Albert I, first monkey flight aboard V-2; mon key apparently died before launch.
- June 14, 1949: Albert II flight, second monkey launched aboard a V-2; instrument recordings indicated monkey was alive until impact; parachute failed.
- September 16, 1949: Albert III flight with monkey onboard; V-2 exploded during launch.
- December 8, 1949: Albert IV flight with monkey aboard a V-2; instrument recordings indicated monkey was alive until impact following parachute failure.
- August 31, 1950: Mouse launched aboard a V-2; mouse died on impact, but camera survived landing, returning film of rodent's response to weightlessness.
- April 18, 1951: First aeromedical *Aerobee* rocket flight from Holloman Air Force Base carried a Capuchin monkey; parachute failed, and monkey died on impact.
- September 20, 1951: Aeromedical *Aerobee* flight #2 with Rhesus monkey and 11 mice on board; rocket reached 44.7 miles and all animals landed unharmed; recovery was delayed, and monkey and two mice died from heat prostration.
- May 21, 1952: Two Capuchin monkeys, Pat and Mike, and a pair of mice successfully recovered following a flight to 36 miles aboard Aeromedical *Aerobee* #3, launched from Holloman Air Force Base.

On November 3, 1949, Charles B. Moore of General Mills made the first piloted flight with a polyethylene balloon. *Source: Winzen Research, Inc. photograph*

5

Early Air Force Biological Flights

After World War II, Soviet dictator Josef Stalin dropped an "iron curtain" across Eastern Europe, and the U.S. wartime ally became a closed society bent on spreading Communism throughout the world. Soviet military research was hidden from western view. Because of this, American military planners could not gauge Soviet military advances and capabilities. In an attempt to obtain information about Soviet activities, United States Air Force planners turned to balloons. Drawing on wartime experience with the Japanese FUGO balloons, the Air Force reasoned it would be possible to use high altitude aerostats to carry reconnaissance cameras across the Soviet Union.

New York University received a contract on June 1, 1951, to design a suitable vehicle. At first, the reconnaissance balloon project was codenamed *Gopher*. Atmospheric conditions above 50,000 feet were still largely unknown, so the Air Force also inaugurated a high altitude weather research project codenamed *Moby Dick*. This became the cover for *Gopher* developmental flights. General Mills soon took over work on the *Gopher* and *Moby Dick* projects, and used *Skyhook* balloons.

When work began on *Moby Dick*, scientific balloon flights were already underway at Holloman to support Dr. Henry's space biology research. The first two such flights, both made on August 29, 1950, were test missions to prepare for the first biological payload. Flight #1 used a 72.8-foot diameter *Skyhook* balloon, and carried a radio beacon provided by Oklahoma A & M University and a pocket-type radiation dosimeter. Balloon Branch personnel launched it from the picnic area in the White Sands National Monument. It rose only 500 to 1,000 feet, then settled back to earth about a half mile away. The envelope had deteriorated in storage, and would not contain the lifting gas.

Fortunately the payload was not damaged, and another balloon was on hand. A few hours later the launch crew tried again. This time the balloon reached 67,000 feet, and was still ascending when the onboard timer released the payload. It descended beneath two six-foot parachutes, but was not recovered until the following week. The beacon batteries died, presumably because of the cold temperatures in the stratosphere, so the recovery crew lost track of it during descent. Records vary as to how much radiation was

recorded on the dosimeter. One report said the instrument recorded 3 milliroentgens; another listed it as 6 to 6 1/2 milliroentgens. With the successful flight, the Balloon Branch was ready to loft a live payload.

Biological balloon flights began under the aegis of the Aero Medical Laboratory at Wright Patterson Air Force Base as part of project RDO 695-72 (MX-1450R), "Physiology of Rocket Flight." Although he was in the midst of the aeromedical *Aerobee* flights, Dr. Henry initiated the balloon project in August 1950 to expose small animals to cosmic radiation for longer periods than were possible with rockets.

Air Force scientists launched the first biological payload with a balloon at Holloman Air Force Base on September 8, 1950. Dr. Henry placed "14 or 16" white mice, another pocket dosimeter, and a pilot's bailout oxygen bottle in a Project Albert capsule suspended beneath a *Skyhook* balloon. The payload weighed about 100 pounds, and the aerostat reached 47,000 feet during a flight that lasted 7 hours. Unfortunately, the capsule's pressure relief valve leaked and all the mice died. The dosimeter recorded 8 to 11 milliroentgens.

Eight days later, the next balloon carried a spectrograph from the University of Denver and another pocket radiation dosimeter. This balloon remained at 97,000 feet for a little over two hours, and was successfully recovered. The dosimeter reading increased 3 milliroentgens during the flight.

The first successful biological flight came on 28 September, when 8 white mice were recovered after a 3-hour, 40-minute flight to 97,000 feet. Search teams found the capsule about three hours after landing, and all the passengers were alive. A pocket dosimeter placed in the capsule with the mice recorded an exposure of 12 to 15 milliroentgens. One of the mice died during the trip back to the base. A necropsy showed it died from pulmonary inflammation that was not caused by the flight. The remaining seven mice lived at least a month after the flight.

This was the last flight to carry a pocket dosimeter for recording the radiation exposure. Pocket dosimeters only register the total radiation exposure, and do not differentiate between helium and hydrogen nuclei, and the less frequent, but more significant heavy

Prior to launch, high-altitude polyethylene balloons are only partially filled with helium, giving them an inverted teardrop shape. As they climb, the helium expands to fully inflate the envelope. This view shows the individual panels, or gores, that are heat-sealed together. *Source: Winzen Research, Inc. photograph*

primary particles. After this flight film emulsion plates became the preferred method of recording cosmic radiation data. Track plates provided a permanent record of a radiation hit, and allowed measurement of a particle's charge and total energy.

The next flight, on 29 November, was a balloon test, and carried 100 pounds of equipment. It only reached 42,000 feet because the balloon was damaged by gusty winds before take off. On January 18, 1951, Henry lofted another Albert capsule carrying mice. At 45,000 feet the balloon burst. The parachute operated properly, and the payload was recovered within two hours of landing. Be-

cause the flight ended at a relatively low altitude there was no cosmic radiation exposure.

Before Dr. Henry launched the first aeromedical *Aerobee* rocket, he tested the nose cone with a balloon flight. This flight took place on January 26, 1951, and took off from the mouth of Rhodes Canyon, about 30 miles northwest of Holloman Air Force Base. The balloon reached 42,000 feet when it began to descend. The recovery team found the nose cone shortly after it landed in the desert about 22 miles northwest of Tularosa, New Mexico. Three months later, Dr. Henry launched the nose cone into the upper atmosphere with an *Aerobee*.

Early Holloman Space Biology Balloon Flights

Date Launched	Altitude, Feet	Payload	Results
8/29/50	1,000	Oklahoma A & M Beacon, Dosimeter	Balloon malfunction
8/29/50	67,000	Oklahoma A & M Beacon, Dosimeter	Recovered on week later
9/8/50	47,000	"14 or 16" mice in Albert capsule	Capsule leak; mice died
9/16/50	97,000	Spectrograph, Dosimeter	Recovered
9/28/50	97,000	8 mice in Albert capsule, Dosimeter	Recovered; all mice survived
11/29/50	42,000	Dummy load test	Recovered
1/18/51	45,000	Albert Capsule with Mice	Balloon burst; recovered, mice survived
1/26/51	42,000	Aeromedical Aerobee Nose Cone	Recovered

The nascent space biology program at Holloman came at a time when researchers were beginning to seriously consider the medical aspects of space flight. In 1950, Dr. Hubertus Strughold of the Air Force School of Aviation Medicine developed the concept of "space equivalence." He realized there is no definite demarcation where the atmosphere ends and space begins. Rather, as altitude increases there are gradations where an unprotected body experiences different physical effects. One of these occurs around 50,000 feet, where atmospheric pressure equals the pressure of water vapor and carbon dioxide in the lungs.

With regard to respiration, a person at this altitude would be in the functional equivalent of outer space, and even breathing pure oxygen at ambient pressure would not sustain life. To survive beyond this altitude, oxygen must be provided under pressure. The next demarcation occurs at 63,000 feet, where water boils at 98.6° and bodily fluids vaporize, so some sort of pressurized garment or sealed capsule must be used.

The significance of Strughold's observation was that, from the effects on the human body, the functional equivalent of outer space begins at altitudes of only 10 to 12 miles. Therefore, it was possible to reach the physiological equivalent of outer space with balloons. In fact, this had been occurring since the 1930s! (Strughold was one of the German scientists recruited to work in the United States after World War II under "Project Paperclip." He had been Director of the *Luftwaffe* Aeromedical Research Laboratory in Berlin. As such, he was involved in experiments involving concentration camp prisoners. In the years immediately after the war his role in such research was overlooked, and he became a senior and respected scientist for the United States Air Force. His wartime activities eventually caught up with him, and people began raising questions. The Air Force removed his name from the

library at the School of Aerospace Medicine, and he was removed from the International Space Hall of Fame in Alamogordo, New Mexico, in 2006.)

On November 8, 1951, a symposium titled "Physics and Medicine of the Upper Atmosphere" was held at the Plaza Hotel in San Antonio, Texas. Participants in this 4-day symposium included Strughold and Wernher von Braun, developer of the V-2. This led to a series of articles in *Collier's* magazine that helped promote public acceptance of space flight. It is interesting to note that the title of this symposium did not mention space, which was still not considered a "respectable" topic for research.

Initially, Holloman personnel supported Dr. Henry's biological flight research on an ad hoc basis. As the pace of activities increased, so did the demands for Holloman support, and a better arrangement was needed. Soon the space biology project officers, who were on temporary duty from Wright Patterson Air Force Base, needed permanent laboratory facilities to prepare their rocket and balloon payloads. The Balloon Branch could assist with launch and recovery, but the base was ill prepared to accommodate monkeys, mice, and fruit flies. The inevitable flight delays also proved costly, as the project scientists from the Aero Medical Laboratory drew temporary duty pay and additional housing allowances while they were away from their home base.

To meet the needs of the growing space biology program, the Air Research and Development Command created the "Aeromedical Field Laboratory" (AMFL) at Holloman in mid-1951. When first activated, the AMFL was subordinate to the Aero Medical Laboratory at Wright Field, and was meant as a field office of the latter. First Lieutenant James D. Telfer, a geneticist, was in charge of the AMFL. At that time, Holloman Air Force Base was under the direction of the Air Force Missile Test Center at Patrick Air Force Base, Florida.

The first AMFL sponsored balloon flight took place on August 16, 1951. Because this was only a test of balloon performance, it carried a 100-pound dummy payload. The Winzen-manufactured *Skyhook* balloon reached 97,000 feet during its 5-hour flight. With this success, Lieutenant Telfer decided to launch a live payload on the next flight.

Drs. Henry and Simons built the Albert capsules for brief flights aboard V-2 rockets, which limited their payload capacity and usefulness for the balloon program. For longer flights with large groups of animals they needed a larger, more flexible capsule. The AMFL contracted the University of Minnesota to build such a capsule. It comprised a 27-inch diameter aluminum sphere that split into two halves held together with 134 nuts and bolts. Animal cages were mounted on the "load ring," which was clamped between the two hemispheres.

The balloon also carried an "instrumentation box" that held a transmitter, altitude indicator, flight termination system, barograph, and low altitude cutdown system. For recovery, the capsule and instrumentation box were cut away from the balloon and recovered by a 24-foot diameter flat parachute. The parachute could be flown either open or packed. Generally, the capsule was suspended from the balloon via an open parachute. Because the parachute was already open, it was virtually guaranteed to work when released from the balloon. This configuration reduced opening shock, because the parachute opened quickly, before the capsule reached terminal freefall velocity. A mechanical timer triggered parachute release at the desired time.

The University of Minnesota capsule first flew on August 23, 1951, with a group of hamsters. For the first flight, the capsule contained just the animal cages and a box of soda lime to absorb carbon dioxide. It was felt the sphere contained enough air at launch to sustain its passengers for the relatively brief flight duration. The first flight with this new capsule was less than propitious. The balloon failed during ascent, at an altitude of 59,400 feet. Because of the relatively low altitude no cosmic radiation exposure occurred, but the hamsters were recovered alive.

The next flight, on 5 September, floated at 97,000 feet for 6 hours and 30 minutes. This flight also carried a group of hamsters in the University of Minnesota capsule. Unfortunately, the capsule was lost during descent, and was not found until three weeks later on the Fort Bliss Artillery Range, which bordered WSPG to the south. Needless to say, none of the animals survived. Two days after the loss of AMFL #3 the next hamster flight took off. This flight lasted 11 hours and reached 94,000 feet. The capsule was recovered near Craig, New Mexico, 45 minutes after landing.

Throughout the early biological balloon flights there were many frustrations. AMFL #7 carried three hamsters and an anesthetized cat with emulsion plates fixed over its head to track cosmic ray hits. Radar showed a maximum altitude of 103,600 feet. The cut-down mechanism failed, and the tracking aircraft lost the balloon 18 hours after launch. About two months later someone found the capsule near Aguilar, Colorado. The flight was repeated with another capsule a week after the loss of AMFL #7, but the balloon burst during ascent and tangled with the parachute. With

the parachute fouled the capsule plummeted to the ground. All four animal passengers died on impact.

During early 1952 the New York University Engineering Department received contract AF 33 (038) 23684 for a capsule capable of sustaining two 15-pound dogs at 90,000 feet for 24 hours. NYU provided three capsules under the terms of the contract. The finished capsules were 28-inch diameter aluminum spheres. Each capsule split into two halves that were sealed by 24 nuts and bolts. On July 16, 1952, the NYU capsule flew for the first time with two dogs. It reached 92,000 feet, but the capsule lost pressure at its peak altitude and the animals died.

On the next flight with the NYU capsule (AMFL #22, on March 18, 1953) the balloon failed at 34,000 feet, and searchers didn't reach the capsule until the next afternoon. They discovered the lines between the externally mounted oxygen bottles and the capsule were broken and both dogs were dead. Prior to the flight, the payload was predicted to weigh 120 pounds. After inflation, this was discovered to be 43 pounds too low, so additional helium had to be added to the balloon. Apparently, the extra handling involved in adding more helium contributed to its failure early in the flight. The oxygen lines broke when the capsule landed on rough terrain in the Sacramento Mountains.

In addition to the AMFL flights, six flights from the Air Force's *Moby Dick* project carried hermetically sealed test tubes of fruit flies provided by the AMFL. Each balloon carried 600 insects. The flights took place between 19 and 26 February 1953, and were launched from Vernalis, California. Of the six one was lost, another failed four hours after launch, and all the fruit flies died on three of the flights. AMFL researchers received live insects from only the third mission. Of the 600 launched, only 12 survived. These were immediately mated, and produced 469 offspring. There were no noticeable radiation-induced mutations among the offspring. Air Force flight crews were particularly interested in this experiment, because as operational aircraft began flying higher and higher, pilots became concerned about the effects of cosmic radiation on their reproductive systems.

When the Holloman Air Development Center became an independent Air Force Research and Development Command center on October 10, 1952, the AMFL came under their jurisdiction. In January 1953 the Air Force expanded Holloman's mission to include biological and medical research. Major David G. Simons, the physician who assisted Dr. Henry with the first two Albert flights, moved to Holloman and temporarily assumed command of the AMFL, because Telfer was due to leave the Air Force in March. Simons personally took charge of the cosmic radiation balloon flights as part of project RDO R 970-001, Biophysics of Cosmic Radiation.

A native of Lancaster, Pennsylvania, Simons came from a family of physicians, and it was taken for granted that he would follow in the family tradition. His father, Sam, and uncles Ike and John, all of them doctors, ran the Simons Medical Clinic on Duke Street in Lancaster. His brother Will (a dentist) also practiced at the clinic. Major Simons graduated from Franklin and Marshall College in Lancaster, Jefferson Medical College in Philadelphia, and performed a 15-month rotating internship at Lancaster General Hospital. His father had also attended the Jefferson Medical College, and it was generally accepted that David G. Simons, M.D., would join the family clinic.

However, Simons received support for his education through the Army Specialist Training Program, and had a two-year service obligation when he finished his internship. As a youth, he spent a great deal of time with Hiram Walker, a part-time student at Franklin and Marshall College who worked as a medical technician at his family's clinic. Walker was a licensed ham radio operator who instilled a fascination for radio and electronics in the young Simons.

When Simons attended Franklin and Marshall College he was a private in the Army. Despite his heavy course load, he still took time to learn Morse code with an eye towards earning a radio operators' license. At the time, though, use of amateur radios was banned due to the war. Later, Simons secured permission to set up a radio station at Lancaster Hospital. He also studied astronomy in his off-duty hours.

When he entered the Army Air Force on August 17, 1947, Simons asked for an assignment that combined his medical training with his interest in electronics. This led to his being assigned to the Aero Medical Laboratory at Wright Field, and his work with Dr. Henry. Simons found his true interests were in medical research. He subsequently attended the Air Force Advanced Course in Aviation Medicine, and became a certified flight surgeon. Following a tour of duty in Japan during the Korean War as Base Surgeon at Yakota Air Force Base, he briefly returned to the Aero Medical Laboratory before being assigned to Holloman.

One of Simons' first acts when he arrived at the AMFL was to change its name to the "Space Biology Field Laboratory." He felt this reflected the nature of the experimental program then underway, because it would lead to eventual space flight. At that time, however, the term "space" was generally subject to ridicule, because it conjured up images of Buck Rogers and other science fiction cartoons.

Colonel John Paul Stapp, M.D., Ph.D. Stapp took charge of the Aeromedical Field Laboratory in 1953. *Source: United States Air Force photograph courtesy of Dr. John Paul Stapp.*

Three months after Simons' arrival, Lieutenant Colonel John Paul Stapp, M.D., Ph. D., arrived to take command of the laboratory. Born in Bahia, Brazil, to Baptist Missionary parents, Stapp was a medical doctor with a Doctorate in Biophysics. The oldest of four sons of the Reverend Charles F. and Louise Shannon Stapp, he was taught at home by tutors until 1922, and was only permitted to speak Portuguese. His father was president of the American Baptist College in Bahia. The Stapp family lived in a supposedly haunted castle that also housed the college. At night, you could hear all sorts of strange noises coming from the attic portions of the castle, hence the legends of ghosts.

As it turned out, the "ghosts" were drunken opossums. There was a rum factory next door, and the opossums were sampling the mash, getting drunk, then running over to the castle. Drunken opossums appalled the Reverend Stapp, but his son was intrigued by them and studied their behavior. He also began spending time with the mission doctor. The Reverend did not approve of his eldest son's growing scientific interest, and forbade the doctor from showing John Paul his medical books. Instead, young Stapp was given religious books, which he later recalled "frightened the hell out of me. Sometimes I wondered if Methodists ever got to Heaven."

When he was 13 John Paul went to live with relatives in Texas, and entered the San Marcos Baptist Academy. Slightly built, nearsighted, and bookish, young Stapp described the San Marcos Academy as a place for "displaced hellions" who delighted in tormenting him. He did not let their taunts get to him. For example, each day the students had to practice close order drill with heavy Springfield rifles. If a student made a mistake during the drill, he had to proceed to the back of the formation by way of "the gauntlet," where the other students removed their belts and whipped him while he made his way past them. Rather than run through like other students, Stapp decided to proclaim his disdain for the practice by walking and showing no reaction to the whippings. Seeing their efforts had no apparent effect on him, the other students soon stopped the practice whenever he had to go through "the gauntlet." He also joined the school band and played the bassoon.

After graduation from San Marcos he enrolled in Baylor University in Waco, Texas, where he earned Bachelors' and Masters' degrees in Zoology and Chemistry. Stapp worked his way through college as a field collector for a biological supply company. "I was always turning over rocks for scorpions, and the sight of a snake gladdened my heart," as he later recalled. In 1934 he entered the University of Texas in Austin, where he received a Doctorate in Biophysics. However, his goal was to become a physician.

While he was in his sophomore year at Baylor, Stapp visited an aunt in Burnett, Texas, during the Christmas holiday. One night, his two-year old cousin crawled too close to an open fireplace and the toddler's clothes caught fire. Stapp nursed his severely burned cousin for 62 hours before the child died. "I decided right then that I wanted to be a doctor," Stapp later said. He entered the University of Minnesota Medical School in 1939, and received his M.D. five years later.

He entered the armed services in 1944, and was assigned to the Air Corps as a Flight Surgeon. During the period of demobilization at the end of World War II, he found himself at an out-processing center in Arizona. One day he had to examine the ears, eyes, noses, and throats of 600 airmen who were being discharged. Stapp described this as "a nightmare relieved only by the thought that I might have been a proctologist."

Stapp's research career with the Air Force began shortly after the end of the war, when he worked on liquid oxygen breathing systems for high altitude use at the Aero Medical Laboratory. Stapp also worked on aircraft ejection seats at Wright Field. The first generation of ejection seats frequently caused spinal compression injuries, so Stapp had plenty of work to do. While working with ejection seats, he became interested in the effects of acceleration on the human body. Traditional wisdom held that the human body could not tolerate more than 18 g's. Stapp was convinced a person could withstand a much higher acceleration, and he set out to prove he was right.

Stapp soon found he enjoyed the company of military research scientists, who were traditionally snubbed by their civilian counterparts. At a meeting of the National Academy of Sciences, he observed that the "mental Cadillac fleet" treated military scientists "like debris." This treatment enraged him so much that when his military service obligation neared its end Stapp opted to remain with the Air Force.

In 1947 he moved to Muroc Army Air Base (which became Edwards Air Force Base in January 1950), where he used their 2,000-foot rocket sled track to investigate human tolerance to acceleration and deceleration. Frequently he was his own test subject, riding a rocket sled he named the "Gee-Whizz." Operating on a meager budget (at best) with only seven contractor personnel from Northrop Aircraft, Colonel Stapp had to find innovative ways to procure supplies for his laboratory. In the late 1940s Muroc was an isolated installation, and medical care for civilian workers and their families was almost nonexistent. Stapp spent his evenings caring for them free of charge. His "curbside clinic" let him achieve results that otherwise would have been beyond his means, for the contractors were so grateful for his kindness they helped him any way they could. Frequently, needed supplies or materials mysteriously appeared on his doorstep.

Officially Stapp was under the authority of Wright Field, a situation he used to his advantage. Some of his experiments were rather risky. By the time his superiors in Ohio found out what he was up to, the experiment was over. If the hierarchy at Muroc tried to interfere, he could rightly respond that he was not under their jurisdiction. Stapp sustained numerous injuries, including a broken wrist, cracked ribs, retinal hemorrhages, sprains, and lost dental fillings as he probed the limits of man's endurance to sudden deceleration in the desert of southern California. By the time he returned to the Aero Medical Laboratory in Ohio to become a Section Chief he had established that humans could tolerate far more than the generally accepted limit of 18 g's—he and other volunteers who rode the Gee Whizz had experienced accelerations of 35 g's.

One of Stapp's first actions upon his arrival at Holloman was to restore the Aeromedical Field Laboratory name to the operation. He felt this more accurately reflected the breadth of research program he had in mind for the nascent laboratory. Of course, he

wanted to continue his research in the biodynamics of acceleration and deceleration. Stapp welcomed the assignment as head of the AMFL because Holloman had a larger, better equipped test track than the one at Edwards. It was originally built to test the launch system for the *Snark* cruise missile, and was 3,500 feet long. Besides his interest in working with deceleration, Stapp also had an interest in stratospheric balloon flights. While at the Aero Medical Laboratory, he proposed a manned balloon ascent to 100,000 feet.

Lieutenant Edward G. Sperry picked up on the idea, and issued a formal Request for Proposal (RFP). Otto Winzen responded on October 13, 1952, with a proposal based largely on his earlier *Helios* work. One of the interesting features of the RFP is that it specified the vehicle had to be capable of landing safely in a wind of 20 feet per second at a site that was 4,000 feet above sea level, which is the elevation of Holloman Air Force Base.

Winzen proposed to use the *Helios* shell, which was on exhibit at the Naval Air Station in Lakehurst, New Jersey. He calculated that fifteen *Skyhook* balloons would lift two pilots in the capsule to 95,000 feet. If a cluster of larger (90-foot) diameter balloons like those used for the *Gopher* project were employed, an altitude of 100,000 feet was expected. Two months later, Winzen submitted a nearly identical proposal to Commander Hoover at the ONR. Again, he suggested using the *Helios* shell. Neither service acted on Winzen's proposals at that time.

With Stapp's arrival, Major Simons became chief of the Space Biology Branch of the AMFL, and he took personal charge of the cosmic radiation research effort. He soon discovered that there were still many technical challenges to be overcome before his research could proceed smoothly. In fact, the first animal flight after Simons' arrival (AMFL Flight #20) showed many things could go wrong on a balloon mission. Seven hamsters were loaded into the capsule and launched at 7:30 AM from Holloman on February 12, 1953, for a planned 24-hour flight.

Two hours after launch the tracking aircraft, a converted B-17 bomber, took off and located the balloon 130 miles east of Holloman. The balloon was heading east with a ground speed of 80 miles per hour. By noon the aerostat reached its peak altitude of 96,500 feet.

The B-17 returned to Holloman to pick up the recovery crew around 3:30 that afternoon. It took them nearly six hours to locate the balloon, which was then 90 miles east of Memphis. Throughout the night the B-17 crew tried to track the balloon. This proved difficult, because the radio beacon attached to the payload package was malfunctioning. Shortly before dawn they followed the radio compass towards the Gulf of Mexico. Upon reaching Florida, the pilots had to turn either east or west. They chose west. Although the radio compass directed them straight ahead, the signal grew weaker. Finally, at 7:35 in the morning, they heard the cut-down signal. Apparently, the steady tone they had been following was not from the balloon, and they had been heading away from the balloon. Realizing the balloon would land before they reached the impact area, which very well could be in the Gulf of Mexico, the aircraft returned to Holloman without a search.

As luck would have it, the balloon landed 5 miles from the Whiting Naval Air Station in Milton, Florida. The Florida base sent a teletype message to Holloman asking what they should do with the capsule. For some reason, the message languished in the Holloman Headquarters building where it was received. Six days later, the message finally made its way across Holloman from the Headquarters building to the AMFL. Simons hurriedly called Florida, telling them to open the capsule and check the hamsters. Miraculously all were alive. At first, they were somnolent, but within a few minutes they awakened and appeared normal.

An AMFL representative reached Florida the next day, and discovered one of the seven hamsters had died during the night. Then, in accordance with instructions from the principle investigator, Dr. Berry Campbell of the University of Minnesota, three were immediately decapitated, and their heads preserved in formaldehyde. The remaining three survivors were caged and shipped back to the AMFL. Enroute one died, and was cannibalized by the others. The night after arrival one of the remaining two died, leaving only one to be returned to Dr. Campbell. Unfortunately it died during shipment.

The series of problems encountered during this flight demonstrated the need for improvements in balloon techniques. Simons also reviewed the scientific return from the successful flights so far, and found that most of the animals flown from Holloman had not received any significant exposures to primary cosmic radiation. Only near the geomagnetic poles, where the Earth's magnetic field converges, do charged particles penetrate low enough for study using balloons. To improve the scientific return from the flights, Simons decided to move the biological payload flights north, where they would receive the desired cosmic radiation exposure.

The first round of northern flights, during June and July 1953, originated from Great Falls Air Base in Montana. AMFL #29, the first flight from Great Falls, landed in Canada. It carried a cat, six hamsters, and 1,000 fruit flies in one of the University of Minnesota capsules on a 20-hour flight. The recovery team reached it within three hours of landing, and all the animals were alive. Unfortunately the cat died within two hours, presumably from the combined effects of excessive anesthesia, rapid pressure change when the capsule was opened, and sudden chilling when it was removed from the gondola. A cosmic ray track plate had been placed above the cat's head to record heavy primary hits and correlate their locations to any observed tissue effects. Despite the loss of the cat, the other animals had been recovered alive, which was good news.

Encouraged by the successful recovery of AMFL #29, Simons placed the hamsters and half the fruit flies aboard the next balloon. He wanted to re-fly animals on consecutive flights to have them accumulate at least 50 hours of exposure time at 90,000 feet. AMFL #30 carried another cat and 10 mice, along with the six hamsters and fruit flies from the previous flight. This time the cat survived, but the hamsters and mice did not. Simons tried again on 20 July, but AMFL #31 was lost over British Columbia and was never recovered. Flight #32 was also lost.

Major Simons returned to Holloman for the next flight, a test of the NYU capsule with two dogs aboard. Because of their anatomy, dachshunds were the preferred species for the dog flights.

The balloon spent 10 hours above 85,000 feet, but the flight ended early due to poor performance. The airplane that was supposed to monitor the capsule's descent developed mechanical problems and had to land shortly after becoming airborne. Because of this, searchers had only an approximate idea of the capsule's landing point. A visual search the next day did not locate the capsule. It was finally found about a week later, just outside the search area.

In late October flights shifted to Pierre, South Dakota. On 26 October a crew from General Mills launched an 85-foot diameter *Skyhook* balloon carrying a University of Minnesota animal capsule. This flight was the first to test an innovative way of cooling the capsule. Technicians at Holloman's Standards Laboratory came up with a water core cooling system. It relied on the known physical principle that as altitude increases, the boiling point of water decreases due to reduced atmospheric pressure. For example, at 90,000 feet water boils at 60° F; at 112,000 feet, the boiling point is only 32° F. The capsule carried a container filled with 2,000 cc of water that was vented to the outside environment. As air circulated around the container, it warmed the water until it reached its boiling temperature. The steam carried away excess cabin heat and cooled the gondola.

After floating for 28 hours and 30 minutes above 90,000 feet, the flight was terminated by ground command. The balloon separated cleanly, and the parachute inflated normally—for about a minute. Then the parachute collapsed into a "streamer," and the capsule plunged to the ground. The crash landing did not affect the overall outcome of the flight, because examination of the wreckage revealed the capsule had depressurized at or near maximum altitude anyway.

There were four more flights from Pierre during November, all of them launched by General Mills personnel. Various problems plagued these flights. On one, some of the animals died from overheating. Those that survived were flown again, but some of these died from pressure changes between the capsule and the outside atmosphere after recovery (AMFL flights 37 and 38). On flight #36 the balloon failed at 30,000 feet, and about half the animals in the capsule survived the landing. In only one flight (AMFL #35), did all the animals survive, but that was because the balloon only reached 2,000 feet.

Of the first 39 Aeromedical Field Laboratory balloon flights, which covered the period through the end of 1953, 26 had live payloads. Only 10 were completely or partially successful. On several flights some of the animals died from hypothermia. Other times, the capsule pressurization system failed. A majority failed due to flight related problems. Most frequently, the capsules were simply not recovered, or were not found until weeks or months after the flight. Three flights, which were categorized as failures, ended early when the balloons burst. In these instances the animals were recovered alive, but did not reach high enough altitudes to receive any significant cosmic radiation exposure. The NYU capsule seemed particularly trouble-prone. Out of half a dozen flights using their capsules none of the test animals survived. Either the capsule failed, or something else went wrong. Even so, it was not a complete failure, because experience using it led to changes in other capsules.

Aeromedical Field Laboratory Space Biology Flights,
1951 - 1953

AMFL Number	Date Launched	Altitude, Feet	Payload
1	8/16/51	97,000	Dummy load test
2	8/23/51	59,400	Animal Capsule w/Hamsters
3	9/5/51	97,000	Animal Capsule w/Hamsters
4	9/7/51	94,000	Animal Capsule w/Hamsters
5	9/18/51	n.a.	Cosmic Ray Film Plates (balloon destroyed at launch)
5	9/19/51	54,000	Cosmic Ray Film Plates
6	11/28/51	n.a.	Cosmic Ray Film Plates (balloon destroyed at launch)
6	11/30/51	86,400	Cosmic Ray Film Plates
7	2/20/52	103,600	Animal Capsule w/Cat, 3 Hamsters, Cosmic Ray Film Plates
8	2/27/52	54,000	Animal Capsule w/Cat, 3 Hamsters
9	3/18/52	92,000	Cosmic Ray Film Plates
10	4/8/52	72,000	Cosmic Ray Film Plates
12C	4/15/52	96,000	Cosmic Ray Film Plates
13	4/24/52	87,000	Animal Capsule
14	5/15/52	87,200	Box w/Fruit Flies
15	6/10/52	94,000	Tandem Balloon Test
16	7/10/52	100,000	Cosmic Ray Film Plates
17	7/15/52	n.a.	Cosmic Ray Film Plates (balloon destroyed at launch)
18	7/16/52	92,000	Animal Capsule w/2 Dogs, Cosmic Ray Film Plates
19	7/18/52	95,700	Cosmic Ray Film Plates
20	2/12/53	96,500	Animal Capsule w/7 Hamsters
n.a.	2/19/53		Moby Dick Balloon w/Fruit Flies
n.a.	2/20/53		Moby Dick Balloon w/Fruit Flies
n.a.	2/22/53		Moby Dick Balloon w/Fruit Flies
n.a.	2/25/53		Moby Dick Balloon w/Fruit Flies
n.a.	2/26/53		Moby Dick Balloon w/Fruit Flies
21	3/12/53	84,000	30 Mice, 6 Hamsters, 500 Fruit Flies, Cosmic Ray Film Plates in Albert Capsule
22	3/18/53	34,000	Animal Capsule w/2 Dogs
23	3/20/53		Test of Command Separation System
24	3/26/53		Test of Command Separation System
25	4/12/53	unknown	Animal Capsule w/Fruit Flies, Black Mice, Hamsters, and Cosmic Ray Film Plates
26	4/14/53	90,000	Cosmic Ray Film Plates
27	4/24/53	85,000	Animal Capsule w/2 Dogs
28	5/5/53	86,500	Animal Capsule w/Hamsters, Mice, Cosmic Ray Film Plates
29	6/19/53	87,000	Animal Capsule w/6 Hamsters, 1 Cat, 1,000 Fruit Flies, Onions, Cosmic Ray Film Plates
30	6/23/53	110,000	Animal Capsule w/6 Hamsters, 1 Cat, 10 Mice,1,000 Fruit Flies, Onions, Cosmic Ray Film Plates
31	7/20/53	85,000	Animal Capsule w/1 Cat, Mice, Hamsters, Fruit Flies, Cosmic Ray Film Plates
32	7/24/53	56,000	Animal Capsule w/1 Cat, Mice Hamsters, Fruit Flies, Onions, Cosmic Ray Film Plates
33	9/21/53	85,000	Animal Capsule w/2 Dogs, Cosmic Ray Film Plates
34	10/26/53	90,000	Animal Capsule w/Hamsters, Mice, Fruit Flies, Cosmic Ray Film Plates
35	11/1/53	2,000	Animal Capsule
36	11/3/53	30,000	Animal Capsule w/Hamsters, Mice, Fruit Flies
37	11/10/53	90,000	Animal Capsule w/33 Mice, Hamsters, Onions, Cosmic Ray Film Plates
38	11/13/53	91,000	Animal Capsule w/36 Mice, 14 Hamsters, 500 Fruit Flies, Onions, Cosmic Ray Film Plates
39	11/16/53	88,000	Animal Capsule w/Botanical Specimens, Cosmic Ray Film Plates

Besides live animals, several capsules carried other biological experiments. These included fruit flies and onion cells. Dr. Jakob A. G. Eugster of Berne, Switzerland, provided one of the more unusual experiments. He sent Simons excised pieces of animal and human skin (his own), which he grafted back in their donors after being flown to high altitudes.

Despite the numerous problems encountered during the first two years of AMFL balloon flights, progress was being made. One of the most important innovations was the development of a capsule cutaway system that could be controlled by ground command. Relying on an on-board timer to release the payload meant it sometimes occurred when the balloon was over rough terrain or bad weather, which usually resulted in the loss of the capsule. With the radio-controlled system, ground controllers could terminate the flight if it looked like the balloon was headed for trouble.

In the first half of 1954, the AMFL conducted a series of flights to test improvements to the balloons and capsules. General Mills conducted these flights for the AMFL. This would be the last time General Mills won a contract for AMFL space biology flights. Results from these flights were favorable, so Simons proceeded with a series of eight flights from the airport at Sault Sainte Marie, Michigan, during the summer. Winzen Research received contract AF 33(616)-2427 to conduct the flights.

Sault Sainte Marie was a good choice for balloon operations. It was far enough north that biological specimens would be exposed to primary cosmic radiation particles. The airport had no commercial traffic and very little private flying. It did, however, have a Civil Aeronautics Agency communications station and a U.S. Weather Bureau station. Winzen arranged with the Sault Sainte Marie City Manager to use the airport. Arrangements included renting hangar space at the airport, and the use of power, water, and a telephone. Military and civilian personnel stayed in a nearby motel.

Winzen provided ten balloons under the contract. They tested the radio beacon with a five-year old 73-foot diameter *Skyhook* balloon on 25 May from their plant at Fleming Field, South Saint Paul, Minnesota. On 7 July 7 they tested the biological capsule system with a 120.8-foot diameter, 1.5-mil balloon with another flight from Fleming Field. Following this flight, Winzen set up operations at Sault Sainte Marie.

The Winzen crew of 7 men arrived on 12 July. They brought a radio truck, two helium trailers, a mobile launch platform, and a 1-1/2 ton stake truck, all of which were on loan from the Navy. Winzen also outfitted a civilian *Navion* airplane as a tracking aircraft. The Air Force provided a C-47 *Skytrain* for tracking. Preparations for the first flight of the series (AMFL #46) began on the night of 14 July, and the balloon was released the following morning. The next flight was three days later. After that, flights occurred every 4 days until the last one of the series (AMFL #53) on 10 August.

This round of flights included several new lines of research. Dr. Herman B. Chase of Brown University flew black mice to evaluate changes in hair pigmentation and hair loss as indicators of cosmic radiation effects. When a radiation particle hits a hair follicle it destroys the pigmentation, and subsequent hairs grow in either gray or white. He could check for radiation damage to their skin by using hair changes as indicators of where to look. Several researchers conducted microscopic examinations of tissue samples from mice and rats. They were looking for signs of radiation damage, particularly on the nervous system. Air Force researchers Drs. Paul Cibis and Hubertus Strughold studied the eyes of mice for radiation-induced opacities. Other studies included flying mice selected and bred for sensitivity to radiation-induced leukemia, and observing other strains of mice to see if cosmic ray exposure affected their longevity or breeding.

Four of the flights carried cynamolgous (or Java) monkeys. They were observed for changes in performance on simple tasks

Major David G. Simons, M. D. (wearing civilian clothes), prepares an animal capsule for flight. This particular flight took off from the airport at International Falls on August 31, 1955, and carried 107 mice and 3 guinea pigs to an altitude of 119,000 feet. *Source: Winzen Research, Inc. photograph*

and overall behavior. Dr. Harry Harlowe of the University of Minnesota conducted these studies. On the first two flights with primates (AMFL flights 46 and 47) the monkeys did not survive. The pair flown on flight #50 not only survived, but they flew again on the next mission. Many of the flights carried animals that had previously flown. The capsules also carried radish seeds, *neurospora* mold spores, fertilized hen's eggs, and cosmic radiation track plates.

Out of the eight biological flights in the summer 1954 series, seven returned good results. One balloon failed during inflation. Another failed at 40,000 feet in the jet stream. All the payloads were recovered, which was a marked improvement over earlier series of flights. In fact, although some of the flights landed in difficult terrain, all but one was recovered within a few hours after landing.

The next round of flights (AMFL #54-60) took off from Holloman. They carried guinea pigs, mice, tissue samples, and *Artemia* (shrimp) eggs. Simons returned to Fleming Field and International Falls, Minnesota, for the next 11-flight series, which went from July 18 through September 20, 1955. These flights carried the same variety of payloads as the recently completed Holloman series. There was one milestone reached with the first flight of the series, AMFL #61, which was launched from Fleming Field.

Over the years polyethylene balloons had grown larger. On July 18, 1955, a two-million cubic foot balloon was used for a biological flight for the first time. It carried a relatively light payload—tissue samples, *Artemia* eggs, and *neurospora* samples—so it reached an altitude of 115,500 feet. The next day, a similar balloon and payload combination reached 120,000 feet.

Beginning 1 August, for the next month flights shifted to International Falls, Minnesota, near the Canadian border (AMFL flights #63-69.) In an unusual move, flight #67, launched on 22 August, carried two capsules. One capsule housed 93 mice for longevity studies; the other one contained 93 mice for neurocytology studies—that is, their brains would be examined for signs of tissue damage from cosmic radiation particles. The capsules remained aloft for 26 hours, and reached a peak altitude of 109,000 feet.

At the time the capsules separated from the balloon, Simons and Dr. Webb Haymaker of the Armed Forces Institute of Pathology (AFIP) were in North Dakota, about ten miles from the Montana border, watching the balloon. They had been chasing the balloon all day across North Dakota in a radio truck loaned by the Navy, accompanied by Lieutenant Irwin Lebish, Dr. Walter Hild, and a pair of drivers (Bob Clark and Chief Serley). Lebish was a veterinarian from AFIP; Hild was from the University of Texas School of Medicine. Using binoculars, Simons saw the capsule fall away. The parachute did not open at first. Everyone held their breath until Simons reported the parachute was open; he estimated the capsule had fallen 25,000 feet.

The crews aboard the *Navion* chartered by WRI and the AMFL C-47 searched for the parachute, but didn't see it land. They began combing the area while the crew in the truck pulled into Garrison, North Dakota, for a meal. Pulling up to a bar on the edge of town, everyone in the truck ordered hamburgers and coffee except for Simons, who ordered soup. Their food had just arrived when a

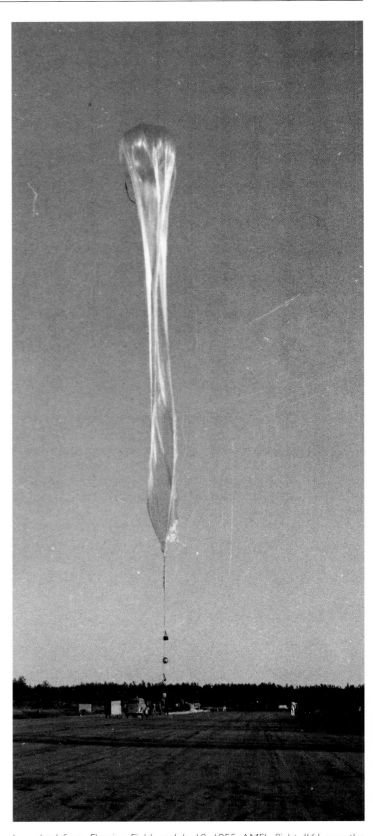

Launched from Fleming Field on July 18, 1955, AMFL flight #61 was the first to use a 2-million cubic foot balloon. *Source: Winzen Research, Inc. photograph*

The payload for AMFL flight #61 included tissue samples, *Artemia* eggs, and *Neurospora* mold cultures. This view of the capsule before it was sealed shows the 134 bolts used to secure the halves together. *Source: Winzen Research, Inc. photograph*

View from the stratosphere. AMFL flight #63 carried a downward-looking camera. It was the first flight launched from International Falls, Minnesota, and reached 117,000 feet. *Source: Winzen Research, Inc. photograph*

Biological capsule for AMFL flight #63. This flight carried 91 mice, Artemia eggs, and Neurospora samples to 117,000 feet. Sixty-five mice survived the flight. *Source: Winzen Research, Inc. photograph*

AMFL flight #68 lifted off on August 31, 1955. This was a 2-million cubic foot capacity balloon. The balloon train comprises (from the top down): the cutaway controls; 20-foot diameter recovery parachute; rectangular radio beacon housing; spherical capsule; and the ballast container. *Source: Winzen Research, Inc. photograph*

The United States Navy had a truck outfitted with special radio equipment for tracking high altitude balloons. Navy officials allowed Winzen Research to use the truck to track Air Force biomedical research flights. *Source: Winzen Research, Inc. photograph*

call came over the radio announcing the C-47 crew had spotted the parachute on the ground. Simons had to leave his soup behind while everyone else grabbed their hamburgers and rushed to the truck.

Two hours after the cutdown, the recovery crew was advised Mrs. Jan Cammermyer found the capsules on her farm, one mile west of Alexander, North Dakota. They were about twenty miles away, and the capsules had an estimated thirty minutes of oxygen remaining. Following directions to the farm, they soon came upon a line of cars along an otherwise empty country road. Rushing to the first capsule, they began removing the 134 bolts that sealed its halves together. Lifting the upper half off, they discovered ninety of the ninety-three mice were alive. When the insulating jacket of the second capsule was removed, the metal sphere felt icy cold. None of the mice in capsule #2 survived. This capsule also carried 40 tissue cultures that were ruined. With help from some local residents they loaded the capsules, parachute, and animals in the back of the radio truck.

At ten o'clock the six men pulled into Alexander. Tired and hungry, they found an open restaurant where they all ordered steaks. Lebish surprised everyone when he walked over to the piano and began playing various jazz and blues songs. Prior to entering the military, Lebish had been a professional jazz pianist in New York. An hour and a half later they left the restaurant, only to discover the truck had a flat tire. Their destination was Minot, which was about 150 miles away. The group finally set out after midnight, totally exhausted. Clark and Serley, the drivers, were so fatigued that Dr. Haymaker had to drive the truck. Slowed by a heavy thunderstorm that made the roads slick and treacherous, Haymaker finally reached Minot as the sun was rising.

A week later Simons and the other scientists prepared two balloons for launch. The first was a 26-hour flight carrying 107 mice and 3 guinea pigs; the second carried ten mice, 1 guinea pig, and 8 tissue cultures for a planned ten-hour flight. The winds were marginal as AMFL #68, the 26-hour flight, was about to be launched. Then, just before release, Simons found a leak in the capsule. The balloon was held, buffeted by the rising wind, while a hasty re-

pair was performed. Ten minutes later Winzen ordered the balloon released. Free of its restraints, the balloon began "circling like a twister in a tornado" and "scooped her 'packages' off the ground," as later written by Dr. Haymaker. AMFL #68 reached 119,000 feet.

AMFL flight #68 landed in a swampy area near Pine Island, Minnesota. *Source: Winzen Research, Inc. photograph*

The Air Force dispatched a Sikorsky *R-5* helicopter to recover the animal capsule from AMFL flight #68. *Source: Winzen Research, Inc. photograph*

AMFL flight #68 caused what turned out to be a humorous incident. At 5:30 PM the FBI in Grafton, Minnesota, contacted the North American Air Defense Command to report an unidentified flying object. A farmer spotted the balloon, and reported a mysterious moving light in the sky to the local sheriff, who notified the FBI. The Air Force scrambled a flight of three *F-84* interceptors. The pilots spotted the object within five minutes and climbed to 40,000 feet, but the object remained out of reach.

August 1st was going to be a very busy day. Early in the morning AMFL #69 began its stratospheric sojourn. An hour later, the payload from AMFL #68 began its descent. Using a theodolite, the scientists watched the parachute bring the capsule back. Then, word reached them that it had landed in an impenetrable wooded bog twenty miles from Pine Island, Minnesota.

Major Simons took off in an *Aeronca* light plane to find the capsule. He landed in a patch of high grass about two miles away, and began hiking over the treacherous terrain. The pilot of another search plane described it as "underbrush so thick that even a jack rabbit would lose its way trying to get through." A helicopter dispatched from Diluth reached the site around noon. Simons had started a signal fire to mark his location, which was only 200 yards from the payload. One of the helicopter crewmembers, Lt. Flatter, was lowered on a cable from the Sikorsky *H-5*. He attached the cable to the capsule, which was hoisted into the helicopter. Twenty minutes later Dr. Haymaker and the capsule were dropped off at the landing strip of the game preserve on Pine Island, while the helicopter returned to pick up Simons and Flatter. (This was despite the fact that the helicopter's tail rotor had hit a tree during the recovery.) With help from the Game Warden, Haymaker opened the capsule. Sadly, none of the mice survived.

AMFL flight #70 landed ten miles northwest of Wilmar, Minnesota. The recovery team reached the capsule almost immediately. *Source: Winzen Research, Inc. photograph*

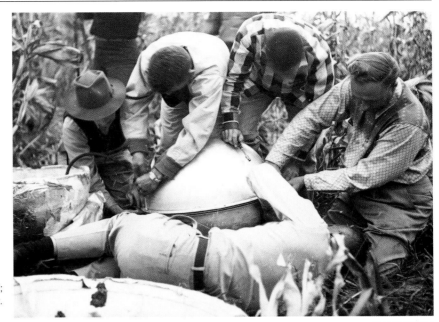

Opening the capsule. David Simons is laying on the ground; Otto Winzen is at the far right. *Source: Winzen Research, Inc. photograph*

The moment of truth—Major Simons lifts the upper half of the capsule as everyone watches. *Source: Winzen Research, Inc. photograph*

Otto Winzen checks one of the animals. All survived their trip to the stratosphere. *Source: Winzen Research, Inc. photograph*

Attention turned to AMFL #69, floating high overhead. On the ground, the crew in the radio truck received the cut down signal from the AMFL *C-47* that was tracking the balloon. Everyone rushed outside to see if they could spot the parachute. Through the theodolite, they saw the balloon with the capsule and electronics box still attached. They waited an hour—the payload remained aloft. Somehow, the cutdown mechanism had failed. Five days later, it was spotted over New Brunswick, headed over the Atlantic.

Two more flights (12 and 20 September) were launched from Fleming Field. These completed the 11-flight series conducted during the summer of 1955.

After dozens of balloon flights carrying biological specimens, the risks posed by cosmic radiation still were not totally clear. Earlier researchers like Dr. Hermann Schaefer of the U.S. Navy School of Aviation Medicine attempted to predict the degree of cosmic radiation exposure and its biological effects based on statistical analysis, and offered rather ominous predictions for prospective space travelers. The balloon flights thus far seemed to refute the dire predictions.

So far, the initial results from the balloon flights indicated their predictions had been overly pessimistic. Mice and guinea pigs showed some gray hairs from cosmic radiation. *Neurospora* and other non-mammal samples showed some effects that may have been linked to radiation exposure, but results from these experiments were inconclusive. The monkeys carried aboard flights 50 and 51 seemed fine. Overall, it seemed that relatively brief exposure to primary cosmic radiation did not pose as great a health threat as first feared, but there remained one more series of tests to see if this was true. A human pilot would have to make the trip.

6

Manned Stratospheric Ballooning Resumes

By mid-1955, it seemed to Colonel Stapp that the animal flights had returned as much data as they could, and it was time to progress to something else. In August, while Simons was conducting the latest series of animal flights, Stapp asked if he was ready to try a manned flight. Simons first answered that he hadn't given it a great deal of thought, but the data collected so far indicated it should not be dangerous from a radiation standpoint. Simons added he would have to do some calculations before he gave a definitive answer. His main concern was constructing a life support system that could sustain a human.

Life support capacity in the biological capsules was expressed in terms of the smallest animal flown, which was a mouse. A guinea pig was two "mouse units," a monkey nearly seven. Simons had already flown capsules with life support capacities of 200 "mouse units." As it turned out, a human worked out to about 500 mouse units, so they only had to increase the life support capacity by a factor of two and a half. Major Simons calculated building such a system would be a relatively straightforward task, so he told Stapp they could do it.

Advances in balloon design also gave Simons reason for optimism. Otto Winzen had recently developed a technique for sealing filaments of various materials into the seams between gores, eliminating the need for externally applied tape to bear the payload weight. Tape had never really adhered well to the polyethylene, so Winzen's innovation was a major breakthrough that increased balloon reliability and strength.

Increased reliability meant Simons was able to re-fly test animals on successive missions with a reasonable assurance of recovery. This increased the length of exposure to cosmic radiation, which increased the scientific return from the flights. Additionally, the recent introduction of 2-million cubic foot capacity balloons to the space biology program made it possible to loft a manned capsule high enough for exposure to primary cosmic radiation. Winzen believed it possible to build even larger balloons with capacities of up to 3-million cubic feet.

Stapp, Simons, and Winzen met to map out the basic design elements of the piloted capsule. As a starting point in their con-

siderations, they looked at cutting one of the spherical capsules in half, and inserting a six-foot cylinder between the hemispheres to create a capsule large enough to hold a human pilot. All three agreed a 24-hour flight above 100,000 feet was possible using a 3-million cubic foot balloon. At such an altitude the capsule would be above 99% of the atmosphere, and well within the realm of "space equivalence" as described by Dr. Hubertus Strughold. If the balloon flew from northern latitudes, the pilot would be exposed to multibillion-electron volt heavy nuclear particles.

Stapp forwarded the idea to the Air Research and Development Command (ARDC). At the end of August Colonel John Talbot, Chief of the Human Factors Division of the ARDC, gave tentative approval for the project. Initially it was described as the manned phase of AMFL Task 78500, "Radiation Hazards of Primary Cosmic Particles."

As the proposal moved further up the chain of command Simons had to change the project objective, since there was, by that time, a feeling that the investigation of cosmic radiation effects did not warrant the risk and expense of a manned program. Cosmic radiation investigation became a secondary goal, and Simons justified the work as contributing to the design of a manned space vehicle. With the change in focus, the project was approved under the auspices of AMFL Task 78516, "Environmental Control in Sealed Cabins." Both tasks, 78500 and 78516, were under the umbrella of Project 7851, "Human Factors of Space Flight."

Winzen Research received a contract for the design, fabrication, and maintenance of the balloon-capsule system on November 9, 1955. The initial estimate for the total project cost was $29,950.00. This may seem low by today's standards, but at that time each biological flight from Holloman cost between $5,000.00 and $10,000.00. In actuality the balloons were not overly profitable for WRI, and the company made most of its money from plastic bags and liners for boxes of milk.

General Mills unsuccessfully bid on the manned balloon contract, and protested its award to their rival Winzen. Holloman's Directorate of Procurement issued a letter to General Mills explaining the award was not meant to reflect any negative feelings about the firm's technical qualifications. Rather, it was a case of Winzen paying closer attention to technical details in their proposal, and having a better approach to the overall project.

Simons first proposed the name *Daedalus* for the project. It turned out this was already in use for a classified atomic-powered airplane project, so Simons had to find another name. He selected the more descriptive title *Man High*. (Eventually the two-word name for the project became *Manhigh*. This is how the project is described in subsequent flight reports, so this convention will be used throughout this book.) The original contract for *Manhigh* called for completion of the capsule by January 31, 1956. Flight testing was supposed to be finished by 15 March, followed by the piloted scientific mission. This schedule proved overly optimistic, particularly when the project suffered delays due to funding limitations. *Manhigh* ran out of money several times during its development. When that happened, Stapp took money from other AMFL projects to keep it going.

The *Manhigh* capsule was eight feet high, three feet in diameter, and had an internal volume of about 50 cubic feet. Made from aluminum, the capsule comprised three major sections: upper dome, turret, and lower shell. The upper dome was a hemisphere

spun from 0.032-inch thick 6061-T6 aluminum alloy. Fabricated from the same material as the upper dome, the lower shell comprised a 45-inch long cylinder attached to a hemispherical end. The upper hemisphere contained the "photo panel." This panel contained two altimeters; oxygen analyzer; voltmeters; an aircraft clock; and indicators for rate of climb, capsule temperature, and outside temperature. A 35-mm camera automatically photographed the panel at either one-minute or five-minute intervals.

The turret—a short cylindrical section eight inches tall—was cast from 220 aluminum alloy, and formed the main structural segment of the capsule. It supported most of the internal structure and equipment, including the seat, instrument panels, oxygen system, radios, and emergency equipment. Six portholes, including two the pilot could open, were built into the turret. There were six attachment points on the turret for the suspension of the capsule from the emergency parachute.

The capsule had two control panels attached to the internal frame. The left side panel contained controls and indicators for the oxygen system and cabin venting controls. The right hand panel contained electrical switches, indicators, and fuses for capsule operation. Most of the switches on that panel had special safety covers to prevent accidental operation.

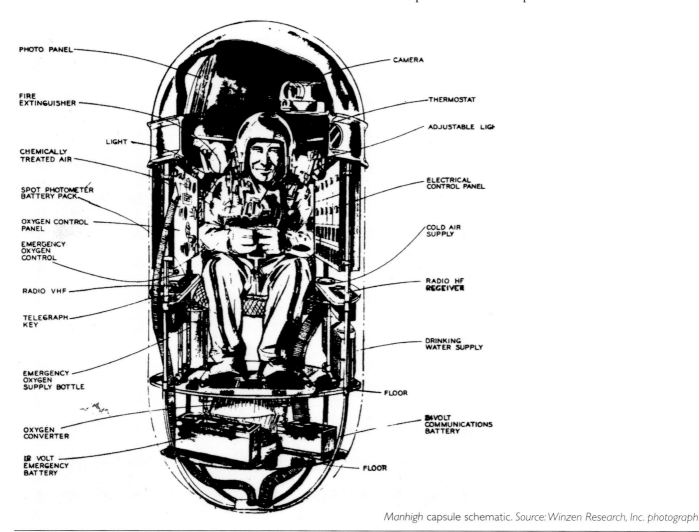

Manhigh capsule schematic. *Source: Winzen Research, Inc. photograph*

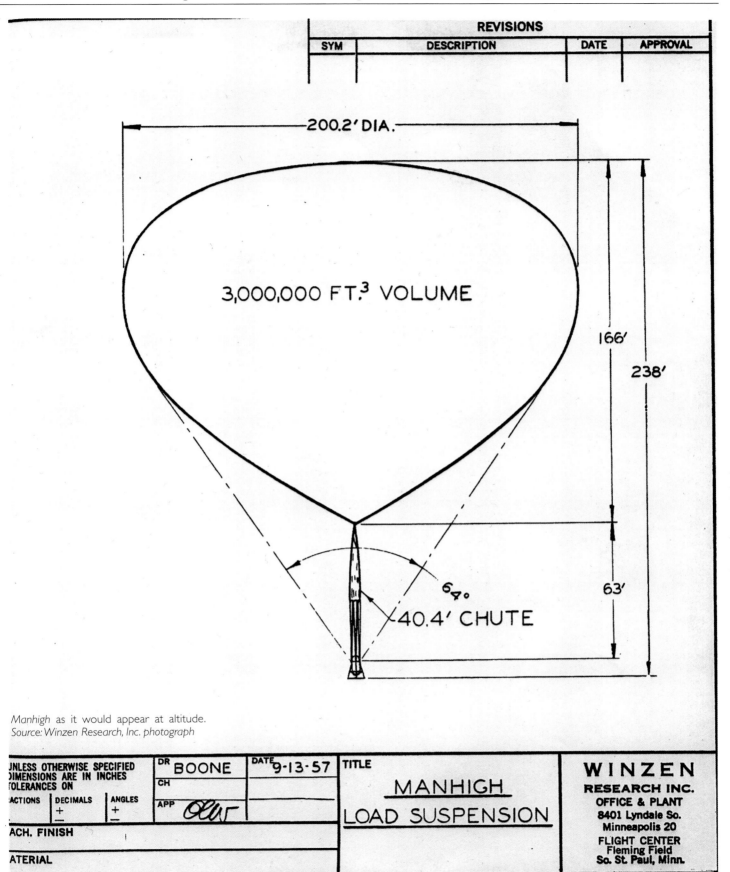

Manhigh as it would appear at altitude.
Source: Winzen Research, Inc. photograph

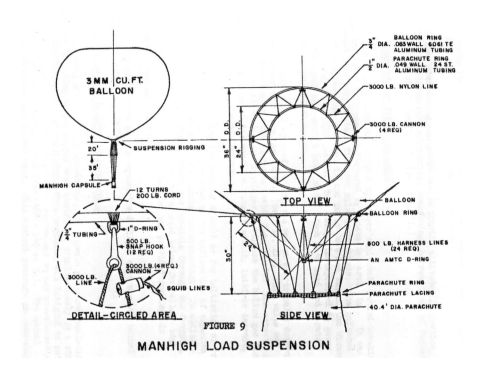

Load suspension system for *Manhigh* capsule. *Source: Manhigh III USAF Manned Balloon Flight Into the Stratosphere.*

Manhigh capsule photo panel. *Source: United States Air Force photograph*

Marman clamps secured the upper dome and lower shell to the turret. The pilot could release the clamps either manually or electrically. Releasing the upper clamp released the upper dome, and allowed the pilot to climb out of the capsule after landing. Releasing the lower clamp released the lower shell, permitting the pilot to bail out of the capsule in flight.

WRI performed several tests to verify the capsule's structural integrity. All welds were X-rayed and examined visually for any defects. Any areas of questionable soundness were routed out and re-welded. During the pressure test, Winzen engineers pressurized the capsule to 15 pounds per square inch (PSI) and verified it did not leak more than 1 PSI over a 24-hour period. The company even conducted flotation tests in the St. Croix River to make sure the pilot would survive landing in a body of water. However, the most extreme trial was the hydrostatic test, where the capsule was filled with 2,700 pounds of water, pressurized to 15 PSI, and suspended from the lugs on the turret. Such a weight subjected the suspension system to the equivalent of a 5-g load.

A tubular aluminum frame attached to the outside of the lower shell supported the capsule in an upright position before launch. Made from one-inch diameter tubing, this structure doubled as a shock absorbing system for landing. Lead acid aircraft batteries mounted on the external frame powered the capsule's systems. Equipped with individual parachutes, these batteries (which weighed 50 pounds each) could be dropped as ballast when expended.

For emergency use, there were two silver-cell batteries beneath the cabin floor. A 24-volt battery provided emergency power for the communications system, while a 12-volt one could power the rest of the capsule for up to six hours.

The black and white paint patterns on earlier stratospheric gondolas were adequate for passive temperature control only during daylight hours. Since *Manhigh* was intended to remain aloft for 24 hours, it needed an active thermal control system. Because the electronic equipment inside the cabin and the pilot himself produced heat, Winzen concluded no heating system was needed. Rather, the problem became one of trying to cool the capsule. Winzen adapted the water core cooling system used for the animal flights. As built for *Manhigh*, the cooling system could remove up to 1,600 BTUs from the cabin per hour. A 20 cubic foot per minute axial type blower circulated air through the cooler core. The major disadvantage of this system was that it only worked at high altitudes. To keep the cabin (and pilot) cool prior to launch and during the initial ascent, a cap of dry ice was placed on top of the upper dome. The blocks of dry ice, which measured 4 x 4 x 1 inch, were held in place with a nylon mesh harness.

The capsule exterior was clad with insulation made from alternating layers of honeycomb paper and aluminized Mylar. There were three layers of the paper, which was 1/2-inch thick, with one-inch honeycomb openings, and four layers of Mylar. Winzen Research developed this insulation to protect the pilot from excessive cooling during ascent and descent; searing solar radiation at altitude during daylight hours; and intense cold at night.

WRI selected Mylar after a series of tests of different materials. They considered aluminum foil coated foam, such as they used on the animal capsules, aluminum foil sandwiched between layers of polyethylene, and aluminized Mylar. A 2/3-size model of the capsule was built to test insulation materials. An electric heater provided a heat load proportional to that of a human pilot in the test capsule. Following a series of three ground tests between January 12 and 16, 1956, the capsule was flown on 9 February. The balloon train included an animal capsule suspended beneath the scale gondola for comparison purposes.

February 9th was the third attempt to launch the payload. During the first attempt, a battery froze in the -20° F temperatures, blocking the launch. On the second try, a strong temperature inversion close to the ground prevented the balloon from rising. The third attempt was successful despite severe weather conditions. At Fleming Field, where the flight began, it was -14° F, and there were high snow banks surrounding the launch site. Learning from the first attempt, which failed due to a frozen battery, WRI installed an electric iron inside the test capsule to keep it warm prior to launch, which occurred at 8:36 AM.

Throughout the day, temperature data from both the model gondola and animal capsule were telemetered to the ground. The 75-foot diameter *Skyhook* balloon made from 2-mil polyethylene reached 85,000 feet, just 400 feet short of its theoretical maximum. In general, the Mylar and corrugated paper insulation on the model worked as well as the 2-inch thick foam that covered the animal capsule. Data continued to come in through sunset and into the night. At 9:20 PM the cut-down signal was broadcast to the balloon. The payload, which was suspended from a 28-foot diameter parachute, apparently separated cleanly from the balloon, but it was never recovered. One interesting note is that the official Winzen flight report uses the name *Daedalus* for the project.

After careful experimentation, the scientists at the AMFL decided to use a three-gas atmosphere inside the capsule. The pilot breathed a mixture of oxygen, nitrogen, and helium. Pure oxygen was rejected because of the fire hazard it created. Simply pressurizing the capsule with a sea-level oxygen-nitrogen atmosphere was not an option either. Nitrogen comprises about two-thirds of the atmosphere at sea level. If there were a sudden decompression while the capsule was at high altitude, nitrogen dissolved in the pilot's blood stream would bubble out, causing the "bends." This extremely painful condition could cripple or kill the pilot.

Pre-breathing oxygen for at least an hour prior to exposure to low pressure will flush nitrogen from the bloodstream and prevent the bends. This would only work as long as the pilot remained in a pure oxygen environment which, as previously mentioned, was rejected due to the fire hazard it presented. Another inert gas was necessary in the cabin atmosphere to eliminate the risk of the bends and reduce the fire hazard. Helium proved to be that gas. A small percentage of nitrogen was left in the cabin atmosphere, but it was low enough to not present a risk in an emergency. Since both helium and nitrogen are inert the body does not consume them, and these gases did not need to be replenished during the flight.

The cabin atmosphere comprised 60% oxygen, 20% helium, and 20% nitrogen. A pressure equivalent to that of 26,000 feet was maintained inside the capsule during the flight thanks to the higher proportion of oxygen in the cabin atmosphere. Opting for the lower pressure than sea level saved weight in the overall capsule design. Because the differential between the cabin and outside pressures at 100,000 feet was not as great as it would have been if a sea level pressure were maintained, the capsule shell could be made from thinner (and lighter) material than would have otherwise been required.

A 5-liter capacity bottle carried enough liquid oxygen to last 48 hours. Actually, the theoretical capability of this supply for a pilot with an average metabolic rate and zero capsule leakage was more than 100 hours. The liquid oxygen bottle and converter (to vaporize the cryogenic fluid) were beneath the floor of the capsule. There was a 205 cubic inch emergency oxygen cylinder under the pilot's seat, and a 90 cubic inch bailout bottle attached to his parachute harness. The 205 cubic inch cylinder could only be utilized through the pressure suit, although exhausted oxygen from the suit could be dumped into the capsule. It provided enough oxygen for 45 minutes of pressure suit breathing; the bailout bottle would last about 20 minutes. However, if used in the cabin, the oxygen exhausted from the pressure suit by these two supplies would provide about seven and three hours of breathable oxygen, respectively. As an absolute last resort, should all the oxygen systems fail, the atmosphere inside the cabin would sustain the pilot for an hour.

An "air-regeneration unit" used three chemicals to remove carbon dioxide and water vapor from the cabin air. The unit comprised thirty nylon bags containing the chemicals arranged in a 12-inch diameter cylinder. Each bag contained all three chemicals. Air first passed through a layer of lithium chloride to remove moisture before it reached the middle layer of lithium hydroxide, which absorbed carbon dioxide. The final step in the process was to circulate the air through a layer of magnesium perchlorate to remove any remaining moisture. Each bag was 18 inches long and 2 inches in diameter. A 25 cubic foot per minute capacity fan drew air from the bottom of the capsule and forced it through the air regeneration unit. Both the cooling and air regeneration units were mounted outside the capsule, on the aluminum frame. Airtight ducts through the bottom hemisphere connected them to the cabin.

A single Firewel Number 1828 regulator controlled both pressure and oxygen content. Should the automatic system fail, the pilot had a manually operated valve that admitted a constant flow of oxygen to the cabin. The regulator automatically maintained any preselected pressure altitude between 12,000 and 40,000 feet. This was adjustable by means of a calibrated knob on the oxygen control panel. The pilot could direct oxygen to either the cabin atmosphere or his pressure suit. In case the cabin pressure rose above desired levels, the pilot could open a manually operated relief valve.

The pilot wore a standard Air Force MC-3 partial pressure suit in case of sudden pressure loss. Above 63,000 feet fluids in the tissues will vaporize. A person exposed to such conditions would swell and quickly suffer circulatory collapse. Partial pressure suits like the MC-3 used mechanical pressure to substitute for air pressure. Inflatable tubes, or capstans, ran along the length of the garment, from the wrists to the shoulders, then down the back to the ankles. The tubes were attached to the suit with interlacing strips of nylon. If the cabin pressure dropped below the equivalent of

43,000 feet, the capstans automatically inflated. When inflated, the tubes expanded against the strips and pulled the garment tight against the skin. An inflatable collar sealed the helmet against the neck to contain breathing oxygen. After a few hours, this collar generally started to chafe the wearer's neck, even if the suit was unpressurized. Gloves containing pressure bladders to keep the hands from swelling completed the ensemble. Although it was individually tailored, this garment was uncomfortable because it was so tight. It was also tailored so it was slightly too short from the crotch to the neck, which added to the discomfort.

Communications equipment included a VHF transceiver, an HF receiver for voice communications, and a telemetry transmitter. The VHF transceiver was the primary system for voice communications. If the voice system failed, the pilot could use the telemetry transmitter to communicate via Morse code. Normally, this transmitter broadcast biotelemetry data from the pilot, and also served as the locator beacon for tracking the balloon.

The pilot's seat received a great deal of attention. Initially, the design incorporated a winch system that let the pilot tilt the capsule to a horizontal position during flight so that he might sleep in a more normal position. This system proved too heavy for flight. It wasn't that the winch itself weighed too much; rather, the problem was the batteries needed to operate it. *Manhigh* would remain upright throughout the flight. This raised serious concerns about pilot comfort. After hours in the capsule seat, would the pilot become so uncomfortable that it would seriously erode his efficiency?

Even contour molded rubber cushions used for long-range aircraft produced "compression fatigue" after 3 1/2 to 4 hours. Something new would be needed, especially since only three pounds had been allocated for the total seat weight. (The contour rubber cushions weighed nearly that much by themselves.) Simons turned to the Wright Air Development Center (WADC) for help. First Lieutenant John H. Duddy of the Design Research Group, Crew Station Habitability Section at WADC, headed the seat development project. He began working on the seat in November 1955, ten days after WRI received the *Manhigh* contract.

Comfort was the major concern, but the seat also had to fit within the confines of a three-foot diameter capsule, and not interfere with the pilot's ability to reach the instrument and control panels. Duddy created a seat made from half-inch nylon mesh over a rigid frame that supported the pilot across the lower buttocks and thighs. His design proved very comfortable, and met the strict weight requirement for the seat. Using nylon mesh had the added benefit of allowing ventilation around the pilot's back. Simons tested the seat by remaining in it for 24 hours in the capsule shell during the mandated claustrophobia test.

In an effort to make the claustrophobia test as realistic as possible, Simons wore the MC-3 suit. The capsule was not pressurized, and he breathed normal air. WRI used a vacuum cleaner to exhaust air from the capsule. Fresh air entered through a three-inch opening in the shell. Simons kept the faceplate of his helmet open. He soon discovered the biggest problem during the test was heat. Temperatures inside the WRI plant, where the test took place, were a comfortable 75 degrees. It was 80° inside the capsule when it was sealed. Wearing the skin-tight nylon pressure suit inside the capsule, Simons felt miserable. Adding to his discomfort, he began feeling congested, so he used the Benzedrex inhaler he had with him. It didn't help much, and he soon had a headache on top of being too hot.

Simons felt perspiration trickling down his face, soaking the collar of the pressure garment. He had several articles and notes for two technical papers with him that he intended to finish, but soon found he was too uncomfortable to focus on them. The cabin temperature reached 86°, so Winzen personnel moved the capsule outside the plant and sprayed it with water from a garden hose. This brought the temperature down somewhat, but it was still too hot for Simons to focus on anything else. He quickly became irritable and resentful towards those conducting the test. The temperature didn't reach a tolerable level until after midnight.

Simons' discomfort did not stop when the capsule cooled. While he was in medical school, Simons had an operation on his left knee. His knee began to ache from the pressure suit. He flexed it, tried standing in the capsule, even tried kneeling in the mesh seat, but nothing helped. The ache continued throughout the night, "deep, incessant, like a toothache," as Simons later recalled.

He peered through the 5 1/2-inch portholes at the sky, looking for Mars. He focused on the capsule, and where equipment should be located. He tried concentrating on anything he could to take his mind off the aching knee. Finally, he managed to doze. After sunrise Simons felt renewed, and worked on the articles and technical reports. Otto Winzen placed some boards over the capsule to shield it from the sun.

Simons took one "No-doze" tablet to see how the stimulant affected him. He reported it made him "much more alert and more comfortable." The discomfort in his knee abated to the point where it was "just slightly annoying, but tolerable." Throughout the test, Simons consumed pemmican and diluted grape juice ("grape water" as he called it). Since earlier polar explorers had subsisted on pemmican for nourishment, he felt it was worth trying for *Manhigh*. "One Pemmican bar remained, but decided to eat more tasty candy bar," noted Simons in his post-test report. Whatever its virtues for consumption when exploring the earth's frigid polar regions, pemmican would definitely not be on the *Manhigh* menu. Finally the test ended, and Simons emerged from the capsule, confident he could complete the flight.

Three days later Otto Winzen spent an hour in the capsule to perform first-hand research as to its comfort, visibility, etc. He also wanted to see how long it would take for carbon dioxide to build up in the capsule without ventilation. During his brief test Winzen's chief complaint concerned the humidity level, and he began experiencing a headache and nausea by the time he climbed out of the capsule. Later that same day Charles R. Stearns, a Winzen consultant from the University of Wisconsin, spent an hour closed in the capsule so he could make recommendations as to instrument panel locations, changes to the seat design, etc. He described the capsule as "roomy," but this was, after all, an empty shell. As a result of his experience, Winzen felt "...comfort of the pilot should be placed above all other considerations. Not only will it make him more efficient during the flight for carrying out scientific observations, but he will be less restricted in case of an emergency."

Stapp then directed that Captain Joseph W. Kittinger also perform a 24-hour test in the capsule. Kittinger was assigned to the Holloman Fighter Test Division, but had become the de facto test pilot for the AMFL, and was the alternate pilot for *Manhigh*.

A Florida native, Kittinger raced powerboats prior to entering the Air Force as an air cadet. Kittinger graduated from the Bolles School, a military prep school in Jacksonville, in 1946. He spent the next several years as a professional hydroplane racer and student at the University of Florida before being accepted for the aviation cadet program in March 1949. Unlike most of his classmates, who couldn't wait to try out the brand new F-80 *Shooting Star*, Kittinger opted for the piston-engine F-51 *Mustang*. (The Air Force no longer used the "P," or Pursuit designation, for its aircraft, so the P-51 *Mustang* of Second World War fame bore an "F" designation for Fighter.) Kittinger's instructor, Captain Daniel Elliott, convinced him to seek training in the World War II vintage fighter while he still had the chance. Kittinger came to agree with Elliott that the *Mustang* was a joy to fly.

Kittinger received his wings and a commission as a Second Lieutenant in the United States Air Force in March 1950. He was then assigned to the 526th Fighter Bomber Squadron at Neubiberg Air Base near Munich, Germany. At first, Kittinger flew the F-47 *Thunderbolt*, another vintage fighter. In less than a year the 526th exchanged their *Thunderbolts* for brand new F-84E *Thunderjet* fighter-bombers.

(l. to r.) Otto Winzen, Joseph W. Kittinger, and David G. Simons pose in front of the *Manhigh* capsule. *Source: United States Air Force photograph*

Kittinger volunteered for a flying assignment with NATO in the spring of 1952. He served as the test pilot for brand new F-84Gs prior to their delivery to the United States' European allies. When this assignment ended, Kittinger requested that he be posted somewhere that he could continue test pilot duty. The Air Force transferred him to the Fighter Test Section at Holloman in July 1953.

One day, Kittinger happened to be assigned to fly a series of parabolic arcs to simulate weightlessness for Simons. For this particular mission they flew in a two-seat F-89 *Scorpion*. Prior to take-off, Kittinger sat down with Simons and carefully studied the desired trajectory. The objective of this day's experiment was relatively simple—Simons wanted to keep his eyes closed during the weightless portion of the flight to see if he experienced any disorientation. Although it was his first time flying such a mission, Kittinger followed the trajectory so precisely that Simons experienced longer periods of weightlessness than he was accustomed from pilots on their first try. Kittinger soon began flying for the AMFL on a regular basis.

On August 15, 1956, Stapp submitted a formal request to Lieutenant Colonel Oakley W. Baron, Director of the Holloman Flight Test Division, for Kittinger's assignment to *Manhigh*. In his request, Stapp stated Kittinger's "special qualifications as a test pilot are essential for proper evaluation of a sealed cabin environment in terms of flight in future aircraft capable of rising above the atmosphere."

Colonel Baron approved the assignment, and added his own comments to the bottom of the page. "Joe – Here's your approval. More guts than brains. Good luck, Baron." Actually, Kittinger had been around *Manhigh* since January, and was present during much of the capsule's construction at the Winzen plant.

Kittinger's claustrophobia test in the capsule included a new element not included in Simons'; Kittinger breathed the oxygen/helium/nitrogen mixture that would be used during an actual flight. Four hours into the test, pressure points from the way his helmet fit became very painful. The only way Kittinger could relieve the pressure was to abort the test, which he wasn't willing to do. He simply endured the discomfort for the rest of the test. On subsequent sessions the helmet became more comfortable, and he didn't have any more problems.

Previous high altitude balloon gondolas had plenty of room to move around, unlike *Manhigh*. Placing a pilot in such a confined space for 24 hours or longer could have disastrous results if the person suffered from claustrophobia. Therefore, the 24-hour test in the capsule was an important early milestone towards clearing someone to pilot *Manhigh*.

In addition to the 24-hour claustrophobia test, Stapp's training program for high altitude balloonists included one parachute jump; balloon training leading to a balloonist's license; a low-pressure, low temperature simulated flight in a test chamber; pressure suit training; and a battery of physiological examinations. Simons questioned the need for the parachute jump, but Stapp was adamant. As a last resort in case of trouble aloft, the pilot could jump from the capsule with a personal parachute. Should the pilot have to bail out, Stapp did not want that to be his first time using a parachute. Stapp wanted the pilot to have the confidence to use the parachute without hesitation in an emergency.

Stapp arranged for Simons and Kittinger to make their parachute jumps at the Naval Air Station in El Centro, California, where the Air Force maintained a small contingent who tested new parachute designs. Simons completed the ground course and performed the one mandated jump. After that, he happily returned to the AMFL. Likewise, Kittinger made the mandatory jump, but found the experience so exhilarating he returned and earned parachutist wings.

By the time the Air Force approved *Manhigh*, the Navy was well along with a manned stratospheric balloon project of its own. In 1954 the ONR appointed an advisory panel to review proposals they had received for manned balloon projects. They decided there was sufficient scientific and operational interest in exploring the stratosphere to justify a manned program. The resulting program was named *Stratolab*, and Winzen Research received the contract to build the gondola. To save money, Otto Winzen convinced the Navy to let him refurbish the *Helios* shell. (The Air Force Aero Medical Laboratory had previously considered using a fiberglass gondola that was similar to the *Helios* shell for their project "Biophysics of Escape." A photograph of Captain Edward Sperry and First Lieutenant Henry Nielson standing in front of the gondola appeared in the August 1955 issue of *The National Geographic Magazine*. The photograph was in an article titled "Aviation Medicine on the Threshold of Space." According to the photograph caption, Sperry and Nielson intended to conduct a series of six flights and jump from the capsule at "extreme altitudes," around 90,000 feet. The capsule was inscribed with the designation *Explorer III* for the photograph, but it apparently was never flown.)

Launching large plastic balloons could be very tricky. Often, the elongated cell of thin plastic film became a sail, and destroyed itself if the winds were even a few miles per hour. Winzen planned to use a 2 million cubic foot balloon for *Stratolab*. At launch, the aerostat was about 300 feet tall. The *Stratobowl* was barely deep enough to protect the craft, so Winzen needed another launch site. He found an open-pit iron mine near Crosby, Minnesota, that fit their needs. The M. A. Hanna Iron Ore Company's Portsmouth Mine was 425 feet deep, and had piles of rocks around its rim that provided additional shielding from the wind.

To test launch techniques, flight characteristics, and the parachute recovery system for the Navy balloon project, Winzen built a mockup of *Stratolab* from steel pipes covered with plastic sheeting. During the first flight attempt with the *Stratolab* mockup at Camp Ripley, Minnesota, the balloon failed. Two months later the Winzen crew moved to the Portsmouth Mine and tried again. This time the launch succeeded. Three more flights were made with the mockup *Stratolab* capsule, the last one on August 20, 1956. Winzen applied the experience gained from the *Stratolab* mockup launches to *Manhigh*, and he decided the Portsmouth Mine would be a good launch site for the Air Force project, as well.

Normal flight procedures for *Manhigh* called for the pilot to valve gas for his descent. As a back-up, the *Manhigh* capsule was suspended from the balloon via an open 40.4-foot diameter parachute. Beech Aircraft used this size parachute, which was manufactured by the Pioneer Parachute Company, to recover target drones. There were three ways to separate the parachute from the balloon: by pilot command; by ground command; or by an on-board timer set to function at sunset of the second day.

The open parachute recovery system had been used for high altitude balloon payloads for ten years. During that time, the parachute proved to be extremely reliable in a variety of settings. Unfortunately, there wasn't any data on balloon behavior and opening shock at high altitudes, so *Manhigh* required a series of flights to study parachute behavior.

The first flight of the *Manhigh* parachute program took place on April 20, 1956, to test this recovery technique and the 40.4-foot parachute. This flight carried a dummy capsule with a 180-pound mass in the seat. After reaching 86,000 feet, the 312-pound payload package was cut away from the balloon. Thirty-seven minutes later it landed five miles northwest of Austin, Minnesota, and was successfully recovered. There were three more parachute test flights. For these flights, the gondola carried tensionometers to measure opening forces, and cameras to observe parachute behavior. These flights also tested the capsule life support system, launch techniques, and tracking procedures.

As a further backup, the pilot had a personal parachute inside the gondola. The pilot wore a parachute harness and X-90 bailout kit, which contained a small oxygen bottle. If both the balloon and capsule parachute failed, the pilot could jettison the lower gondola shell and bail out once he was below 15,000 feet. The report issued by Winzen Research covering testing of the parachute systems stated "the gondola parachute system is strictly for emergency use, and the personnel (sic) parachute for emergency-emergency use only." The 20 April flight also tested the lower shell jettison technique to make sure the pilot could egress in an emergency. Two minutes after the capsule separated from the balloon and the recovery parachute opened, a pyrotechnic squib fired to release the marman clamp that held the lower shell to the turret. A lanyard connected the lower shell to the turret so it did not fall to the ground. The shell separated cleanly.

The AMFL requested help from the Parachute Branch at the WADC with the personal parachute system. Francis Beaupre had developed a parachute system for high altitude use. On March 17, 1957, an anthropomorphic dummy was dropped from 90,000 feet with this special parachute. The test was a success, but ground testing revealed a problem between the WADC parachute and *Manhigh*. The WADC parachute was packed in a backpack type container. When Simons wore the backpack inside the capsule, it took up so much room that his knees were against the shell, and he could not reach all the control panels. Since it was a third line of defense ("emergency-emergency") device, *Manhigh's* planners opted for a chest-pack type of parachute that could be hung from the wall of the capsule and clipped to the pilot's parachute harness if needed.

Winzen finished the developmental *Manhigh* capsule in the fall of 1956, and it was ready for its first test flight with a colony of mice and hamsters. There were enough animals on board to place the same demands on the air regeneration system (500 "mouse units") as a human pilot. This flight used a 3-million cubic foot

balloon made from 1.2-mil plastic; the same as planned for the manned mission. Everyone arrived at Crosby in October, looking forward to a successful flight. Everything was ready, except the weather.

According to data from previous years, they should have had at least two days of good weather during the last half of October. This year was different. Days turned into weeks as they waited for the right weather conditions. Every day the team waited, they racked up more motel and per diem expenses that ate into the project budget. Thanksgiving came and went with no flight. Finally, in mid-December, just as they were ready to give up, there was a favorable forecast.

Early on the morning of December 17, 1956, the Air Force Weather Officer, Captain Fountain, stated that conditions would be ideal around midnight. A large Arctic high pressure air mass was headed their way and should be centered over Crosby, giving them three to four hours of calm weather for launch. Capsule preparations began around 1:00 PM, and were finished around 5:00. The air mass moved a little faster than anticipated, and the calm conditions arrived an hour later, just after the sun set.

It was 20 degrees below zero as the Winzen crew laid out the balloon on a canvas ground cloth. Everyone did their best to keep warm as they went through the process of preparing the balloon for flight. The extreme cold increased the time needed to prepare the balloon by about half an hour. At last, Otto Winzen gave the signal for the ground team to release the balloon at 7:55 PM.

At first the ascent was followed by a Beech Bonanza leased from the University of Minnesota. Kline Bower of WRI was the observer on board the aircraft. Simons rode in a twin Beech aircraft piloted by Glenn Hovland, listening to the tone of the capsule radio beacon as the balloon reached 97,000 feet. Communications during the ascent proved problematical. One of the receivers didn't work, and there was a lot of interference on the radio channels they were using. Code signals could only be copied every nine minutes from the main beacon.

Carrying laboratory animals in the capsule would not only test the life support system, but would also provide additional specimens for cosmic radiation studies. Suddenly the signal changed. Something happened to the balloon, and the capsule was plummeting back to earth. Later analysis indicated the temperature of the helium inside the balloon had dropped to -90° F., which was below the freezing point of the plastic. The balloon actually shattered. Fortunately, the parachute opened and slowed the capsule enough that it wasn't damaged upon landing. From the tracking aircraft, Simons spotted the flashing tracking light on the capsule's top and noted the location on a map before returning to Eau Claire. At approximately midnight Simons, Winzen, and Herbert Ballman (another WRI employee) rented a Hertz van. They then drove to Rice Lake, which was near the landing point, and grabbed a few hours' sleep in a motel.

Early the next morning, the recovery team trudged through knee-deep snow to reach the capsule and its occupants. A local farmer lent them his tractor and a trailer to recover the capsule. They found the capsule along the edge of a woods; the parachute was draped over a tree. The air regeneration system fan could be heard running inside the capsule. Capsule, parachute, and other equipment were loaded on the trailer and taken to the van. The next stop was a nearby gas station, where permission was obtained to open the capsule indoors at a warm temperature. Two animals had not survived, but their deaths were determined not to be flight related. Otherwise, all the animals and the capsule were in fine shape.

While Winzen tested the *Manhigh* capsule, Simons and Kittinger continued their training program. During 1956 Winzen developed the *Sky-Car* system to support low-altitude scientific research and ballooning instruction. The *Sky-Car* comprised a cylindrical frame gondola made from steel tubing suspended from a polyethylene balloon. Depending on the desired altitude, balloon size varied from 31.5 feet (13,500 cubic-foot capacity) to 39.34 feet (27,000 cubic-foot capacity). The balloon train included a 40.4-foot diameter parachute like the one being used for the *Manhigh* capsule as a backup in case the balloon malfunctioned.

The gondola had seats for two people, but had enough room to accommodate a third person. It was 56 inches in diameter and 40 inches tall. For flight a canvas cover was laced around its exterior, and it had a plywood floor. Instrumentation included the following:

Altimeter
Rate of Climb Indicator
8-Day Aircraft Clock with Sweep Second Hand
Magnetic Compass
Drift Meter
Controls for Balloon Cutaway

The radio gear was packaged separately in a box that could be dumped overboard as ballast if necessary. For shipping, the balloon, parachute, and other necessary equipment could be packed into the gondola.

Simons and Kittinger used the *Sky-Car* to earn their Civil Aeronautics Agency balloonist's license. To earn a lighter-than-air Pilot's Certificate, a candidate had to complete six instructional flights of not less than two hours' duration, one controlled flight to an altitude of 10,000 feet, and a solo flight lasting at least an hour.

Although they were at relatively low altitudes, flights in the *Sky-Car* posed a certain element of risk. On one training flight Bernard "Duke" Gildenberg, the Balloon Branch meteorologist, accompanied Simons and Kittinger. Gildenberg's prowess at predicting balloon trajectories and reading weather charts had become almost legendary at Holloman. He became a critical member of the *Manhigh* team, and was even considered as an alternate pilot, hence his training in the *Sky-Car*.

Early one morning Simons, Kittinger, and Gildenberg were flying the *Sky-Car* over the desert near Holloman. Simons had already completed his training; Kittinger and Gildenberg were practicing touchdowns and takeoffs. After several hours of flying the winds picked up to a brisk 15 miles per hour. Their landings became harder due to the increased winds, so they decided to stand with their knees flexed to better absorb the shock of impact on

the next touchdown. When the gondola landed it abruptly stopped, and all three pitched forward. Simons slammed into Gildenberg, fracturing one of his ribs. This ended his aspirations of piloting *Manhigh*.

With its head start on *Manhigh*, *Stratolab* became the first to carry American balloonists to the stratosphere since *Explorer II* in 1935. *Stratolab* comprised high altitude flights with the resurrected *Helios* gondola, and flights to the lower stratosphere (around 40,000 feet) with the *Sky-Car* open basket. Even before the first unmanned test with the *Manhigh* capsule, Lieutenant Commanders Malcolm D. Ross and M. Lee Lewis made the first manned *Stratolab* flight in the *Sky-Car* gondola. Riding in the open gondola, they ascended to 40,000 feet on August 10, 1956, to photograph condensation trails from jet aircraft. Secondary objectives were to make physiological measurements of the pilots and test their pressure suits. Ross and Lewis made the first flight in the *Stratolab* gondola on November 8, 1956, and reached 76,000 feet.

Early in the spring, WRI conducted two more test flights with the developmental capsule in April 1957. WRI flight #749 took place on 14 April. This flight carried a colony of guinea pigs and mice. Flight objectives included testing the life support system and emergency parachute. The developmental capsule was modified so the air regeneration and cooling systems were mounted on the exterior, just as they would be for the manned flight.

Shortly after midnight on the 14th, the AMFL delivered the test animals to the WRI plant. They were sealed in the capsule, which was then pressure checked. Once all the pre-flight checks were completed, the capsule was placed on the back of a truck for the trip to the Winzen Flight Operations Center at Fleming Field. The capsule arrived at Fleming Field at approximately 4:30 AM. Winds were from the north at 5 MPH—nearly ideal for the balloon launch.

Otto Winzen directed the placement of the capsule on a wheeled dolly at about the spot where the balloon would pick it up once it was released. The Air Force C-47 took off thirty minutes before the scheduled launch time and orbited above the balloon. The position of the aircraft was synchronized with the balloon launch so that the takeoff could be photographed from the air. Captain Kittinger piloted the C-47. Simons talked with Kittinger over the radio to make sure the airplane was in the proper position.

Thirty seconds before launch, Simons fired a green flare into the sky to notify outlying camera positions that the launch was imminent. Fifteen seconds to go, and Simons fired a second flare. Winzen gave the order to release the balloon at 7:18 AM. The capsule lifted cleanly off the launching cart and climbed smoothly into the clear sky. After launch Kittinger landed, and the rest of the tracking crew boarded the aircraft. WRI provided a *Navion* that was also used to track the balloon from the air.

The balloon climbed to 103,500 feet as it drifted eastward across Wisconsin. By 1:30 PM it was over the western shore of Lake Michigan. Although the balloon was starting to slowly lose altitude, and the capsule pressure showed a slight drop, it was allowed to continue. Kittinger followed the balloon across the lake; the single-engine *Navion* turned south to skirt the large body of water, and headed to the expected landing point.

An hour and a half later the balloon reached the eastern edge of the lake, traveling between 52 and 55 miles per hour. If it continued on its current path, all the way across Michigan, it was heading towards Saginaw Bay. Once the *Navion* was within range the cutdown signal was broadcast to the capsule. Nothing happened.

Despite repeated attempts to cut down the payload, it stubbornly remained aloft. All that could be done was to wait for the on-board timer to release the capsule. The balloon was nearing Saginaw, Michigan, when the timer cut the capsule away from the balloon at 5:36 PM. The parachute blossomed almost immediately. Dropping at 32 feet per second, it headed towards a populated area of Saginaw. The capsule barely missed a house as it landed in someone's back yard at 6:10 PM. Kittinger landed at the Tri-City Airport, and the recovery team headed to the capsule's landing site, which was about five miles away. City police and fire department personnel helped load the capsule on the back of a truck for transport to the airport. Simons opened the capsule and found that other than one guinea pig and a few mice, all the animals were in good shape.

The next test flight, on 27 April, also used the developmental capsule and reached 111,800 feet. This flight did not carry animals; it was primarily a test of the parachute system. As a secondary test objective, the capsule dropped fifty pounds of ballast at 5,000 feet to measure its effect on the balloon. The flight began at 6:50 AM from Fleming Field. At 11:03 AM the onboard timer cut away the capsule. The capsule landed in a tree about four miles northnorthwest of Webster, Wisconsin. Mr. Jack Hughes, a local farmer, provided a tractor with a trailer to carry the payload to the nearest road.

Tensionometers on the last two flights recorded parachute opening shock levels from 2.45 to 3.76 g's—well within tolerable levels for a human pilot. These flights concluded the *Manhigh* test program; it was time for a flight with a human pilot on board.

Knowing the limited nature of *Manhigh's* budget, Simons intended to perform the 24-hour scientific mission after the test flights. He calculated the project had just enough money left for the one flight, so he figured this would be his only chance. Including the planned flight, *Manhigh* cost nearly ten times the original contract amount ($235,590.00). Simons later concluded that nearly $70,000 of the cost was due to not having funding in place when needed. Despite the limited budget, Stapp did not feel it was prudent to proceed to the full-scale scientific flight without a test flight with a human on board. He told Simons:

"Animal tests are fine, Dave, but I don't think that's enough. The animals did nothing up there but breathe, eat, and defecate. They didn't talk on the radio, shift around in a 180-pound mass, fidget in a pressure suit, try to grab scientific observations out of those saucer-sized portholes, or do any of the things you will have to do when you go up. To put the *Manhigh* system up now for a full-scale flight without at least one manned test flight first would be like trying to send a new fighter plane into combat without wringing the bugs out of it."

Simons reluctantly agreed with Stapp. There was a chance the ARDC would terminate *Manhigh* after the mission, deciding the program had served its purpose. On the other hand, Stapp reasoned there was a good chance they would fund the full-scale research mission after a successful test flight. After all, the Air Force was used to a series of test flights with new aircraft before they became operational.

Simons was eager to fly the *Manhigh* capsule, and offered to make the ascent as an engineering test without the full agenda of scientific observations. This would, he argued, serve the dual purpose of testing both the capsule and pilot prior to the full-scale scientific flight. Stapp reminded Simons that he was a doctor, not a test pilot. He also pointed out that if they had even a relatively minor mishap that resulted in Simons being injured, it would definitely end any hopes of the full-scale scientific mission. Since the capsule was still untested in an actual manned flight Stapp did not want to risk the project's chief scientist, so he directed that Kittinger pilot *Manhigh I*.

Manhigh Major Systems and Their Backups

System	Primary	Emergency Backup	"Emergency-Emergency" Backup
Recovery	Venting Gas	40-foot parachute	Individual parachute
Artificial Environment	Capsule Atmosphere	Partial Pressure Suit	N/A
Capsule Separation	N/A	Electrical Release, Upper or Lower Shell	Manual Release, Upper or Lower Shell
Parachute Release on Landing	N/A	Mechanical Release	N/A
Oxygen System	5-Liter Liquid Oxygen Converter	45-Minute Pressure Bottle	15-Minute Pressure Bottle
Air Regeneration	Independent Blowers in Air Regeneration and Cooling Systems	Either Blower Will Operate Both Systems	Capsule Atmosphere Breathable for 1 Hour
Electrical Power	Main Battery Pack	External Battery Units	Internal Silver Cell Batteries
Manual Decompression	N/A	Two Manual Decompression Valves	Open 1 or 2 Portholes
Communications	Voice – VHF	Morse Code – HF	Portable Tape Recorder on Board
Tracking	Visual, Airplane Fixes, and Theodolite	ADF on Capsule Telemetry Beacon	Omnirange Readings from Capsule
Altitude Determination	Altitude Beacon, Double Theodolite	Photo Panel Record on Film, Radar	Barographs on Board

7

Manhigh I

Kittinger moved his training into high gear. He spent hours at a time sitting in the *Manhigh* capsule at the Winzen plant, memorizing the locations of every switch, dial, and gauge. (Having outgrown its Fleming Field facility, the Winzen Research plant was by that time located on Lyndale Avenue South in Minneapolis. Fleming Field became their flight operations center.) Working with Don Foster, Winzen's chief engineer, Kittinger figured out his every move for maximum efficiency within the capsule's tight confines.

Kittinger's least favorite aspect of preparing for the flight was pressure suit training. He had to endure sessions in a test chamber at WADC at a simulated altitude of 100,000 feet with the suit pressurized, as well as lengthy tests in the capsule while wearing an unpressurized garment. The pressurized suit was particularly uncomfortable, and restricted his mobility. On one capsule test, the temperature inside the cabin reached 80° F. Like Simons during his claustrophobia test when the temperature rose, Kittinger became irritable, and his efficiency dropped. After a couple of hours the temperature dropped to a more comfortable level, and Kittinger completed the test. Clearly, temperatures that might otherwise be tolerable wearing a flight suit soon became intolerable for someone wearing a skin-tight partial pressure suit.

While preparing for the flight, Kittinger recognized he faced a problem that was unique to high altitude ballooning. Kittinger described this problem as "time remoteness." In a conventional aircraft, if a problem developed at a high altitude, the pilot could usually descend quickly to an altitude where there was sufficient oxygen to sustain him. With *Manhigh*, even if the capsule was cut away from the balloon, it took at least half an hour to descend under the cargo parachute. If he had to abort the mission and land by conventional means (ie venting helium), the descent would take several hours. Kittinger also realized that if any problems developed during his flight nobody could reach him to provide help. In other words, he would be on his own to manage any life threatening emergencies.

Other than offering advice, the only action that ground control could take would be to cut the capsule away from the balloon and bring it back via the emergency parachute. Kittinger and Simons both worried that someone on the ground might overreact

to a manageable problem with the flight and trigger the release. There was also the possibility that a spurious radio signal would cut away the balloon. This happened several years earlier during a flight from Holloman when a local radio station played "The Tiger Rag," and a portion of the song matched the coded cutaway signal. Following that incident the cutaway coding signals were changed to prevent this from happening again, but the prospective pilots still worried about the system.

Simons also worried that Kittinger would find some excuse to jettison the lower shell and bail out from maximum altitude. After qualifying for his parachutist's wings, Kittinger openly speculated that it would be possible to make a controlled freefall from 100,000 feet. He spoke about the possibility with such enthusiasm that Simons feared Kittinger might actually try it. Such an action would reduce the lower shell, with the cooling and air regeneration systems, to a crumpled pile of scrap metal, and would absolutely end *Manhigh* before Simons had a chance to make his flight. Simons took his concerns to Stapp, who instructed Kittinger that the only acceptable reason for jettisoning the lower shell would be an uncontrollable fire in the cabin.

Manhigh I used a 2 million cubic foot balloon, rather than the 3 million cubic foot behemoth planned for the scientific research flight. The smaller balloon was fabricated from 2-mil polyethylene; the larger one used lighter 1.5-mil material so it could reach a higher altitude. With the smaller balloon, *Manhigh I* would not quite reach 100,000 feet. While not as high as the altitude planned for the research flight, it would still be higher than anyone had ever reached using a balloon.

Because it used the sturdier balloon, *Manhigh I* employed the launch arm, or *Skyhook* launch method, rather than the vertical inflation and launch technique. Winzen developed a technique for launching *Skyhook* balloons where the balloon is laid out on the ground, and only the small portion of the envelope containing the lifting gas is exposed to the surface winds. Upon its release, the balloon undergoes a lot of stress due to dynamic deformation. A 3-million cubic foot balloon made from 1.5-mil material could probably not withstand such punishment. The 2-mil balloon was much tougher, and could survive a surface launch. This meant the launch

Captain Joseph W. Kittinger in the *Manhigh* capsule seat. *Source: United States Air Force photograph*

did not need the protection afforded by the mine in Crosby. *Manhigh I* could be launched from the airstrip at Fleming Field, which was only ten miles from the Winzen plant. This simplified preparations for the Winzen crew because they didn't have to transport their equipment all the way to Crosby.

The *Manhigh I* balloon was made from 60 gores of 2-mil plastic with 120 integral heat-sealed load bands. Each load band had a tensile strength of 500 pounds. When fully inflated, the balloon was 172 feet in diameter. The balloon was the so-called "natural shape" FIST (filament stressed) design, which resembled an upside down onion when inflated. The University of Minnesota Physics Department developed the natural shape while working on the *Skyhook* program. It provided equal stress along the load bands when the balloon was fully inflated.

Kittinger would be the first to try out the "final" *Manhigh* gondola, which was the third one built for the program. For this 12-hour test mission, it carried the control instrumentation and life support equipment that would be used for the 24-hour scientific flight. *Manhigh I* carried one less 12-volt battery and less experimental equipment than proposed for the full-up mission, so it weighed a little less.

All that was needed for launch were clear skies and calm winds shortly after daybreak. The forecast for 2 June looked favorable. Captain Kittinger began final preparations for the flight at 11:00 PM the night before launch. After a physical examination by Stapp and Simons, Captain Erwin Archibald taped a miniature microphone to Kittinger's chest that would register both his heartbeat and breathing rate for transmission to the ground. With the microphone in place, Technical Sergeant Edward Dittmer helped Kittinger don the MC-3 pressure suit. While Kittinger completed his arrangements, Winzen technicians finished preparing the capsule. They filled the liquid oxygen tank and loaded bags of chemicals into the air regeneration unit. The electrical and communications systems also received checks.

Manhigh I required eight radio frequencies. The *Manhigh* capsule carried commercially available radio equipment, which meant all communications between Kittinger and the ground would be

The truck carrying Kittinger and the capsule arrived before dawn. Looking through the portholes, Kittinger saw the launch crew working among a layer of fog. *Source: Photo courtesy of Dr. John Paul Stapp*

Manhigh I Weight Breakdown

Balloon	
Balloon with valve and all accessories	953 lbs
Parachute	45 lbs
Radio control for balloon release and termination	14 lbs
Total	1,012 lbs
Capsule	
Shell	150 lbs
Air conditioning and regeneration	141 lbs
Oxygen system	62 lbs
Photo panel, recording camera, strobe light	50 lbs
Control panels and wiring	45 lbs
Internal batteries	40 lbs
Internal structure	30 lbs
Communications gear	60 lbs
Altitude recording and telemetering	20 lbs
Total	598 lbs
Ballast	
External batteries	196 lbs
Steel shot	50 lbs
Total	246 lbs
Crew	
Pilot	160 lbs
Personal equipment	65 lbs
Food and water	15 lbs
Total	240 lbs
Experiments	
Equipment for experiments	50 lbs
Cameras and film	20 lbs
Total	70 lbs
TOTAL WEIGHT OF AEROSTAT	2,166 lbs

Manhigh I Radio Frequencies

Frequency	Use	Code
118.5 megacycles	Voice special	A
122.8 megacycles	Voice unicom	B
122.1 megacycles	Voice CAA communication	C
121.5 megacycles	Emergency	D
122.5 megacycles	Tower	E
1724 kilocycles	Aerostat transmitting only	F
3123 kilocycles	Aerostat receiving only	G
6700.5 kilocycles	Aerostat receiving only	H

publicly accessible. This was not necessarily a bad thing, however, because it also meant that in an emergency, civilian airports and aircraft could communicate with *Manhigh*. To ensure some measure of privacy and economize on the length of transmissions, Kittinger followed a prearranged checklist for status reports. The reports covered such topics as altitude, capsule temperature, cabin pressure, battery voltage, and quantity of liquid oxygen remaining.

Kittinger boarded the capsule at 12:30 AM. He climbed into the nylon mesh seat mounted in the interior frame suspended from the turret and upper dome assembly. Once he was comfortably seated, the assembly was lifted by a crane, the lower shell placed beneath him, and he was then lowered into the shell. Winzen technicians placed the marmon clamp around the turret/lower shell joint and sealed the capsule. Under the terms of their contract with the Air Force, Winzen was responsible for launching, tracking, and recovering the *Manhigh* capsule. As a practical matter, though, the flight can be seen as a cooperative venture of company and Air Force personnel.

Captain Archibald, who was the project physiologist, added helium to the sealed capsule atmosphere, and increased the air pressure inside it by 6 PSI. The capsule was allowed to stand for 30 minutes to make sure there were no leaks. During this time, all electrical and mechanical systems received one final check. The capsule maintained the pressure, so Kittinger opened the relief valve. Archibald then added oxygen to further reduce the partial pressure of nitrogen, and achieve the proper balance of gases for the flight. These preparations were completed about 3:30 AM, and the capsule, with Kittinger inside, was placed on a truck and driven to the launch site. Before leaving the Winzen plant, a cap of dry ice was placed on top of the capsule. Placing Kittinger in the capsule so far ahead of time gave his body time to flush some of the dissolved nitrogen from his bloodstream.

Wisps of vapor streamed from the dry ice on top of the capsule as the truck traveled to the airport. When he arrived, which was around 4:30 AM, Kittinger peered through the small portholes in the turret. Illuminated by the harsh glare of portable floodlights, he saw a surreal scene as the crew worked among a layer of ground fog. The workers laid out a canvas ground cover, then unpacked the balloon. With the balloon stretched out on the ground, the ground crew began filling it with helium.

The Winzen team included Otto's wife, Vera. She supervised the women who built the balloons at the plant, and was Vice President of the company. Mrs. Winzen had become the world's foremost expert on balloon construction techniques and held four patents. She was the daughter of a Detroit photographer whom Otto met through Jean Piccard. Besides supervising balloon construction, Vera managed much of the company's daily operations. Because of her family background, she also became the company photographer.

Whenever possible, Vera always brought some of her "girls" to balloon launches so they could see the results of their labor. Thanks to such policies as having a comprehensive training program, task rotation, and frequent breaks, her "girls" built a solid reputation for superior performance. No Winzen balloon had ever failed due to manufacturing defects. Mrs. Winzen and Donna McCormick performed the final inspection of the balloon prior to flight.

Ed Lewis, who supervised the Winzen launch crew, directed the other crewmembers as they attached the capsule to the cargo parachute risers. The parachute was then connected to the balloon load ring. The 36-inch diameter load ring was attached to the base of the balloon. A slightly smaller (24 inches in diameter) parachute ring was laced to the apex of the cargo parachute. Both rings were made from 1/2-inch aluminum tubing. Twenty-four 30-inch lengths of 3,000-pound strength nylon line connected the rings. Four explosive cutters arranged 90° apart could sever the lines to release the capsule and parachute from the balloon.

"We're almost ready, Joe. Everything okay inside?" asked Simons.

Winzen Research workers lay out the *Manhigh I* balloon in the early morning mist. *Source: Photo courtesy of Dr. John Paul Stapp*

Manhigh I balloon during inflation. The two-million cubic foot balloon was filled via the two red tubes. *Source: Photo courtesy of Dr. John Paul Stapp*

As the balloon inflated, the ground crew fed it through a roller. *Source: Photo courtesy of Dr. John Paul Stapp*

The launch trailer had a dynamometer that measured the lift of the balloon. Using this device, the launch crew could make sure the balloon contained the proper amount of helium for the desired rate of climb and altitude. *Source: Photo courtesy of Dr. John Paul Stapp*

"No sweat," replied Kittinger.

Simons suggested that Kittinger secure his cameras and other equipment in case the balloon jerked the capsule at take off. By 6:20 AM everyone was ready to launch *Manhigh*. The capsule gleamed in the reflected sunlight of the rising sun. A final weather check showed the winds were about 2 knots, and conditions were ideal. Stapp gave Otto Winzen an "okay" signal to indicate all was well. Green flares were fired into the sky at launch minus 30 and 15 seconds. Winzen then told the ground crew to release the balloon, and Kittinger lifted off at 6:23 AM. Kittinger quipped "Good-bye, cruel world," as he took off. *Manhigh I* lifted off smoothly, and Kittinger barely felt a thing as he began his journey to the fringes of the atmosphere. Captain Kittinger was supposed to remain aloft for 12 hours, half of that time at ceiling altitude.

A fleet of aircraft supported *Manhigh I*. The Air Force provided two helicopters and the AMFL C-47. Winzen chartered a North American *Navion* as a tracking aircraft. Glenn Hoveland, an experienced balloon chaser, piloted the Winzen aircraft. Stapp, Simons, and Dittmer flew in one of the helicopters; the other transported the Winzens, Captain Archibald, and others back to the Winzen plant, since the radio communications center was located at the Winzen plant. Captain Hank Fronkier piloted the C-47; Captain Drury Parks, a zoologist from the AMFL, accompanied him, and supervised aerial tracking of the balloon. Captain L. B. McGrady commanded the helicopters.

Five minutes after takeoff Simons, Stapp, and Dittmer took off in one of the helicopters to follow the balloon. With Winzen heading back to the plant, this separated the three people responsible for the flight, and put the two senior military officers away from the main communications center. For the earlier biological flights it was usual practice for Simons, the senior officer present, to be in one of the tracking aircraft, so this was a logical extension of past practices. He and Stapp wanted to follow the balloon across the countryside. If Kittinger had to bail out, or encountered any other difficulties, they figured he would need medical assistance as quickly as possible, so they stayed beneath the balloon.

At first *Manhigh I* ascended at a rate of 400 feet per minute. If the balloon climbed too fast, then aerodynamic drag and fluttering of the plastic could tear it apart. Therefore, the rate of climb was one of the most important parameters Kittinger had to watch. As *Manhigh* climbed the ascent rate reached 500 feet per minute, which was nearly ideal.

Within a few minutes of taking off Kittinger noticed the capsule pressure was not dropping as fast as the atmospheric pressure. This created a pressure differential between the atmosphere inside the capsule and the outside air that should not have occurred until the balloon was above 26,000 feet. Since nobody had ever flown the capsule, nor had it been tested in a vacuum chamber to simulate high-altitude conditions to observe the rate of pressure equalization, Kittinger decided to continue with the flight.

The command helicopter was directly beneath *Manhigh I*, so Simons had the pilot land in a nearby pasture. Simons tried to raise Kittinger on the radio, but there was no response. After several attempts Vern Baumgartner, who was manning the radio at the Winzen plant, chimed in and told Simons they had not heard anything

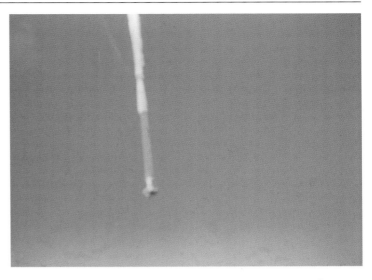

Manhigh I during ascent. *Source: Photo courtesy of Dr. John Paul Stapp*

from the capsule for several minutes. Simons asked if they had checked the emergency frequency.

Baumgartner replied they were checking it, then told Simons it sounded like Kittinger was sending Morse code, but it was difficult to hear. Simons switched to the emergency frequency and strained to decipher the pulses. Grateful for his experience as a ham radio operator, Simons pieced together Kittinger's message: "N-O S-W-E-A-T." Kittinger had not used Morse code since his days as an aviation cadet, so his messages came through haltingly and slowly. However, Simons was used to listening to hard to read signals from across the globe.

About 20 minutes after launch, Kittinger told ground control he was going to check the other channels on the VHF communications system. While changing channels the selector knob failed, so he could no longer transmit voice communications to the ground. The receiver still worked, so Kittinger could hear instructions, but he had to use the backup Morse code system for his replies. Once again, Kittinger reassured everyone on the ground: "A-L-L-S W-E-L-L N-O S-W-E-A-T."

Kittinger initially climbed at a rate of 400 feet per minute. *Source: Photo courtesy of Dr. John Paul Stapp*

In between Kittinger's Morse code signals, Stapp monitored his heart and breathing rates. Channel F (1724 kilocycles) was used for telemetry and emergency Morse code transmissions. Normally, the pilot's heartbeat and respiration were broadcast four out of every five minutes, with one minute of altitude data. When it was used as a Morse code (or CW) transmitter, it could not be used for telemetry. Stapp found that Kittinger's pulse and breathing were both slightly elevated from the radio problems, but otherwise he was fine.

Approaching an altitude of 45,000 feet, Kittinger braced himself. Pre-launch weather charts indicated there was a jet stream of 100 miles per hour, which was the limit of what the balloon could stand. Entering the jet stream would stress the balloon to its limits. Adding to Kittinger's concerns was the knowledge that even a material as flexible as the polyethylene used for the balloon became brittle in the frigid temperatures outside his capsule. He had seen balloons fail at this point in their flights before. Most balloon failures occurred at this point in the flight. Sometimes, watching through binoculars, it looked as though a giant scythe cut off the

Kaman *H-43 Huskie*, one of the helicopters used to track Kittinger. *Source: Photo courtesy of Dr. John Paul Stapp*

top of the balloon. One flight in particular stood out in his mind, during which the balloon shattered, then wrapped itself around the emergency parachute, and the payload plummeted to earth.

Suddenly there was an abrupt tug as the balloon entered the air stream. The force was so violent it nearly turned the capsule on its side! Using a mirror mounted outside one of his windows, Kittinger peered at the balloon. What he saw was truly frightening. The wind beat at the balloon, and contorted it into a grotesque concave shape. Knowing the limitations of the polyethylene, he waited for the balloon to shatter as *Manhigh* began a quick dash towards the east, carried by the 100-mile per hour wind. Then he climbed through the jet stream, and things settled down.

Inside the capsule, Kittinger felt a growing sense of frustration. Having to tap everything out in Morse code took him away from other tasks. Simons continued tracking the balloon from the helicopter, having the pilot land periodically. At 8:07 AM Kittinger reached 95,200 feet. Simons asked for a status report of the capsule. Kittinger was having trouble receiving transmissions from the ground because he was near a commercial broadcasting station operating on nearly the same wavelength.

Kittinger began laboriously tapping out the report. It took ten minutes for him to report on such subjects as capsule pressure, oxygen percentage, altitude, and so forth. Everything seemed normal until item seven, the oxygen quantity remaining in the supply tank. Simons transcribed the coded message. "I-T-E-M S-E-V-E-N..." The report stopped. After a brief pause, it resumed. "I-T-E-M S-E-V-E-N H-A-L-F." Archibald, who was at the plant, asked Kittinger if he was sure about the reading. Since he'd been airborne for only an hour and a half, the tank should have been nearly full. "D-O-U-B-L-E C-H-E-C-K-E-D. H-A-L-F F-U-L-L. W-H-A-T G-I-V-E-S," replied Kittinger.

Simons tried to raise the Winzen plant, but the helicopter was too far away for a clear radio signal. He told the pilot he had to get to a telephone. The pilot found a small gas station and landed on an adjacent road. Simons sprang from the helicopter, ran into the gas station, and asked for a phone. He quickly dialed TUxedo 1-5871, the number for the plant, and spoke to Otto Winzen.

Looking through one of the portholes, Kittinger could see the balloon through an upward looking mirror. *Source: Photo courtesy of Dr. John Paul Stapp*

As Kittinger floated overhead at 95,200 feet, Winzen personnel on the ground watched him through a telescope. *Source: Photo courtesy of Dr. John Paul Stapp*

Winzen advised Simons that Archibald had just asked for another status report—the liquid oxygen supply was down to two liters, only 40% of the original supply. Since the cabin pressure remained steady there was not a leak in the capsule, Winzen opined. Simons decided he and Stapp should head back to the communications center at the plant, so they took off again.

Twenty minutes later the helicopter landed at Wold-Chamberlain Field in Minneapolis. Simons ran to a phone and called the plant again. Archibald answered, and told him the oxygen tank was only a tenth full, which should last three hours provided no more drained out.

"Won't it keep on draining?" asked Simons.

"I don't think so," replied Archibald, who went on to explain that they had advised Kittinger to switch his oxygen supply from the cabin to the pressure suit. Cabin pressure held steady, indicating the problem was in the pressure controller. After that test, Kittinger manually replenished the oxygen supply to the cabin. Since he'd increased the oxygen content of the capsule atmosphere, he selected a pressure altitude of 28,000 feet inside *Manhigh*. When the internal pressure dropped to the equivalent of 30,000 feet he added more oxygen. Thus, Kittinger maintained a breathable atmosphere inside the capsule, but the situation was still urgent. Half a liter of liquid oxygen would barely be enough to last him through the descent.

At 8:54 Stapp advised Kittinger that he had just enough oxygen left for the descent, with nothing to spare, and ordered him to begin his return. Everyone waited to hear Kittinger report he was on his way back to the ground. Finally, the Morse code signal came through, "C-O-M-E A-N-D G-E-T M-E."

Come and get me? Navy *Stratolab* balloon crews and some pilots flying at extreme altitudes had reported a feeling of detachment from the earth, like they belonged more with the sky above than the ground below. They just wanted to keep flying higher and higher. This was called "breakaway phenomenon." Had Kittinger succumbed to this mysterious condition? Would he remain aloft until his oxygen ran out?

Taking the microphone in hand, Stapp's reply was clear and unambiguous: "Captain, if you don't start your descent immediately, we will cut you away from the balloon and bring you back with the parachute." Once more, everyone waited for Kittinger's response. "V-A-L-V-I-N-G G-A-S." Kittinger complied with the order; his initial response had been a joke. He opened the 14-inch diameter valve at the apex of the balloon for one minute and released helium. He then waited for five minutes to see how the balloon responded. At first there was little effect, so he opened the valve again. Finally, he began descending. Then, since the balloon gas was warmer than the surrounding air, it began lifting again. This was a condition called *superheat*, where the sun heated the helium and increased its buoyancy. He released more gas, and gingerly began his descent. The problem Kittinger faced was that whatever descent rate he established in the stratosphere would double as he passed through the tropopause.

He established a steady descent rate until reaching 62,000 feet, when the balloon leveled off. He released more helium and began dropping again. During the descent Kittinger held the valve open for a total of 34 minutes, all of that time above the tropopause. While Kittinger released helium, the C-47 sat on the ramp at Wold-Chamberlain Field alongside the command helicopter. A bank of high clouds had moved in, and nobody could see the balloon from the ground.

Around 11:30 AM, Kittinger reported he was at 53,000 feet. The radio beacon provided a bearing towards the balloon, so the C-47 crew took off, crisscrossing the sky in search of *Manhigh*. Captain Fronkier was careful to not fly into the clouds to avoid colliding with the balloon. The command helicopter followed. By 12:15 PM Kittinger was below the tropopause. Everyone strained to spot the balloon. Finally, around 12:30 PM, Simons spotted the inverted teardrop shape of the balloon. It was fifteen miles away.

The helicopter sped to catch up with the balloon. When he was 400 feet above the ground, Kittinger released three batteries to slow his descent. *Manhigh* was traveling over a wooded area, so Kittinger had to carefully select his touchdown point. At 12:57 he landed about 80 miles southeast of the launch area on the bank

View from the recovery helicopter as Kittinger brought *Manhigh* in for a landing. *Source: Photo courtesy of Dr. John Paul Stapp*

After he landed Kittinger released the balloon. Used balloons were particularly useful to farmers, who used the plastic to package frozen meats, or as tarps for equipment. *Source: Photo courtesy of Dr. John Paul Stapp*

Major Simons was the first to reach the capsule after it tumbled into Weaver Creek. *Source: Photo courtesy of Dr. John Paul Stapp*

of Indian Creek, a little north of Weaver, Minnesota. At the instant of landing Kittinger released the balloon, and the capsule toppled backward into the shallow creek. The liquid oxygen tank was empty.

Almost immediately the command helicopter landed nearby. Simons and Stapp both jumped out, then scrambled down the creek bank to check on Captain Kittinger. Simons got there first, and found one of the small windows on the turret open. Peering inside he called to Kittinger, who grinned back at him. A few minutes later other personnel arrived to help right the capsule, and remove the upper dome. Captain Kittinger, who had just reached the highest sustained altitude ever recorded, climbed out of the capsule.

Other than a few bends in the aluminum frame undercarriage, the capsule looked as good as new. The ground team carried the capsule out of the creek as Kittinger clambered up the bank. He stood there grinning, his pressure suit stained dark from perspiration. A quick examination showed he was in fine shape following his trip above 98% of the atmosphere. Later, Stapp and Simons

conducted a more thorough physical examination and preliminary debriefing back at Wold-Chamberlain Field in Minneapolis.

Kittinger reported he was not able to make as many observations through the windows because he had to focus on the code key. At ceiling altitude he spotted what he thought was Lake Michigan. A layer of clouds obscured his view of the ground, but there were no clouds along the horizon, and the cloudless area was shaped like the lake. The moon was brighter than usual, but otherwise looked just like it did on a clear night.

Winzen took the capsule back to their plant, where Ed Lewis quickly diagnosed the problems that disrupted *Manhigh's* initial flight. Someone accidentally reversed the oxygen supply and vent lines to the pressure controller. Instead of supplying oxygen to the cabin, the controller dumped most of it overboard. The communications problem proved to be nothing more serious than a loose selector switch. If there had been a screwdriver on board, Kittinger could have easily fixed this problem and resumed normal communications.

After the capsule was righted, Simons helped Kittinger remove the upper dome. *Source: Photo courtesy of Dr. John Paul Stapp*

Kittinger emerges from the capsule. *Source: Photo courtesy of Dr. John Paul Stapp*

The crew from the helicopter helped Kittinger climb down from the capsule. *Source: Photo courtesy of Dr. John Paul Stapp*

Once he was clear of the capsule, Kittinger climbed up the bank of Weaver Creek. *Source: Photo courtesy of Dr. John Paul Stapp*

Simons helped Kittinger remove the helmet of his pressure suit. *Source: Photo courtesy of Dr. John Paul Stapp*

Kittinger and Simons discuss the flight. *Source: Photo courtesy of Dr. John Paul Stapp*

With the flight over, Kittinger wriggled out of the skin-tight pressure suit. *Source: Photo courtesy of Dr. John Paul Stapp*

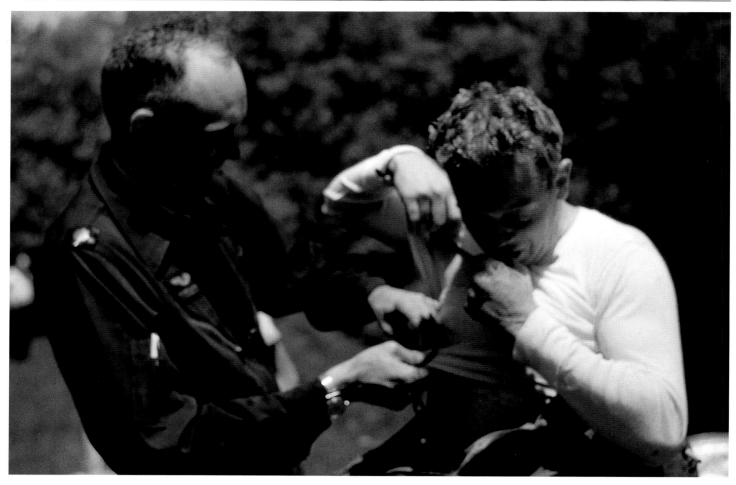

Simons disconnects the microphone that registered Kittinger's pulse and breathing rates. *Source: Photo courtesy of Dr. John Paul Stapp*

Stapp and Kittinger in the recovery helicopter after the Manhigh I flight. *Source: Winzen Research, Inc. photograph*

8

Manhigh II

WRI corrected the problems that plagued *Manhigh I*, and Simons eagerly looked forward to making his own flight as soon as possible. Granted, *Manhigh I* had expended just about all the remaining money under the contract, but the federal fiscal year started on 1 July, and Simons hoped to receive additional funding from the ARDC for his flight. Then, *Manhigh* hit a problem that threatened to end the project. In the summer of 1957 the national debt reached its legal ceiling, and government agencies received orders to curtail their spending. Air Force research programs were particularly hard hit. The Air Force would not provide funding to continue *Manhigh*, at least not at that time.

After the close call with the oxygen system, Colonel Stapp ordered a 24-hour low-pressure, low-temperature test in an altitude chamber before the capsule could be cleared for another flight. Together, the simulated flight and manned mission would cost $14,000 more than was available in the budget. After two years of effort and a test flight, Simons would have to mothball the project and hope for additional funding when the economic climate improved. With the external frame repaired, the capsule sat in a corner of the Winzen plant looking ready for flight. Reflected light gleamed off its Mylar insulation like a beacon, beckoning Simons to take it into the stratosphere again.

Otto Winzen tried to argue with Simons that halting everything just as they were on the brink of the 24-hour mission, only to attempt to resurrect it at a later date, would likely double the cost for the flight. Further, he declared, to stop work just as the AMFL was about to perform the scientific flight would negate all that had been achieved thus far. Simons replied he recognized these facts, but the lack of funding left him no choice. He knew full well that *Manhigh* was likely dead because of the high costs associated with restarting it.

Simons glumly set about the task of gathering project documents at the Winzen plant when Otto and Vera Winzen called him into their office. The company's accountant was also present. At first, Simons didn't have any idea why they summoned him, and was particularly perplexed as to why they were smiling. Then, the Winzens announced their company would fund the ground test

and subsequent flight, because they felt the goodwill and publicity were worth a $14,000 investment. Simons was delighted. *Manhigh* was back in business.

The simulated flight was set for 26 July at WADC. The test chamber resembled a gigantic pressure cooker or bean pot. Vacuum pumps could remove air from the chamber to simulate an altitude of 85,000 feet. It also incorporated infrared lamps and a refrigeration system to create extremes of heat and cold, simulating the temperature conditions of the stratosphere.

For three days before the test Simons consumed a low-residue diet. One of the operating limitations of the MC-3 pressure suit was that it did not have any provisions for defecation. Hence, the low-residue diet was needed to preclude the pilot having a bowel movement during either the 24-hour test or the flight.

On the night of 26 July Simons donned the pressure suit and climbed into the capsule. Everyone followed, as closely as possible, the procedures and preparations for an actual flight. The preparations even included having blood collected, just as he would prior to the flight. Actually, this served a useful purpose—it provided "baseline" data so that any changes from the flight could be gauged. Doctors had observed binucleated lymphocytes in the blood of workers at the University of California Radiation Laboratory. They attributed this phenomenon to repeated exposure to low levels of radiation, and wanted to see if cosmic radiation exposure would produce similar effects. This meant they needed to study Simons' blood chemistry before the flight, so he tolerated having his fingers punctured for the experiment, even though he wasn't leaving the ground.

Major Simons boarded the capsule a little past 11:00 PM, and Captain Archibald prepared to introduce helium and oxygen to its atmosphere, just as he'd done for Kittinger's flight. At first, the capsule would not hold pressure due to a problem with a fitting on the air conditioning unit. Attempts to repair the fitting with Simons on board the capsule proved unsuccessful, so he climbed out. During this break from the test he ate a light meal that included some potato soup from a vending machine and an egg sandwich. Around 2:00 AM Simons reboarded the capsule, but this time the high-pressure relief valve in the liquid oxygen converter proved faulty, and once again *Manhigh* would not pressurize. He remained in the capsule for eight hours this time before it had to be opened again.

While waiting for the valve to be replaced Simons laid down to rest. He ate lunch at 2:00 PM, then prepared to restart the test. Finally, at 5:00 PM, nearly 18 hours later than originally planned, the capsule was pressurized, and the simulated flight began. As the huge vacuum pumps steadily removed air from the chamber, Simons noted the cabin pressure responded as expected. At the time, the temperature inside the capsule read 72°, which was uncomfortably warm for someone clad in an MC-3 pressure suit. By 8:30 PM the temperature reached 79°. Simons considered asking that someone put some dry ice on the lid of the chamber, but he felt too tired and lethargic to bother asking. Although he was thirsty, Simons was even too tired to make the effort to get anything to drink at that time. He just sat back in the seat, grateful that nobody was asking him to do anything. A half-hour later, the temperature still hovering around 80°, he summoned the strength to drink a pint of water and took two salt tablets.

To simulate the effects of having *Manhigh* float in the stratosphere overnight, ground controllers turned on the refrigeration system in the chamber, and the temperature inside the capsule began to drop. His underwear and pressure suit soaked with perspiration, Simons became uncomfortably cold as the temperature in the capsule dropped to 44° by 4:00 in the morning.

Throughout the simulated flight Simons tried to perform the same tasks he would during the actual mission. He used the cameras (which were loaded with film), even though there was nothing to photograph except the walls of the chamber; measured the brightness of the "sky" with a spot photometer; and used the 5-inch diameter telescope mounted on the side of the capsule. The telescope was added to the capsule after *Manhigh I*. Simons had a motorized control that could move a mirror on the telescope so he could look at different objects in the sky.

One of the experiments being conducted during the simulated flight was an analysis of steroid levels in Simons' urine to observe his reaction to stress. Every twelve hours he collected a sample for later analysis. Shortly before the 8:30 AM sample, Simons developed severe diarrhea pains and intestinal cramps. Stapp later opined the blueberry pie he ate the previous afternoon (during the valve repair) caused the diarrhea. Simons concluded it was from the potato soup he got from a vending machine. Whatever the source of his problem, the MC-3 suit had no provision for eliminating solid wastes. Adding to his discomfort, Simons found he could not urinate without defecating. This left two choices—either terminate the test, or endure the growing discomfort. Unwilling to end the test early, Simons chose the latter option. He restricted his diet to chocolate drops without any liquid, hoping they would give him energy without stimulating his bowels.

At 4:00 PM, Simons could not tolerate the pressure in his bladder any longer, and the test ended. After the technicians removed the upper dome from the capsule, Simons probably set some sort of record running to the bathroom and getting out of the pressure suit. Fortunately he had managed to stay in the capsule long enough to have everyone agree it was ready for the stratospheric

flight. This incident pointed out the need for emergency provisions against such an event during the flight, so a small bottle of paregoric, aluminum hydroxide gel tablets, and a plastic bag were added to the list of capsule equipment. *Manhigh II* was scheduled for mid-August.

The simulation at WADC incorporated a new tool to evaluate the effects of the flight on the pilot. Working with Captain George Ruff, an Air Force psychiatrist, Simons developed a self-assessment tool to evaluate his performance. The self-evaluation was relatively simple, based on a 0 to 100 scale, with the top score representing peak performance. The pilot also assigned a letter code to describe the temperature in the cabin. "A" stood for average, or comfortable; "H" indicated hot; "TH" was too hot; "C" represented cold; and "TC" was too cold. Simons scored himself anywhere from 35% at 2:30 AM to 100% at 10:30 AM during the chamber test. Everyone decided to use this self-assessment during the flight.

While Simons completed final preparations for *Manhigh II* personal tragedy struck. Early in the year, his father was diagnosed with inoperable stomach cancer. Throughout the remainder of the winter and into the spring Simons traveled home to Lancaster, Pennsylvania, to visit his dying father whenever he could. His last visit took place on Fathers' Day, shortly after *Manhigh I*. Although they became estranged when Major Simons opted for a research career in the Air Force, rather than joining the family practice, the senior Dr. Simons took great interest in his son's upcoming flight. Sadly, he did not live long enough to see *Manhigh II*. With less than a week before the mission, Major Simons received the dreaded phone call. His father had died—from heart failure, his body weakened by the fight with cancer. On his return to Minneapolis following the funeral, Simons had time to reflect on his father's ideals and dedication to medicine. Simons arrived back at the Winzen plant with a renewed sense of determination to complete the 24-hour scientific flight.

Three days before the flight, Simons once more began the low-residue diet regimen. He was allowed to have lean beef, liver, chicken, and fish. Permitted vegetables included one serving per day of tomatoes, peas, or carrots. Foods to be avoided included whole grain breads, rich desserts, fried foods, milk, cheese (except cottage cheese), large amounts of fat, and tough cuts of meat. Miss Beatrice Finkelstein of the WADC suggested a high-protein low-residue diet comprising foods that would be almost completely absorbed from the gastrointestinal tract. Because he was having blood drawn so frequently for the cosmic radiation studies, Simons added iron tablets to his diet. He started taking aluminum hydroxide capsules to slow his bowels on 15 August, the day before his scheduled takeoff.

Major Edward F. Smith and a detail of six Air Police were the first to arrive in Crosby on 15 August. Their arrival in town caused quite a stir; they landed in a helicopter in the middle of the town park. They were assigned to provide traffic control and VIP escort during the launch.

At noon on the fifteenth Simons took a seconal tablet, and went to bed at a motel near the Winzen plant, because Stapp wanted him fully rested for the flight. Three times during the afternoon Eunice

Hugoniot, who Simons began to refer to as "Miss Vampira," woke him to draw blood. Simons got out of bed at 6:00 PM and went with Stapp to a restaurant. He had a 12-ounce piece of lean steak, 1/3 serving of Julienne potatoes, a bowl of thin beef soup, a roll with butter, and two teaspoons of lime sherbet. Throughout the meal, Simons longed for some fresh fruit or a salad. Once dinner was over he and Stapp left the restaurant for the WRI plant.

Upon their arrival at the plant, Gildenberg informed them the weather did not look promising. Despite the gloomy forecast, everyone proceeded with the preparations just in case the weather unexpectedly improved. By 11:00 PM the sky was clouded over, with a prediction of rain squalls and gusty winds for the morning. The flight was postponed for 24 hours just as Simons was about to board the capsule. The next day the weather didn't improve, so the flight was again delayed, this time until 19 August.

Once more Simons went through the ritual of going to bed at noon, rising at six, eating a low-residue dinner at the restaurant, then driving to the plant. Stapp let Simons drive from the motel to the restaurant. During the drive, Stapp noted he talked volubly about the insidious psychological effects of the seconal, and showed a slight slowing of reflexes. At the restaurant, Simons broke his diet regimen and had a small salad with Roquefort dressing with his dinner. Stapp went along with it because he figured it wouldn't cause any problems during the next 36 hours. After the meal Stapp observed his alertness improved, and he talked with less intensity. There was a delay in getting their check at the restaurant, which made them 20 minutes late arriving at the plant.

During their drive to the WRI plant Simons and Stapp did not think the weather looked very promising, and they told Gildenberg so when they arrived. Gildenberg answered tersely that it would be fine for launch in the morning, and he showed them the weather map. By the time of the launch there would be a system of high pressure with clear weather in the area. There was a storm system to the southwest, but Gildenberg calculated it would not reach their area until at least six to eight hours after Simons landed. Stapp and Simons let the matter drop.

Neither doctor knew Gildenberg worried there was a chance the storm front would move faster than anticipated, and might reach them while *Manhigh* was in flight. Even if this happened, Gildenberg thought it would pose only a minimal risk. If it moved that fast, by the time Simons wanted to descend the storm should have passed beneath him, and it would be safe to land. Since Simons would be safely above the storm clouds as they moved through the area, Gildenberg figured it was worth the gamble to proceed with the flight, so he did not mention this possibility.

While it may sound callous to have taken such a gamble, Gildenberg didn't have any other choice. August 19th presented the only chance to launch the flight for the next several weeks. Gildenberg remembered the first attempt at launching a *Manhigh* capsule, when weather delayed the flight for nearly two months. Knowing the severe budget limitations of *Manhigh*, Gildenberg feared such a delay would kill the project. Therefore, he decided to take a calculated risk.

With the go ahead from Gildenberg, Simons began his final preparations for the flight. These included shaving as closely as possible, particularly around his neck. He did this to try to reduce irritation from the pressure suit collar later in the flight. (As a time-saving measure, years earlier Simons adopted the habit of using two electric razors so he could shave in half the time.) A microphone was taped over the fifth interspace of his chest to register his heartbeat. Kittinger wore such a microphone for both heart and breathing sounds. For *Manhigh II*, the microphone was used solely for heart sounds. Simons wore a pneumograph around his chest that transmitted a sound signal each time he inhaled and exhaled. Packets of emulsion to record cosmic radiation particle hits were taped to the right side of his chest and forearms before he donned the suit. India ink tattoo marks on his skin marked the corners of the plates. This way, recorded "hits" in the emulsion could be correlated to any hair or skin changes that occurred.

"Simons was in high spirits, and appeared rested and in excellent condition," as he climbed into the capsule seat at 10:00 PM, wrote Stapp in his Flight Surgeon's Report. "There was much handshaking and conviviality as the capsule was put together and buttoned up." Just before the capsule was sealed, Colonel Stapp, never one to miss an opportunity for a pun, reached in, shook his hand, and said: "Major, you will soon reach the high point of your

Major David G. Simons in the *Manhigh II* capsule. *Source: United States Air Force photograph*

career." Winzen handed him a box containing two cheeseburgers, a roast beef sandwich, and a cheese, bacon, and tomato sandwich.

Other foods already packed onboard included 2 standard IF-8 inflight rations, 4 cans of fruit juice, 6 candy bars, 1 can of nuts, and 2 1/2 quarts of water. The juice and nuts were packed in a metal tray on the floor of the cabin. Simons had to use a metal rod to move the tray within reach, and then it was difficult to get at its contents. Someone calculated being inside the *Manhigh* capsule was like being in a telephone booth with five suitcases.

Manhigh II carried one particular piece of equipment not found on the first flight, a recording barograph necessary to establish an official altitude record. Setting an officially recognized record also required the presence of an official judge from the National Aeronautic Association. *Life* magazine, which signed an agreement for rights to the story of *Manhigh II*, underwrote the expenses involved.

Simons found two notes inside the upper hemisphere. One, left by Otto Winzen, read: "Have all the fun you want, but don't jump up and down." This was a reference to Simons' enthusiastic nature. The second, from his children, had a map of the moon on one side and the inscription "When you reach this, come home" on the back, along with their names.

All mechanical controls within the capsule were color coded. The windows were blue; parachute release levers red; capsule shell release buttons yellow. The interior was a pastel green. For *Manhigh I*, the inside of the upper dome was white, which Kittinger reported created an uncomfortable glare, so the color was toned down for the second mission. Bright red plastic covers protected the plumbing and electrical terminal outlets. The instrument panels were black with white labels.

A "2-clo" suit lined the seat. The term "2-clo" referred to the insulating qualities of the garment, which was determined to be the equivalent of two sets of clothing. Mr. Norman Childs, who worked under the direction of Mr. Don Huxley of the Clothing Branch at the Aero Medical Laboratory, designed and fabricated the suit. Having it on the seat meant Simons could don it within the tight confines of the capsule if he got cold during the flight.

Simons ate the first cheeseburger, then closed the faceplate on his helmet and began breathing pure oxygen. This was the first step in the helium flushing process, which had been modified since *Manhigh I*. For the first flight, the procedure was based on several assumptions, and built around an analyzer that had a limited range to measure the partial pressure of oxygen in the cabin. Preliminary tests showed the oxygen content would increase as a matter of course as the flight progressed. A leak in the capsule would result in a greater rate of increase in oxygen, proportional to the leak rate. The *Manhigh I* procedure provided a relatively low partial pressure of oxygen at ceiling altitude at the start. Thus, the low partial pressure of oxygen at the start of the flight gave Kittinger a way of checking the capsule leak rate at altitude.

Manhigh II carried a Beckman analyzer, an instrument that could measure oxygen content from zero to 760 millimeters (mm) of Mercury. (Normal atmospheric pressure at sea level, which is 14.7 pounds per square inch, will support a column of Mercury 760 millimeters high.) During the low-pressure test at WADC the failure of the relief valve in the liquid oxygen converter led to the discovery that the capsule regulating system could maintain both cabin pressure and partial pressure of oxygen. With the improved analyzer, the desired balance of gases in the cabin could be maintained throughout the flight.

Using the Beckman analyzer, Archibald revised the procedure for flushing nitrogen from the cabin atmosphere. *Manhigh II*'s revised procedure comprised several additional steps from those used by Kittinger for the first flight. During step one, Simons breathed oxygen through the pressure suit mask to begin flushing nitrogen from his bloodstream. To conserve the supply inside the capsule, the oxygen came from an external supply. Excess oxygen from the mask exhausted into the cabin, so Simons continuously monitored the Beckman meter. The Firewel valve was open to prevent cabin pressure from building up. Once the partial pressure of oxygen reached 190 mm Archibald shut off the external supply, and Simons took off the helmet faceplate.

Archibald introduced helium to the capsule until the atmosphere was 5 PSI over the outside air pressure. Everyone waited 20 minutes to see if there was a leak. At 11:50 PM Simons reported the capsule atmosphere had held steady, and he opened the Firewel vent to release the excess pressure. Meanwhile, the temperature inside the capsule climbed to 80°, leaving Simons feeling listless. He

Enroute from the Winzen plant to the launch site in Crosby, Minnesota, the driver of the truck carrying the *Manhigh II* capsule stopped in an all-night gas station for fuel. *Source: New Mexico Museum of Space History*

frequently repeated words, and had long pauses between sentences. Yet, he rated himself at 95% on the self-evaluation. The dry ice cap was placed on the capsule to try to reduce the temperature.

The helium made his voice rise in pitch, but after a few minutes of squeaky-voice communication, Simons noticed he subconsciously lowered his voice pitch by muscular control. On the tape recorder he carried in the capsule Simons said:

"I've been sweating a great deal due to the warm temperature in here. They've got the ice caps on. Now I feel better. I'm going to concentrate on drying off here. I still feel pretty warm, but by putting the dryer on and putting it in the suit in various places, I'll see if I can start to cool off."

The capsule was loaded on the truck at midnight. Simons took two aluminum hydroxide tablets and ate the second cheeseburger. He closed the Firewel valve, resecured the faceplate, and began breathing oxygen again. The truck left the WRI plant at 12:41 AM. Simons monitored the Beckman analyzer until the partial pressure reached 375 mm, which occurred at 1:15 AM. At that point, the capsule atmosphere was 50% oxygen and 33.6% nitrogen. Simons closed the Firewel valve and opened the faceplate.

Because the Portsmouth Mine was 140 miles away from the WRI plant, the trip to the launch site took longer than it had for Kittinger's flight. Enroute, the truck pulled into an all-night gas station for fuel. Simons sat patiently in the capsule as the attendant filled the gasoline tank. He described the ride as "a jolting experience," and feared the Beckman analyzer, "the most important instrument onboard," might be damaged. "Checks after several hard bumps assured (him) that the meter should survive the trip to the mine." Major Simons also worried the sandwiches might spoil without refrigeration. He ate the roast beef sandwich at 4:30 AM.

Despite the bouncy ride, Simons managed to doze for 10 to 15 minutes at a time. The caravan arrived at the mine at 5:10 AM. "Although it was still dark when we arrived at the pit, a new phase of activity required my participation in making final preflight adjustments and checks. Sleep was gone, and interest in activity soared," recorded Simons. He went on to further describe the preparations:

The Winzen launch crew laid out the balloon on the road leading to the base of the mine. *Source: Photo courtesy of Dr. John Paul Stapp*

"The VHF and HF radios were rechecked, the heartbeat and respiration monitor adjusted, the telescope mirror installed, and the drive system tested. By this time, the cool night air and the dry ice had made the capsule almost uncomfortably cool, particularly because my skin was still damp under the pressure suit from the hot period following capsule closure. While helping with checks and taking pictures of the activity, I frequently wished I could do more to expedite things, and insure that the flight would soon be on its way."

Captain Archibald began the final step in adjusting the cabin atmosphere — he introduced helium again, raising the capsule air pressure by 5 PSI. As this was underway, the WRI team began laying out the balloon. The WRI crew comprised Ed Lewis, Herbert Ballman, Vern Baumgartner, Bob Enderson, Don Foster, Leander Rademacher, Clarence Olsen, Donna McCormick, Vera Winzen, and Otto Winzen.

Manhigh II used a 3-million cubic foot "natural shape" balloon made from 1.5-mil DE 2500 polyethylene resin. Fully inflated, the balloon was 200.2 feet in diameter. It comprised 70 gores. Five-hundred pound load-test glass filament bands were heat sealed

Arrival at the launch site. *Source: Photo courtesy of Dr. John Paul Stapp*

Balloon inflation begins. *Source: Photo courtesy of Dr. John Paul Stapp*

As the gas bubble formed in the top of the balloon, it assumed the familiar upside-down teardrop shape. The red inflation tubes are clearly visible. *Source: Photo courtesy of Dr. John Paul Stapp*

The launch crew moved the capsule into position beneath the balloon as they inflated it. The *Manhigh II* balloon had three inflation tubes. *Source: Photo courtesy of Dr. John Paul Stapp*

in the seams between gores, which gave the balloon a maximum strength of 35,000 pounds. There was a 14-inch diameter electric valve built into the apex of the balloon. Simons used this valve to release helium to control the ascent or begin his descent. A gear reduction motor operated the valve through an electric clutch. When Simons released the switch that opened the valve, it would snap shut automatically. This same failsafe design closed the valve if the system lost power. Electrical leads to the valve were sheathed in polyethylene, and suspended externally over the balloon and through the emergency parachute.

Inside the cabin, Simons opened the Firewel vent again to bleed off the excess pressure in the capsule and ate the last sandwich at 8:00 AM. There were five spectators reported along the north wall of the mine. Evaporating dry ice fogged over the capsule windows, so Simons couldn't see the activities underway to prepare the gigantic balloon. Stapp and Winzen kept him informed via radio of the progress towards his launch. The winds were starting to increase, causing some concern, but so far they were within limits.

Everything proceeded smoothly until just before launch. During inflation a plastic sleeve encased the lower portion of the balloon. This kept the plastic organized, and prevented it from being caught by the wind and becoming a huge sail. As the envelope rose, the launch team discovered the band around the top of the sleeve had torn loose. This type of problem was unprecedented. *Manhigh II* could not fly with the band in place, since it constricted the lower portion of the balloon. When the balloon approached its ceiling altitude the band would keep it from fully inflating, and it would burst.

Lending a sense of urgency to the situation, the winds above the pit were reaching dangerous levels. Much more, and they would dash the capsule against one of the jagged walls before it cleared the pit. The band had to be removed without delay. There was no way to lower the balloon to bring the band, which was 30 feet off the ground, in reach. Someone had to cut away the band, but who could perform the task, and how would they get to it? Word was sent to the mine headquarters that they needed a tall ladder.

The 425-foot deep Portsmouth Mine near Crosby, Minnesota, shielded the balloon from surface winds during inflation. *Source: Photo courtesy of Dr. John Paul Stapp*

With launch only minutes away, the end of the reefing sleeve that contained the balloon fabric during inflation tore loose, leaving a constricting band around the balloon. The balloon could not fly with this band in place. *Source: Photo courtesy of Dr. John Paul Stapp*

Once a ladder arrived from mine headquarters, Vera Winzen climbed it and carefully cut away the constricting band, saving the flight. *Source: Photo courtesy of Dr. John Paul Stapp*

This photo clearly shows the 40.4-foot diameter emergency parachute between the balloon and the capsule. *Source: Photo courtesy of Dr. John Paul Stapp*

Prior to launch, the Manhigh II aerostat towered 350 feet into the air. *Source: United States Air Force photograph*

Just before launch, Otto Winzen had the ground crew move *Manhigh II* closer to one side of the mine to provide as much protection from surface winds as possible. *Source: Winzen Research, Inc. photograph*

The moment of release! *Manhigh II* was underway. *Source: Photo courtesy of Dr. John Paul Stapp*

The slightest nick with a knife or pair of scissors would render the 1.5-mil envelope useless. The task fell to Vera Simons. She had more experience handling the delicate material than anyone at the launch site, so she was least likely to cut the wrong piece of plastic. A ladder was found and secured with guy wires so she could climb it. Members of the ground crew steadied the ladder as high as they could reach. She carefully climbed the ladder then reached out with a pair of scissors in one hand. A snip, and the band no longer constricted the balloon.

At Otto Winzen's instruction, ground crews edged *Manhigh* deeper into the mine to gain as much protection from the wind as possible. The balloon, which towered 350 feet above them, swayed slightly as they moved the capsule. Waiting until the balloon was directly above the capsule, Winzen yelled, "Let her go!" at 9:22 AM, CDT. *Manhigh II* was underway.

The wind caught the balloon almost immediately, and sent the capsule careening towards the wall of the mine. Peering through

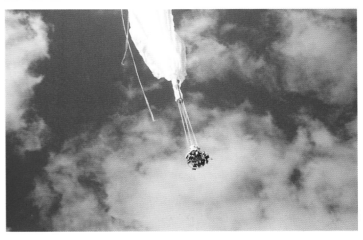

Once clear of the mine walls, *Manhigh II* climbed quickly towards the stratosphere. *Source: Photo courtesy of Dr. John Paul Stapp*

Although Otto Winzen had the ground crew move the capsule deeper into the mine to protect the balloon from the surface winds in the minutes before launch, once it was airborne, the wind pushed it towards one of the walls. Simons narrowly missed being dashed against the wall. *Source: Photo courtesy of Dr. John Paul Stapp*

the tiny windows, Simons saw he was headed for the rust-streaked, jagged face. The ground crew held their breath, fearing a crash just as the flight started. Simons swung to within a yard of one of the cliffs. Then, everyone breathed a collective sigh of relief as the capsule cleared the lip of the mine. Seeing that he was clear and was at last airborne, Simons felt both a tremendous thrill and a sense of responsibility now that the flight was finally a reality.

It turned out *Manhigh II* lifted off just in the nick of time. Surface winds steadily increased after Simons cleared the mine. Had the balloon been launched even a few minutes later, Simons would have almost certainly hit the mine's wall.

At first, the balloon climbed at a rate of 1,200 feet per minute, which was too high. Winzen advised Simons to vent helium and bring the ascent to 1,000 feet per minute. Over the next twenty-four minutes, he opened the valve six times for a total of three minutes. Simons spoke into a small tape recorder to record his observations.

The already chilled capsule became cooler as it ascended, and soon Simons' fingers became stiff with cold, which interfered with his ability to manipulate the spot photometer and cameras. At 10,000 feet the automatic pressure control valve began to reduce the air pressure inside the capsule. The pressure continued to drop until *Manhigh* reached 24,000 feet, after which it held steady. Up to 30,000 feet the sky looked like it had during many of the flights Simons made previously in jet aircraft. Above that point, however, he was in new territory.

"Forty-nine thousand, just coming up on fifty thousand feet. The sky is beginning to darken very, very markedly at this time... much more so than I had ever noticed it before. It is especially noticeable when you look up at the balloon. In fact, it almost looks black," radioed Simons to the ground. At 54,000 feet he commented on how the balloon formed a triangular shape, with very little flapping by the folds of plastic.

Reaching 68,500 feet, Simons recorded "(the clouds) are beautiful. You can just see for miles and miles. The ground detail is already beginning to fade. By the time you get out to 45 degrees there is a continuous haze, particularly from 30 degrees

Two and a half hours after launch, Simons reached 102,000 feet. *Source: Manhigh II*

magnetic." To the west he observed a build up of clouds, "right up to the tropopause." *Manhigh* carried an electric thermister to measure outside air temperature. It comprised two heated wires on a rotating arm. As the arm revolved the wires cooled. The amount of current consumed to reheat the wires indicated the air temperature. Simons turned on the thermister waver motor.

As *Manhigh* ascended to 75,000 feet the rate of climb reached 1,200 feet per minute again. Winzen advised Simons to vent some helium to retard the rate. He opened the valve for 30 seconds. Outside the capsule, the sky appeared increasingly dark as *Manhigh* drifted westward across Minnesota at about 20 miles per hour.

Atmospheric pressure drops by half every 18,000 feet. So, when the balloon approached 85,000 feet, it should have appeared about half full. Comparing the reading from the Wallace and Tiernan pressure gauge to the appearance of the balloon, it became apparent the gauge was off by a wide margin. As it turned out, personnel from the Bureau of Standards had recalibrated it so it read nearly 30% high. According to the Wallace and Tiernan instrument, *Manhigh* was above 100,000 feet, which was near the theoretical maximum for the balloon, but it still was not half full yet. The balloon continued to climb, well past the altitude it was capable of. Finally, as the gauge indicated an altitude of 130,000 feet, the inflation ducts on the balloon began to swell, showing it had reached its maximum altitude. As measured by ground-based radar, *Manhigh II* was 102,000 feet above the earth. Simons had been aloft for two hours, eighteen minutes.

As he floated above 99% of the atmosphere, Major Simons could see 400 miles in any direction. To his east he spotted Lake Michigan; below him, he saw a strip of green winding through the brown landscape. It was the Missouri River. A line of thunderstorms loomed southwest of him. Every time he moved inside the cabin he felt the entire aerostat vibrate. The temperature inside the cabin was a comfortable 52° F, despite the fact that the capsule wall was nearly 100° on the side facing the sun.

He spent the day making observations with both the unaided eye and the five-inch telescope, taking photographs, and measuring sky brightness with a spot photometer. Simons found it difficult to use the telescope to observe ground features because the balloon slowly rotated, first in one direction, then in the other. An F-89 *Scorpion* aircraft flew beneath him to see if he could observe it or its contrails. Weather conditions were not conducive for the formation of contrails from the jet, so he could not see it.

Noticing Simons' voice seemed sluggish, around 2:00 PM Stapp suggested he eat a candy bar to maintain his blood sugar level. Inside *Manhigh*, Simons rated himself at 95%. Condensation formed inside the upper hemisphere from the super cold dry ice that topped the capsule. The condensation froze until late in the afternoon, when the dry ice melted. With the dry ice cap gone, water began dripping on Simons and the photo panel. Condensation collected on the windows, too, as the ice inside the cabin melted. Simons directed the hose from the air conditioning unit towards the windows to dry them off.

Looking outside, Simons tried to match the sky to a series of color charts he carried. "I tried to compare the color charts to the sky color, the green...one was too green, the other too purplish violet, because the sky has the blue of an ocean blue, pure clean lapis lazuli blue, at the interface between the dark purple sky above and the white typical of looking through the atmosphere horizontally toward the horizon. The color above this is deep indigo, intense, almost black. In fact, the point is, what little color is there is very deep and intense, although there isn't very much. It is nearly black," he recorded shortly before 3:00 PM.

As the sun approached the horizon the balloon began to cool, and *Manhigh* lost altitude. While the altimeter could not provide the actual height, changes in altitude could be measured. "We have now lost from 135,000 feet down to 127,000, and obviously are descending even on the meter. So we shall use dribble ballast," reported Simons. Based on what the altimeter showed, he calculated

As the day progressed, Simons noticed a line of thunderstorms approaching from the west. *Source: Manhigh II*

Manhigh was at 98,000 feet, so he dropped six pounds of ballast to reverse the trend.

The cabin wall on the side facing the sun was 120°; the temperature in the cabin was 75°. At takeoff, the water core cooler was only about two-thirds full. Now, as the flight progressed, it was not operating at peak efficiency because it was only partially filled. With the cabin so warm, Simons knew he would perspire under the pressure suit, which would leave him feeling chilled later in the night when the capsule cooled.

Throughout the day the VHF radio link between Simons and the mobile command post had been excellent. Now, it occasionally shifted frequencies and had to be manually adjusted. This hinted at a slight malfunction that could get progressively worse until the radio broke down completely. The HF radio beacon (the backup method of communications used by Kittinger), which also broadcast pulse and respiration data, failed around 4:30 in the afternoon. If the VHF radio failed, Simons would not be able to talk to the ground (and vice versa). Should this happen, he would be truly isolated during the night, and on his own to deal with any other problems that might come up. "Are you willing to see it through the night alone if the radio fails?" asked Winzen.

Simons took a quick mental inventory of his situation. Throughout the day the balloon had maintained its altitude. If it had even the smallest leak, he would have had trouble remaining at the ceiling altitude. Other than the high temperature, which he knew would abate after sundown, the capsule systems were working well. So far the flight was going smoothly, and he had complete faith in the capsule and balloon. "May I please remain aloft for the night?"

Taking the microphone in hand, Stapp reminded Simons that if the radio failed he would be alone, particularly during the night. Like Kittinger had prior to his flight, Simons realized there was little the people on the ground could do to help him anyway, so he decided the possibility of a radio failure did not really matter.

Simons was willing to take the chance that the VHF radio would continue working. After weighing all the factors, everyone decided to let the flight continue.

About 7:00 PM, Stapp noted Simons again sounded fatigued. Stapp suggested he eat two more candy bars. Adding to his fatigue, the capsule temperature was 76 degrees, which drained his energy. In spite of the heat stress and physical fatigue, he still rated himself at the 95% level, and continued his observations.

The sun set at 8:50 PM. Watching the sunset was particularly moving, as was the setting of Venus, with a brilliant display of colors. Stars burned brilliantly without twinkling. There was a quarter moon. During the day, the storm front had been heading his way, much faster than predicted. Now, Simons could look down and see thunderstorms churning beneath him, with lightning flashing through the clouds. Although he was comfortably above the storm clouds, Simons watched them with concern. "The clouds were becoming sirens, beautiful but dangerous. Although fascinatingly lovely to watch, especially important for their fine detail and

During the night the line of thunderstorms continued to build, and stalled beneath the capsule. *Source: Manhigh II*

fantastic forms, like gigantic cauliflowers or brains lighted from within, the thunderheads posed a threat. The aerostat was steadily losing altitude, inexorably approaching the thunderheads," recalled Simons in his post flight report. Besides cooling the capsule and relieving his heat-related discomfort, night cooled the balloon, causing it to descend.

With the clouds blocking the ground the balloon cooled more than expected, and began dropping closer to the storm. Simons worried about lightning striking the 300-foot wire antenna that hung beneath the capsule. After discussing the situation with Otto Winzen, Major Simons dropped two expended batteries (100 pounds) about an hour after sunset to slow the descent, and level off at 80,000 feet. Since thunderheads were not known to reach above 45,000 or 50,000 feet at that latitude, Simons felt safe. He could float comfortably above the storm until morning. Within the capsule, the heat continued. In fact, it was not until 10:00 PM before the temperature began to drop, and midnight before he felt any relief from the heat.

Part of the reason the temperature remained high was that Simons shut off the cooling system at 9:00. He did this in anticipation of the cold night ahead. All the windows frosted over, and Simons had to either wipe them with a tissue, or use the exhaust hose from the air regeneration system to clear the ice. As the balloon descended, it rotated. Simons used the air hose to keep one window clear, which gave him a panoramic view of the sky and clouds. Attempts to observe the same spot as the capsule rotated by cleaning windows as they came into position didn't work, because they would frost over again after only five to fifteen seconds.

In his 10:30 report Simons indicated his back hurt, and his left knee was giving him trouble. In addition, he reported feeling hungry, thirsty, and most of all, tired. The period from evening through several hours past sunset should have produced some of the most interesting observations of the flight. Unfortunately, the high cabin temperatures sapped Simons' energy and ability to focus. Despite this situation, he rated himself at better than 95%, partly because he didn't want to give any reason for terminating the flight. He did manage to observe Mrkos' comet, which he described as "very pretty," and the aurora borealis.

Around 11:30 he advised ground control he was going to sleep for a while. Simons slept until a little past midnight. While he slept *Manhigh* continued to descend, so he dropped another battery after he woke up. Stapp asked him to eat something to bring up his blood sugar level; Simons complied by eating three candy bars. Over the course of the next few hours Simons napped several more times.

During the night the thunderstorms stalled beneath him. Simons realized why Gildenberg had seemed moody the night before. The meteorologist had obviously been wrestling with whether to let the flight proceed or not. Simons understood the situation and did not fault Gildenberg. Given the same situation, Simons would have made the same decision, for he knew they faced a "now or never" proposition with the flight.

Simons dropped another battery at 2:30 AM, then reported the cabin temperature was down to 40° F. Since his undergarment was soaked with perspiration this was uncomfortably cold. He decided to put on the 2-clo suit, which took 25 minutes in the tight confines of the capsule. Movements inside the capsule had to be made very carefully. In the frigid stratosphere, the balloon could easily shatter if subjected to any sudden shocks or stresses. With the insulated suit on Simons made some more observations with the telescope, then settled in for another nap.

A little past 4:00 AM Simons was startled awake as the capsule abruptly dropped 500 feet. Lightning flashes filled the cabin with light. He had descended to 68,000 feet. Looking out the windows he could not see any stars, which meant the thunderheads towered much higher than previously thought. Suddenly the balloon gave a strong twist! He was dangerously close to the storm! Watching the lightning, Simons dropped two more batteries and rose to a higher, safer altitude.

Looking to the eastern horizon, Simons noted the first faint glow of the impending sunrise. Temperatures inside the capsule were down to 32°, which made it difficult for Simons to operate the photometer and cameras. In spite of the cold, he felt energized as he looked forward to the start of a new day. On the ground, all the vehicles and aircraft were placed on standby, but they could not be dispatched because of the thunderstorms.

When the sun broke across the horizon at 6:05, Simons saw a green flash through a slit in the clouds. Basking in the sun's warm, friendly glow, Simons felt a sense of security and well being unlike anything he'd experienced thus far during the flight. Winzen suggested that Simons eat one of his IF-8 rations. It consisted of ham and eggs, peaches, and a nut roll. As he ate, Simons began feeling that he should be heading towards space; that he belonged there. Such emotions quickly evaporated once he became engrossed in making observations and performing other flight-related tasks. Because the beacon wasn't working, Simons took bearings from several omnirange stations on the ground, and radioed this information to the control van. By plotting the bearings on a map, his location could be determined.

After sunrise the balloon warmed, and eventually rose to 100,000 feet. Still, the storm continued below him. During the early morning hours, Simons began having trouble with the VHF radio as the voltage from the remaining lead-acid batteries dropped to just over 10 volts. Simons switched on the emergency batteries. He could see the western edge of the storm and the ground beneath, and reported the view "gives one a feeling of being in heaven, above the world, where you can look down over the edge and see the poor faltering mortals. It's a strange sensation, a quiet world, peaceful, bright, and dark at the same time."

The temperature inside the cabin had climbed to 55°. Although it was still cold, Simons shed the 2-clo suit, because he expected the capsule to warm as the day progressed. He also turned on the water core cooler to keep things comfortable as long as possible.

Manhigh still drifted above a tongue of clouds that extended to the west from the main storm system. Gildenberg advised that, in order to clear the clouds as rapidly as possible, the balloon should gain some altitude, where there was a stronger westward wind. At 9:50 Simons dropped the last lead-acid battery and switched completely to the emergency batteries, which could only power all the systems in the capsule for about six hours. This gave a deadline of

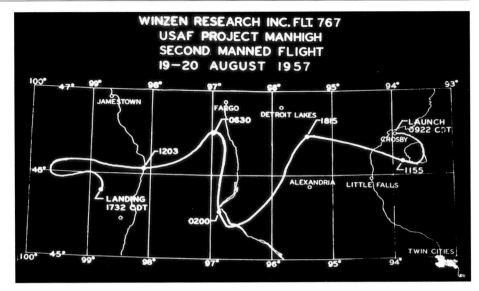

Manhigh II ground track. Source: Photo courtesy of Dr. John Paul Stapp

3:50 PM for the system that powered both the air regeneration and air cooler blowers.

About an hour later Simons noticed it took an unusually long time to make a set of omnirange readings. He repeatedly forgot to make the 180° correction in his readings, and even lost track of what he was doing in mid-task. Unable to concentrate, he passed it off as fatigue and was not concerned.

When Stapp asked him to report his respiration rate, Simons replied it was 44 breaths per minute. Normal respiration is about 12-18 breaths per minute. At the time, Simons didn't see anything unusual about his breathing, which told Stapp Simons' judgment was impaired. When asked to report the carbon dioxide level in the cabin, he replied it was 4%, well above the safe limit. Partly because the flight had gone longer than planned, and partly because

the lithium hydroxide in the air regeneration system had cooled during the night, which reduced its efficiency, the carbon dioxide level in the cabin began to rise. Four percent was well in the range of producing such symptoms as mental confusion and inability to concentrate.

Throughout the flight Simons had been in charge of the balloon. Now, due to the toxic effects of the carbon dioxide building up in the cabin, his judgment could not be counted on. Per pre-arranged and agreed upon procedures, Stapp and Winzen took control of the flight. Simons was told to take only those actions directed to do so by personnel on the ground.

Since the balloon had drifted clear of the storm, Winzen told Simons to open the balloon vent valve for ten minutes to begin his descent. While doing this, Simons put on his faceplate and

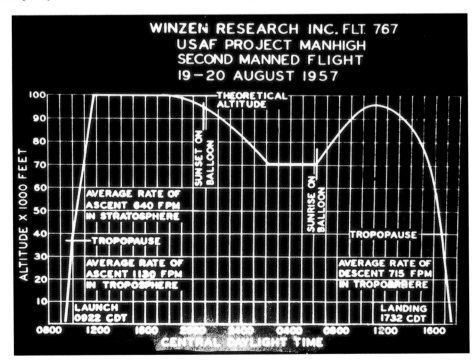

Manhigh II altitude profile. Source: Photo courtesy of Dr. John Paul Stapp

breathed pure oxygen through the suit. After ten minutes on the suit, he opened the faceplate for ten minutes. Simons continued this procedure—ten minutes with the faceplate closed, ten minutes with it open—throughout the next hour. This gave the air scrubber time to work. By 11:25 AM the amount of carbon dioxide stabilized at an acceptable 2% level. A half-hour later, it was down to 1/2%.

Despite repeated valving for a cumulative time of 46 minutes, the balloon stubbornly refused to descend. An hour and a half after Simons first opened the vent valve, *Manhigh* remained at the same altitude. Simons suspected *Manhigh* was either caught in a strong temperature inversion, or the balloon was superheating in the sun. He continued valving for up to ten minutes at a time. Finally, around 12:45 PM, he began to descend.

Unfortunately, the balloon soon began to rise again. Winzen suggested *Manhigh* was caught in a wave motion of air near the storm front. Another theory was that the balloon was picking up heat as it descended. Whatever the cause, this yo-yo motion continued until 2:00 in the afternoon, when Simons finally managed to establish a steady rate of descent. The balloon was down to 86,000 feet; temperatures inside the cabin had reached 80°. Despite the extreme discomfort from the heat, Simons turned off the cooling system. He presumed the air moving past the capsule would have a cooling effect, and he needed to conserve battery power for the air regeneration system, because the 3:50 deadline for keeping everything running was approaching. As a further energy conservation move, Simons asked permission to turn off the radio intermittently.

Descending through 75,000 feet, Simons felt a burning pain in his shoulder. The telescope was adjusted so that the sun was focused on his pressure suit, which began to smolder. Simons quickly adjusted the mirror so the image would no longer be directed through the optics and into the cabin. The temperature inside the cabin remained at 80°, which drained Simons. Still, he had to remain alert and focused to retain control over the aerostat. Feeling hungry, he fished out the can of nuts and munched on them throughout the rest of the descent.

The descent rate was 310 feet per minute, which was slower than it should be, so Simons released some more helium. Winzen wanted Simons to establish a 400-foot per minute descent rate. This would take him through the tropopause quickly, which was necessary, because there was a 90-mile per hour jet stream that could carry him into the storm if he lingered too long.

At the same time, Winzen did not want the balloon to drop too fast when it reached the tropopause. When a balloon reaches the tropopause, around 40,000 feet, the descent rate established in the stratosphere doubles. This is exactly what happened. Because the balloon was slow to respond to repeated valving Simons released too much helium, and ended up descending faster than desired. Emerging from the tropopause, Simons was descending at 1,000 feet per minute. Dropping that fast, it was going to be a hard landing.

At 25,000 feet Simons opened one of the windows. The cool outside air felt particularly refreshing as it entered the cabin. Simons dropped one of the external emergency batteries as *Manhigh*

Manhigh II on the ground as viewed from the recovery helicopter. *Source: Photo courtesy of Dr. John Paul Stapp*

passed through a cumulus cloud layer a few thousand feet above the ground. Several minutes later he dropped the last 100 pounds of ballast. This slowed the descent, but he was still coming down fast. There was only enough battery power left to fire the explosive squibs that released the balloon after touchdown. Simons braced for a hard landing.

Finally, 32 hours and 10 minutes after launch, Major Simons landed in an alfalfa field ten miles northwest of Frederick, South Dakota. Everything in the cabin that could come loose did. Releasing the balloon required an upward throw of the switch, and the landing was so hard Simons' hand slipped. The capsule toppled over and was dragged fifty yards before he could find the switch to cut away the balloon.

Smelling a burning, acrid odor, Major Simons feared the highly toxic bromine fire extinguisher in the cabin had discharged. (The odor turned out to be the lithium hydroxide in the air regeneration system.) He held his breath, quickly released the upper hemisphere, and clambered out. Winzen and Stapp landed nearby in a helicopter. As Simons stood alongside the capsule, the farmer who owned the field and his young son came running over. "Oh look Daddy! A helicopter! I've always wanted to see one of those!"

An exhausted but happy David Simons after his epic flight to 102,000 feet. *Source: Photo courtesy of Dr. John Paul Stapp*

Otto Winzen discusses the just completed flight with Simons while Colonel Stapp draws blood. *Source: Photo courtesy of Dr. John Paul Stapp*

shouted the boy, ignoring the physician who had just ventured to the edge of space, and the capsule that carried him there.

Stapp and the rest of the recovery team surrounded Simons, checking to make sure he was okay, and congratulating him on completing the flight. Blood was drawn from Simons' arm for the cosmic radiation studies. Stapp observed he split his lip during landing, and had a thick growth of beard after 43 hours in the pressure suit. Along the angles of his jaw, particularly on the left side, there were raw spots from the helmet neck seal. Stapp and Simons boarded the helicopter for a flight to Fargo, North Dakota. As the helicopter took off Simons tried to tell Stapp about the landing, but quickly became unintelligible and fell asleep.

Simons was immediately catapulted into the limelight. General Sam Anderson, commander of the ARDC, personally awarded

him the Distinguished Flying Cross, and announced his promotion to Lieutenant Colonel. He appeared on the cover of the September 2, 1957, issue of *Life*, and his personal account of *Manhigh II* was the lead story. The headline for the story read: "A Journey No Man Had Taken," with the subtitle: "Balloonist Invades Space, Brings Back Vivid Record." *Manhigh II* was hailed as an amazing adventure on the road to space.

To his dismay, Simons learned soon after his flight that the "vivid record" brought back did not include many of the tape recordings of his inflight observations. His tape recorder had malfunctioned during much of the flight, and the tapes that covered significant portions of his sojourn were either blank or filled with static. Fortunately, he had written down many of his most important observations as a backup. Even worse than the blank tapes,

One of the differences in the capsule between the first two flights was the addition of a five-inch telescope. This photograph shows the mirror Simons used to "point" the instrument towards different portions of the sky. *Source: Photo courtesy of Dr. John Paul Stapp*

Even in a South Dakota alfalfa field, *Manhigh II* attracted a crowd of curious onlookers when it landed. *Source: Photo courtesy of Dr. John Paul Stapp*

though, the WRI accountant informed him that after *Manhigh II*, the project was completely broke. There wasn't even enough money to pay someone to transcribe the data tapes and logs, so for the time being, everything would have to be placed in storage.

The Air Force did fund his attendance at the 6th Congress of the International Astronautical Federation (IAF) in Barcelona, Spain, to present a scientific paper describing his flight. Simons arrived in Europe on 2 October, a few days before the Congress started. Two days later, he noticed everyone seemed excited as they gathered around radios and newspaper stands. Unable to speak the language, it took Simons a few moments to find out what was going on. The Soviet Union had just launched the world's first artificial satellite, *Sputnik*.

American reaction to *Sputnik* ranged from concern to outright fear in some Washington circles. Their achievement meant the Soviets had a rocket large enough to lob a nuclear warhead halfway

around the world. It also signified the level of Soviet technology was far higher than many western experts previously believed. Space suddenly became a new arena for competition between Communism and Democracy. Spending for space related projects rapidly increased.

During the IAF Congress in Barcelona, Brigadier General Don Flickinger, head of human factors research at the ARDC, contacted Simons, and instructed him to stop by Command Headquarters in Baltimore on his way back to Holloman. Flickinger assembled the Air Force's top space medicine experts to discuss how soon they could launch a human into space. At the meeting, Flickinger pulled Simons aside and told him to plan on a third mission in 1958. Simons realized that, as a necessary preliminary step before a third *Manhigh* flight took place, the data from his mission would have to be analyzed. Lieutenant Colonel Simons intended to get started as soon as he returned to the AMFL.

Although he was exhausted, Simons took time after his flight to grant a media interview. *Source: Winzen Research, Inc. photograph*

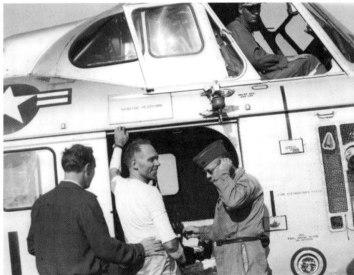

Major Simons boards the recovery helicopter. He was so fatigued from the flight that he fell asleep shortly after the aircraft took off. *Source: Winzen Research, Inc. photograph*

9

Manhigh III

The Soviets followed their first satellite with a second *Sputnik* on 3 November. What made this flight even more of a space spectacular, *Sputnik II* carried a dog named *Laika*. Unfortunately for *Laika*, the Soviets did not have a means of returning her to earth. For years afterward Soviet authorities insisted that *Laika* survived nearly a week in orbit before she was painlessly put to sleep. Actually, thermal insulation that protected her cabin tore loose when the nose cone separated, and she died after only a few hours in space from the heat.

Regardless of *Laika's* fate, the message to the world was that Soviet space technology matched or surpassed anything available in the West. After all, Russian rockets had orbited two satellites, something the United States had not achieved even once. Making matters even worse, both Soviet satellites were much heavier than anything announced by the Americans. To many observers around the world, it appeared the Soviet Union was ahead of the United States in what became a race for space superiority.

American prestige suffered another blow on December 6, 1957. The first American attempt to launch a satellite, with the Navy's *Vanguard* rocket, ended in disaster. Two seconds after lift-off the first stage engine faltered. *Vanguard* settled back on the pad and collapsed in a massive explosion. The six-inch diameter test satellite lay on the ground, battered and burned. Some journalists referred to the unsuccessful test as "Flopnik."

After *Sputnik II*, the Army Ballistic Missile Agency requested permission to attempt a satellite launch. They were given the green light to proceed. Finally, on January 31, 1958, the U.S. Army launched the first American satellite, *Explorer I*, with a *Jupiter-C* rocket. The *Jupiter-C* was based on the Army's *Redstone* missile. Wernher von Braun, who headed the *V-2* missile program in Germany during World War II, led the team that developed the *Redstone* and *Jupiter-C*.

When World War II ended, von Braun and over a hundred of his rocket group surrendered to the United States. American forces also captured enough components to assemble nearly 80 *V-2* missiles for launch from White Sands Proving Grounds. In the years immediately after the war, the German rocket scientists helped American crews launch *V-2s* from the New Mexico desert. They eventually relocated to Redstone Arsenal in northern Alabama, where they continued developing rockets for the Army. The *Redstone* was the first large liquid-fuel rocket they created in America. It had a range of 200 miles. To transform the *Redstone* into a space

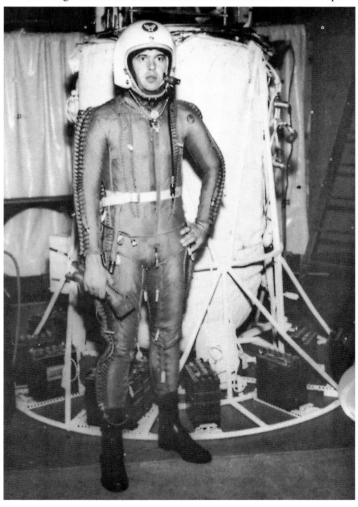

Lieutenant Clifton McClure standing in front of the *Manhigh III* capsule.
Source: United States Air Force photograph

launch vehicle, von Braun added three upper stages of solid-fuel rocket motors.

Despite the Army's success with *Explorer I*, President Dwight D. Eisenhower believed America's space research needs could best be met by a civilian agency. President Eisenhower submitted a request to Congress on April 2, 1958, calling for the creation of such an organization. The existing National Advisory Committee for Aeronautics (NACA) formed the nucleus of the new agency. On 10 July 10 President Eisenhower signed the National Aeronautics and Space Act into law. It created the National Aeronautics and Space Administration (NASA), which absorbed the NACA and its laboratories; the Navy's *Vanguard* satellite program; Army and Air Force lunar programs; and Air Force large rocket motor programs. (Later, those elements of the Army Ballistic Missile Agency working on large boosters under Wernher von Braun became part of NASA.) The civilian agency was scheduled to officially come into being on 1 October.

With the new national emphasis on space research, *Manhigh III* became a testing ground for eventual space missions. Advocates for high altitude ballooning believed it offered a closer approximation of space flight than could be created on the ground. A person could be sustained in a sealed cabin on the ground like the "space cabin simulator" developed by Hubertus Strughold at the Air Force School of Aviation Medicine. But there were stresses,

particularly psychological ones, encountered during high altitude balloon missions that could not be duplicated on earth. *Manhigh* aeronauts faced such psychological stresses as isolation and "time remoteness." A ground simulation could be aborted, and the subject reached quickly in case of trouble. This was not the case during *Manhigh* flights, a factor that added a depth of psychological stress that could not be duplicated on the ground.

As described by the Air Force in their pre-flight Fact Sheet, "(the) purpose of the *Manhigh III* flight, conducted by the Air Research and Development Command (ARDC) of the United States Air Force, is to continue research in the field of space medicine. It will involve the investigation of human reactions under space equivalent conditions with special emphasis on the psycho-physiological area of interactions." The Fact Sheet went on to state: "(the) flight is a necessary stepping stone in the Air Force program of putting man into space."

In an effort to make the flight as scientifically productive as possible, a panel of experts on the ground directed the pilot's observations and activities while aloft. The panel included specialists in space medicine; physiology; meteorology; astronomy; cosmic radiation; atmospheric physics; and capsule design. The pilot was supposed to transmit a report every 30 minutes, and blocks of time were set aside for individual researchers. According to the pre-flight Fact Sheet:

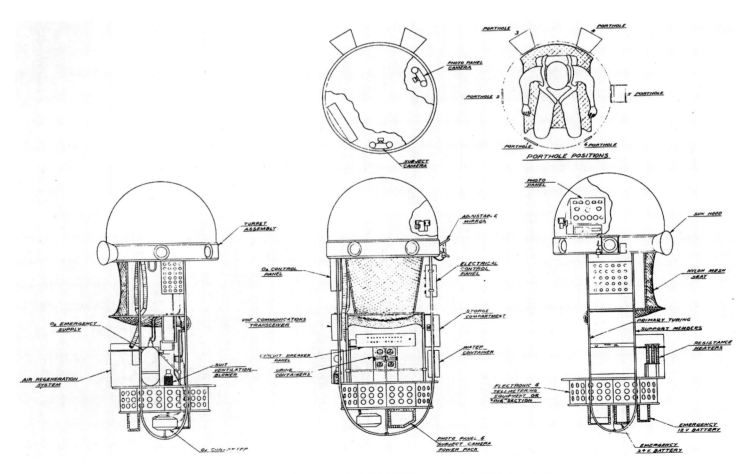

Manhigh III capsule schematic. *Source: Manhigh III USAF Manned Balloon Flight Into the Stratosphere.*

"As the pilot is not an expert in the various fields mentioned above, he acts as the eyes and the hands of the panel members who interrogate him while he conducts the experiments."

One of the findings from *Manhigh II* was that the pilot was probably least able to objectively judge his condition. Throughout the flight, Simons consistently evaluated his performance as better than 90%, despite the debilitating effects of heat, fatigue, and carbon dioxide buildup. Once the deadly effects of carbon dioxide took their toll on Simons, Dr. Stapp was not aware because the HF radio had failed. Had the telemetry system been working, Stapp would have noted Simons' rapid respiration sooner. Because of this, Simons decided better physiological data was necessary. *Manhigh III* included instruments to transmit the pilot's electrocardiogram, breathing rate, and basal skin resistance, or BSR, to the ground. The BSR measured the skin's conductivity, which would tell how much the pilot perspired to provide an indicator of stress. These data were continuously transmitted. The pilot had to periodically report his body temperature to the ground.

Simons and Ruff reworked the self-assessment in an effort to make it more objective and comprehensive. Dr. James Henry, the physician who launched monkeys aboard *V-2s* and *Aerobees*, also contributed to the revised evaluation. Instead of only giving himself an overall score, the pilot had to make subjective assessments of his alertness, drive, tension, comfort, and efficiency. Within each category, the pilot had to describe his feelings. For example, in the alertness area, the pilot described himself as feeling "keen alert," "average," or "sleepy." Choices for "drive" were "eager," "enjoy activity," and "don't care." Tension choices comprised "relaxed," "calm," and "uneasy." The comfort area referred to the temperature, and offered five choices from hot to cold. Only in the category termed "efficiency" was the pilot asked to assign a numeric value to his performance. Simons hoped to cross-index the physiological and psychological data against the pilot's actual performance to develop data for predicting how someone would respond to space flight.

Winzen received the contract for the mission in February 1958, and work proceeded rapidly. The third flight required a totally new capsule. Drawing upon the first two missions, many systems were revised. The air regeneration system and radio beacon, which had previously been mounted externally, were moved inside the capsule to clean up its exterior. Outwardly, *Manhigh III* was a foot taller than the previous capsule. Despite the fact that it was larger, improvements in capsule systems kept it at nearly the same weight as its predecessor.

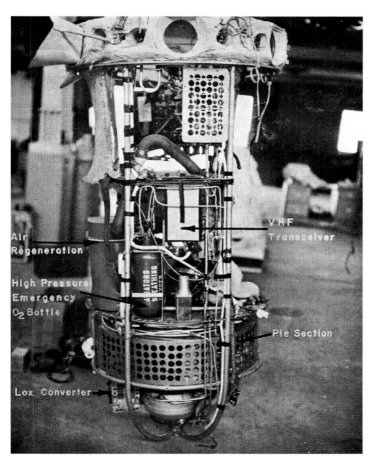

Interior shot of the *Manhigh III* capsule showing the location of the air regeneration unit directly beneath the pilot's seat. *Source: Manhigh III USAF Manned Balloon Flight Into the Stratosphere.*

Manhigh III instrument panel. *Source: Manhigh III USAF Manned Balloon Flight Into the Stratosphere.*

Structurally, the capsule followed the pattern of the previous ones—that is, it comprised an upper hemisphere, lower body shell, internal frame, and turret. An external aluminum frame supported the capsule prior to launch, and doubled as a crushable landing gear. In a departure from previous capsules, the turret was machined from stainless steel.

The *Manhigh III* capsule used the same emergency parachute system as before, with one significant difference. When a cutaway signal was broadcast from the ground, a tone sounded in the pilot's headphones. He had thirty seconds to override the cutaway. This would, presumably, prevent an inadvertent cutdown.

By the time Winzen received the contract Stapp had been promoted to Colonel, and transferred to Wright Patterson Air Force Base as head of the Aero Medical Laboratory. Lieutenant Colonel Rufus Hessberg took his place at Holloman. Prior to his move to the AMFL, Hessberg headed the Biophysics Branch at the Aero Medical Laboratory. As it turned out, he was no stranger to *Manhigh*. During Simons' balloon flight, Hessberg was dispatched from Wright Field and rode in one of the tracking planes as a paramedic in case of an emergency.

Besides being moved inside the capsule, the air regeneration system was completely redesigned. Instead of having three separate chemicals to remove moisture and carbon dioxide from the cabin atmosphere, *Manhigh III* used a single chemical system. A blower circulated cabin air through a canister filled with 16 pounds of potassium hydroxide, which absorbed both moisture and carbon dioxide.

The goal of redesigning the air regeneration unit was to create a simpler, lighter system. Initially, a system where cabin air bubbled through a solution of potassium hydroxide was examined, but

The *Manhigh III* capsule with the "Major Ferriby" camera package. Technical problems with the camera package kept it from flying on the mission. *Source: Manhigh III USAF Manned Balloon Flight Into the Stratosphere.*

the nozzles kept clogging. In any event, such a system was deemed not feasible for use in a weightless environment. Since *Manhigh III* was supposed to investigate design elements for future orbital spacecraft, it was rejected. Solid potassium hydroxide was tried next. This chemical had the advantage of being able to remove carbon dioxide and water vapor from the air.

As cabin air passed through bags containing potassium hydroxide, the chemical absorbed moisture. Eventually, a concentrated solution of the hydroxide would drip from the bags. The solution was collected in a pan. Air entering the regeneration unit passed over the solution, which continued to absorb carbon dioxide. From a pilot safety perspective, there was one potentially serious drawback to having a solution of potassium hydroxide inside the cabin. It was very caustic, and would burn the pilot's skin if any leaked out of the unit. Therefore, the unit was designed so that the caustic solution would not flow out even if the capsule toppled over. The pilot also had valves at both ends of the unit he could close prior to landing to further ensure there would be no leakage. During ground testing of a system using potassium hydroxide, it was noted that air leaving the unit was ten degrees warmer than air entering it. At the time, no special notation was made of this.

Manhigh III represented a reversal in design philosophy regarding temperature control. Rather than build a capsule that would heat up and require cooling, *Manhigh III's* designers tried to create a gondola that was normally cool, and required heating during the night. Alternating layers of aluminized mylar and honeycombed cardboard covered the earlier Manhigh capsule to insulate against extremes of temperature. *Manhigh III* had an improved insulation system topped by a white coverlayer. *Manhigh's* designers believed this would be enough to keep the capsule cool, and they removed the water core heat exchanger and added a heater. Another major departure from previous *Manhigh* protocols was that this design was not test flown with animals; the first time it left the ground it carried a human pilot.

Following the precedent established for the first two flights, Lieutenant Colonel Simons nominated two individuals for this ascent. His initial choices were Otto Winzen as primary pilot, and an AMFL physiologist was his alternate. The alternate pilot was likely Captain Eli "Lack" Beeding. The Air Force Technical Report on *Manhigh III* presents a detailed description of the pilot selection process for the flight, with one exception—names were withheld. In a later account of the flight, Simons revealed Winzen's consideration as primary pilot. Evidence points to Beeding as the alternate, as will be explained shortly.

They both began the same evaluation and training processes as Kittinger and Simons, with a few changes. Because of his civilian status, Winzen did not have to perform the parachute jump. The David Clark Company in Worcester, Massachusetts, manufactured the MC-3 pressure suits worn on the first two flights. For *Manhigh III*, the David Clark Company received a contract to modify the suits to provide greater ventilation and comfort during prolonged wear. The pilots also underwent thorough eye examinations by Dr. D. V. L. Brown of Chicago. Dr. Brown would re-examine the pilot after his flight to detect any changes caused by heavy cosmic radiation particles. Captain Ruff evaluated the candidates at the Stress and Fatigue Section at the WADC. His examinations included psychiatric interviews and psychological evaluations that incorporated a subject-terminated session in an anechoic, lightless chamber.

Unfortunately, both candidates were eliminated from consideration in June. After that, General Flickinger suggested that candidates be screened to meet the qualifications anticipated for future space pilots. Since there were no space pilots at that time, qualifications for space men of the future would be tested by *Manhigh*.

Simons indicated in the *Manhigh III* report that two more candidates were considered. He described the first two candidates (Winzen and an unnamed Air Force officer) as having been directly connected to the *Manhigh* project. A Fact Sheet released by the Air Force on the third flight mentions Beeding as the primary pilot, which would have been logical following Winzen's elimination from consideration. According to Simons' account, the next two candidates were assigned to the AMFL, but not *Manhigh* directly. One of them was Captain Grover Schock; the other was eliminated about two weeks after his nomination. Schock became primary pilot, and two more officers were evaluated. The final two had no prior connection to *Manhigh* or the AMFL. They were Captain Harry R. Collins and First Lieutenant Clifton M. McClure. For the last two candidates, the screening process included:

- Preselection interview to determine motivation and scientific background;
- Four-day medical evaluation at the Lovelace Clinic in Albuquerque, New Mexico;
- High-altitude chamber and partial-pressure suit indoctrination;
- A 24-hour claustrophobia test in the *Manhigh* capsule;
- A 24-hour simulated flight in the test chamber at the WADC;
- One parachute jump;
- Earning a CAA balloon pilot license;
- A full day of tests by a clinical psychologist and psychiatric interviews;
- A session in a soundproof, unlighted chamber;
- Physiological stress testing that included centrifuge runs, one hour in a "hot box" ($155°$ F and 85% humidity), and a "cold presser" test that comprised immersion of the subject's feet in ice water for 7 minutes while his pulse and blood pressure were monitored.

After going through this grueling series of tests, Captain Collins became Schock's backup. Lieutenant McClure remained involved with the project, partly to provide further "baseline" data for the evaluation process, and partly as insurance should anything happen to Schock or Collins. All that remained to clear Schock for *Manhigh III* was his CAA Balloonist's License. Time was critical for this last qualification.

In the fall, the upper atmospheric winds over the northern United States shift, which would carry a balloon over the Great Lakes, or even to the Atlantic Ocean during a 24-hour high altitude flight. Duke Gildenburg figured they probably had until the end of September, maybe the first week of October, before the weather over Minnesota deteriorated for the season. Further complicating matters, the ARDC instructed the AMFL to finish *Manhigh* as soon as possible. Any lengthy postponements could very well result in the program's cancellation, with or without a third manned flight.

In August, the White House announced NASA would have the responsibility for America's manned space flight program. This effectively ended Air Force aspirations for a manned space flight effort, which meant there were no compelling reasons to continue *Manhigh*. The Air Force still had the *X-20 Dyna Soar* on the drawing boards, but at that time it was still a suborbital research aircraft. With the *Manhigh* hardware already paid for, the ARDC allowed the program to proceed, as long as it could be concluded quickly. Postponing the flight until spring, when the weather would again be favorable, was out of the question.

Schock was still working on his license in early August. With time growing short, he needed an all-day flight that included multiple tasks to maintain any hope of beating the deadline. On 13 August Schock took off from Fleming Field in a *Sky-Car* balloon with Otto Winzen on a flight that would complete his training. According to everyone's plans, by the time Schock landed all he would need to receive his license was the solo flight. When they took off at 7:30 in the morning winds were from the southeast at two knots. Schock had to complete six landings, ascend to 10,000 feet, accumulate as much flight time as possible, and convince Winzen he could handle a gas balloon.

At first, the *Sky-Car* headed towards Minneapolis. When they climbed, their course shifted from northwest to northeast. Passing by Stillwater, Minnesota, two hours after takeoff, Schock and Winzen found themselves following the course of the upper St. Croix River. Schock made their first landing near the river, about ten miles north of Stillwater. He made another landing ten minutes later, after which they crossed into Wisconsin. The winds began to pick up, and they were traveling at 20 miles per hour over the ground.

Clouds also built up around them, so they decided to postpone the climb to 10,000 feet until later in the flight. The clouds cleared enough for Schock to make the climb at 1:30 PM. He had trouble descending, and eventually reached 11,800 feet. By 2:00 PM he had established a steady descent, so he and Winzen concentrated on navigation. They were over terrain covered by lakes, hills, and forests.

Captain Schock made three more landings during the afternoon. Storm clouds began building again as they approached Lake Superior. Around 5:00 PM he made the sixth and final touchdown of the flight. Lake Superior was only three miles away. With Lake Superior so close, Schock and Winzen looked for a landing spot. On their first landing approach there were too many ground obstructions, so they released ballast and tried to find somewhere else. Lake Superior was only a mile away. At last Schock found a suitable clearing. In preparation for the landing, Winzen lifted the cover over the switch that triggered the balloon cutaway once they touched down. Unexpectedly, the explosive cutters fired. They were about one hundred feet above the ground.

The *Sky-Car* gondola plummeted to earth. Sergeant Dittmer had been following the balloon in a truck, and he arrived on the scene almost immediately after the crash. Both men were gravely injured. Winzen sustained fractures of the collarbone, two ribs, two vertebrae, right wrist, and lower arm. He also had a dislocated bone in his right foot. Schock had numerous broken bones, severe internal injuries, and he cut his jaw badly. Dittmer, an experienced medic, stopped Schock's bleeding. His quick action saved Schock's life. A nearby resident saw the crash and called for an ambulance. Fortunately the ambulance station was only a few miles away, so they arrived quickly. Although he survived his injuries, Schock would never pilot *Manhigh*.

With the primary pilot eliminated, Collins, an experienced parachutist, moved into his slot. McClure, a 25-year old Air Force pilot with a master's degree in ceramics engineering, became his backup. Collins had encountered some difficulties qualifying for the flight. During his initial physical examination his blood cholesterol level was too high, and he failed the Double Masters Two-step test. He was also too large to fit in the capsule comfortably. Collins returned to his unit, but requested a re-evaluation of his physical condition. The high cholesterol level appeared to be caused by medication, and he passed the cardiac examination. Both the previous problems were deemed transient, and he returned to the *Manhigh* program. Then, following the 24-hour chamber test at the WADC, doctors determined his cholesterol level was still too high, so he became the backup pilot. McClure was now the primary pilot.

First Lieutenant Clifton McClure piloted the third *Manhigh* mission. *Source: New Mexico Museum of Space History*

Born in Anderson, South Carolina, on November 8, 1932, McClure's nickname was "Demi." He received this nickname because he was the "first Democrat born on the night Franklin D. Roosevelt was elected President." After graduation from Anderson High School, he earned a bachelor's degree in materials engineering from Clemson University. He went on to receive a master's degree in ceramics engineering from Clemson in 1954.

Upon his graduation he received a commission in the Air Force, and attended flight school. McClure became a *T-33* instructor pilot at Laughlin Air Force Base, followed by Bryan Air Force Base, both in Texas. Many pilots tried to avoid such assignments, but McClure relished being an instructor because he could get as many flight hours as he wanted. McClure's other interests included astronomy, and he was sure it was only a matter of time before humans ventured into space. While at Bryan he met Colonel Stapp, who suggested he apply for an assignment at Holloman. After an assignment at the Solar Furnace Project Office at White Sands

Proving Grounds, McClure finally managed a transfer to Holloman and the AMFL.

As he endured the testing required for *Manhigh*, McClure impressed everyone with his enthusiasm and curiosity. The doctors also noted his physical condition and stamina. On one test he displayed an "exceptionally high maximum breathing capacity." For *Manhigh III*, the 24-hour claustrophobia test introduced a new procedure. The subjects had to perform three tasks at least twice every half-hour. They had to extinguish a small light, called the "panic light," whenever it came on; maintain a mock cabin pressure gauge at a certain reading; and advise the control center whenever a blinking bulb representing an oxygen meter did not flash with its usual frequency. McClure did much better than Collins on these tests, consistently responding in less time.

During a press conference held in Minnesota, one of the reporters asked McClure why he volunteered for such an assignment. "The way I look at it is this; I was brought up to believe in

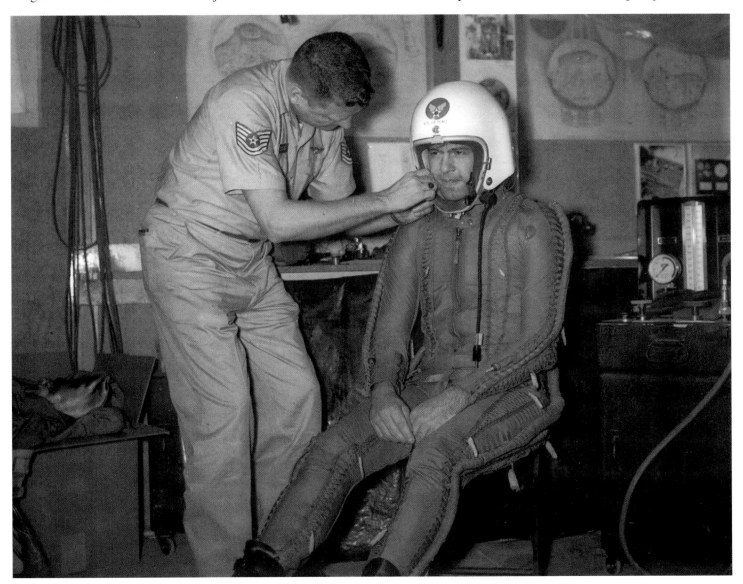

Technical Sergeant Edward Dittmer helps McClure don his partial pressure suit. *Source: New Mexico Museum of Space History*

McClure in the capsule seat. *Source: New Mexico Museum of Space History*

the country I live in. I feel you have to put more into it than you take out of it if it's going to continue as it is. I want my son to have a chance to study anything he wants to, as I have had. I think the least we can do is to approach the problem without being afraid of the supreme sacrifice." He told the reporters: "I'm afraid I'm not afraid. Anything of this sort has its serious side, but I think it's also going to be quite a bit of fun."

Although he was designated as the primary pilot, McClure had not completed one important qualification for his flight—he still needed to earn a balloonist's license. Here, like it had so many times before, weather held up progress. *Stratolab* veteran M. Lee Lewis had recently retired from the Navy, and joined WRI as their chief of operations. He was McClure's instructor pilot for the *Sky-Car*. Duke Gildenberg set the end of September as the deadline for a flight from Crosby.

Weather was so bad around Minneapolis that Lewis looked westward for favorable conditions for the *Sky-Car* flights. Finally, on 25 September 25 Lewis and McClure set out for Bismarck, North Dakota, for the latter's first training flight. Meanwhile, Gildenberg noted the east to west shift in high altitude winds was starting. McClure only had a matter of a few days to complete his training. On 27 September 27 the weather cleared enough over Fleming Field for another *Sky-Car* flight, so they dashed back to Minnesota. The next day, which was a Sunday, looked favorable, and McClure at last qualified for a balloonist's license on 28 September.

McClure just before he was sealed in the capsule. *Source: New Mexico Museum of Space History*

The *Manhigh III* team gathered the next day and reviewed the situation. The seasonal shift had taken place, but Gildenberg remained hopeful. Weather predictions looked marginally favorable for a flight on 1 October. Everyone packed up and headed to Crosby. To make the pre-flight process less stressful, most of the final preparations took place at the launch site. WRI arranged to use a garage at the Portsmouth Mine for capsule preparation. McClure slept in a nearby hospital so he wouldn't have to make the four or five-hour journey from the Winzen plant to the launch site sealed in the capsule. He would receive his final physical exam and don the pressure suit in the mine office.

The night before the planned launch the winds were unsuitable, and Gildenberg did not see any chance for improvement by morning. If launched, McClure would land in the vicinity of Hudson Bay, where there were storms. McClure went ahead and began suiting up just in case the winds changed. By 10:30 PM, however, the forecast had not improved. The flight was scrubbed.

Gildenberg predicted there was only a negligible chance they would have satisfactory weather any time during the entire month. His best estimate was that they might have several opportunities during November, but that was questionable because of the seasonal wind shift. After that, they were definitely done for the season.

Rather than risk having the ARDC cancel *Manhigh III* because of the delay, Hessberg and Simons considered other launch options. The *Stratobowl* was examined, but wind conditions there were not favorable. That left Holloman Air Force Base. New Mexico was too far south to gather any significant cosmic ray data, but the flight could still serve as a control to judge the effects of the other flights. By 3 October the entire operation relocated to New Mexico. The Holloman Balloon Branch would conduct the launching rather than the Winzen Research crew.

Key personnel met at Holloman on Sunday, 5 October, to discuss the revised operating plan. Monday did not look promising, but Tuesday seemed better, according to Gildenberg. McClure returned to the "night shift," taking a seconal at noon, and arising at 6:00 PM to prepare for a dawn launch.

Early on the morning of 7 October McClure sat in the capsule, ready for flight. The ground crew had some problems with one of the reefing sleeves around the balloon, which delayed the launch. Holloman had no natural protection like the iron mine at Crosby, so the launch had to be made from one of the base runways. This was not a problem around dawn. The desert air is usually calm at that time of day, but the wind picks up quickly after sunrise. By the time launch preparations were finished the morning winds had started. Just ten minutes before launch, the three million cubic foot balloon began whipping around, and finally careened into the ground. There was a gentle, almost imperceptible "pop" as the bag tore. Winzen had only manufactured two balloons to manned flight specifications for the project—now only one was left.

Everyone agreed to try again the next day. That night, McClure boarded the capsule a little past midnight. Just like Kittinger and Simons, he had a personal parachute in the cabin. McClure tried to convince Colonel Hessberg the parachute was unnecessary, but the AMFL commander was adamant. If there was a serious emergency, he wanted McClure to have every possible chance of survival.

This parachute, which was specially rigged for high altitude use, hung from the capsule support structure between the pilot's knees. Unfortunately, it was hanging so the closing pins pointed up; in other words, so they could fall out if loosened. With all the handling and jostling the parachute had received during the past few days, the pins had worked themselves loose. About three hours after he boarded the capsule, Beeding asked McClure to report the partial pressure of oxygen in the cabin. As he turned to read the gauge he brushed against the parachute, and it popped open "with a muffled flump." Finding his lap full of fabric, he faced a serious dilemma.

Should he report the problem or not? McClure had the microphone in hand, ready to tell Beeding and Hessberg what happened, but then he hesitated. With the launch only a few hours away, McClure did not know if the balloon had already been laid out for inflation. If so, it could not be held until another day. The balloons were so fragile they could not be repacked once they were unrolled. If they opened the capsule and had an Air Force Rigger repack the parachute, it would delay the flight for several hours, by which time the winds would have picked up. A launch attempt under those conditions would likely destroy the balloon like it had the day before. This was the last balloon, and there were not funds or time available to procure another. So, rather than risk aborting the mission by reporting the open parachute, he decided to remain silent and repack it inside the capsule.

When he was undergoing parachute training the previous summer, McClure had one of the riggers show him how to pack a chute. However, parachutes like his were generally packed on long tables, not in the tight confines of a three-foot diameter capsule. McClure carefully dictated every step of the procedure into his on-board tape recorder. This way, if something went wrong later in the flight, at least there would be a record of his actions.

Every so often he had to stop packing the parachute to respond to questions from the ground crew. From the outside, people could see McClure's helmet through the portholes. They noticed he seemed to be moving around a lot, but nobody walked up to the capsule to look inside. Beeding asked if he was hot inside the cabin, and McClure told him he felt fine.

It was difficult, tedious work, but McClure finally closed the parachute container and inserted the closing pins. Pausing to examine his handiwork, he discovered he had inserted the pins backwards. Before repacking the canopy, he had vowed to himself that he'd only make the flight if it was properly packed. McClure pulled the ripcord to release the canopy and repeated the task. This time he secured the container properly, just as the truck carrying the capsule left the AMFL for the launch site. The process had been very taxing, and he was perspiring heavily. Satisfied, he finally sat back to relax as the capsule was being moved to the flight line. Launch was 20 minutes away.

The dry ice cap placed on the capsule after McClure boarded was nearly gone. Normal flight preparations included replacing the cap before launch to keep the pilot cool during the ascent. This time, though, someone forgot to have the dry ice on hand. During the previous day's launch attempt, McClure reported feeling cold prior to the launch attempt, so the feeling was it probably wasn't necessary. Without the added cooling of the dry ice, he continued to perspire.

Potassium hydroxide reacts with moisture to produce heat, and McClure was perspiring so heavily he saturated the air that was blown through the regeneration unit. The unit soon began blowing hot air into the cabin. Compounding the problem, without the water core cooling system that had been present in the earlier capsule, there was no way to dissipate the heat at altitude. Although the David Clark Company had modified the pressure suit for improved ventilation, much of McClure's torso was still covered by impermeable pressure bladders, so the body's normal way of cooling—evaporation of perspiration—was blocked.

On the flight line, preparations went smoothly. Soaked with perspiration McClure felt cold, and he zipped up the 2-clo suit that lined the seat. The heat coming out of the air regenerator hadn't built up in the capsule yet. There were no problems with any reefing sleeves this morning, and Gildenberg told them they should be okay from a wind standpoint until at least eight o'clock. Balloon Branch personnel, WRI representatives, reporters, and the panel of experts watched as an Air Force truck pulled up with the capsule. The panel rode in a bus equipped with a speaker that could be plugged into the adjacent communications trailer. This let them monitor all the communications between the ground and the capsule. The communications trailer had a microphone for use by whichever panel member's experiment was underway at the time. The panel of experts convened for *Manhigh III* comprised:

- Psychiatric Consultant, Captain George Ruff;
- Aviation Physiologist, Captain Eli Beeding;
- Flight Surgeon, Lt. Colonel David Simons;
- Sky Luminance Experiment, Dr. S. Q. Duntley;
- Stability Experiment, Mr. George Nielson;
- Meteorologist, Mr. Duke Gildenberg;
- Cosmic Radiation Experiments, Dr. Herman Yagoda; and
- Astronomer, Mr. George Nielson.

In addition, Vera Wizen, Lee Lewis, Don Foster, and Vern Baumgartner from WRI were present to answer questions on capsule or balloon systems.

One major experiment package would not be flying on *Manhigh III*. Major Carl Ferriby of the Reconnaissance Laboratory at the WADC created a sophisticated camera package intended to hang beneath the capsule. Nicknamed the "Ferriby Package," it weighed 248 pounds, and contained a variety of cameras using different filters. Major Ferriby hoped to compare the photographs to visual observations made by the pilot. Unfortunately the package proved too complicated, and could not be readied in time for the flight.

McClure took off at 6:51 on the morning of 8 October, about six hours after he boarded the capsule. From his perspective inside the capsule, McClure later described the takeoff as "smooth

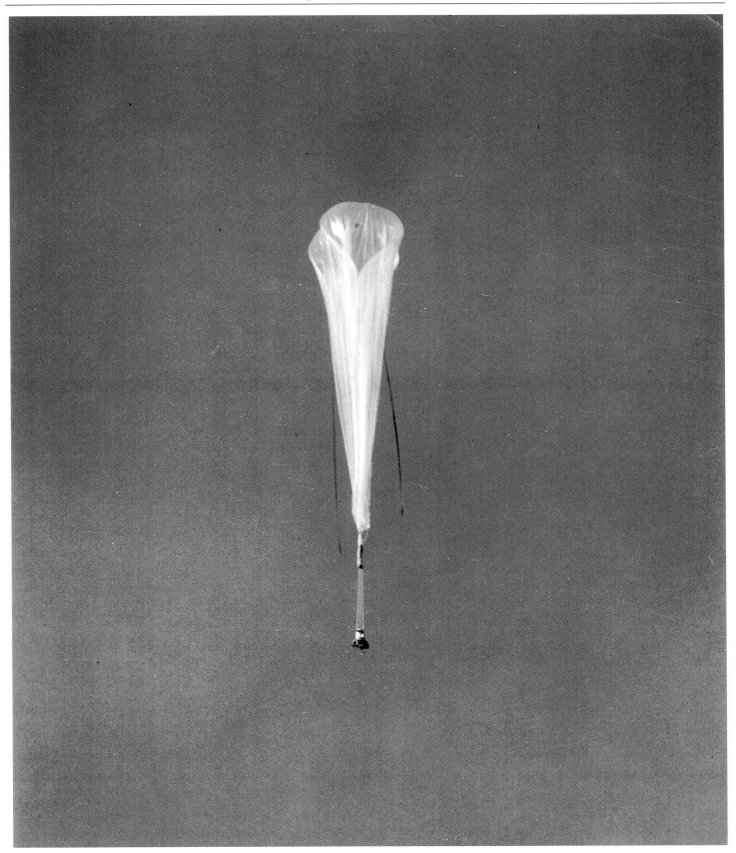

Manhigh III launch. Source: New Mexico Museum of Space History

and uneventful." Actually, the launch occurred slightly sooner than McClure expected, and he was still fastening his seat belt for the first 500 to 1,000 feet of the ascent.

As he climbed past 24,000 feet, he reported the temperature in the capsule was 89° F. He also told ground control he was uncomfortably warm. At 55,000 feet the cabin temperature gauge read 94°. Everyone agreed something was wrong with the gauge; the capsule temperature could not possibly be that high, so the flight proceeded. After examining drawings of the capsule, they discovered the thermometer was mounted on top of the air regeneration unit, which led to the conclusion it indicated the temperature of the unit itself, not the true cabin air temperature. About 10:00 he reached the ceiling altitude of 99,700 feet. *Manhigh III* drifted over the Sacramento Mountains that bordered the Tularosa Basin.

During the climb, McClure noticed above 85,000 feet the sky lost its coloring, and became "a completely dark void." As he later described, "(the) main sky-aspect change from this altitude to ceiling was in the horizon zone. This area got narrower and of higher contrast with the dark sky above it as we ascended higher." After filing his routine pilot's report at ceiling, Captain Ruff came on the radio and talked to him about his feelings thus far. In his post-flight pilot's report, McClure described a sense of "insecurity," because his normal references and support were gone. He also had a "reverent" feeling.

Ground control asked McClure to have a snack between 11:40 and 11:50 AM so they could evaluate his trajectory. McClure was aware of hunger and "extreme thirst." In the excitement of repacking the parachute, preparing for the ascent, and launch, he had forgotten to eat or drink anything since the previous night. McClure had a tube of chicken, two Oreo cookies, and a can of juice. The juice "tasted especially refreshing and cool." He put his hand to his face after holding the cool can and noticed his skin felt warm.

His light meal finished, a reporter interviewed McClure via radio. The interview exhausted him, and he slumped back in his seat when it was over. At 12:15 McClure collected sky brightness measurements with the spot photometer. He reported the spot photometer readings left him "really exhausted." Captain Beeding, the physiologist for the flight, told him to relax for a while. McClure noticed he was breathing fast, and that his heart rate was up. At first this did not cause any concern. During the physical testing, McClure's pulse rate had shown wide fluctuations.

McClure tried to drink some water. His water supply was in a container with a rubber drinking tube and a hand operated pressure bulb. Pumping the bulb forced water out of the container and through the tube. He placed the tube in his mouth and pumped the pressure bulb for 20 or 30 seconds. Nothing happened. In ground tests, this had been sufficient to make water flow from the container. He checked the valve position and pumped the bulb for about two minutes. Still nothing came out of the tube. Then, observing the tube, he realized the problem was a vapor lock caused by the reduced pressure in the cabin. Finally, he got a "pitifully small amount of water." It took about three minutes for him to get a mouthful.

At one point he considered puncturing the container with a knife and collecting the water in a cup. Because of the location of the water tank, McClure realized this would be difficult at best, so he continued trying to coax water from the container using the hose. All at once water gushed through the tube and almost choked him. Realizing the vapor lock problem was not solved, McClure drank as much water as he could, in case the flow stopped again.

Because the balloon was moving northwest faster than anticipated, the command group and panel of experts decided to move. One of the AMFL C-47 aircraft had been outfitted as a flying control center. The command group included Hessberg, Simons, Beeding, Vera Winzen, Lee Lewis, and Don Foster. Everyone boarded the C-47, and took off shortly after McClure made his sky brightness measurements.

Moving the flight to Holloman allowed a new experiment to be added to the flight plan. McClure was supposed to watch a ground-launched missile destroy a target at 80,000 feet. An aerial interception like that had never been observed from above. McClure began monitoring the countdown at 12:45, and was in contact with the C-47. He tried to orient himself by the White Sands dune fields, San Andres Mountains, and the lava beds near Carrizozo while he loaded film in the camera. McClure noted just holding the camera up to the window was tiring. Fifteen minutes later the missile firing was canceled.

By that time, it became evident that something was seriously wrong in the capsule. McClure's speech was sluggish, and his pulse rate was up to 140 beats per minute. Asked about his temperature, McClure replied it was 101°. A half-hour later, it was up to 102.3°. Measuring the cabin temperature with a mercury thermometer, he reported it was 96 degrees! McClure removed the cotton sock from the second thermometer in the psychrometer and verified the reading. Beeding asked if he had turned on the heater, so McClure verified the switch was in the "OFF" position. He held the hose from the air regenerator to his face and got a blast of very hot air.

Due to communications difficulties, the command group did not get this critical information until 1:50, nearly twenty minutes after it was received. Ten minutes later, McClure reported his temperature was 103.4°. Colonel Hessberg decided to terminate the flight, at first asking McClure to descend to 55,000 feet, where the atmosphere would be much colder, and hopefully cool the capsule. McClure tried to argue the point, saying that he only felt "a little warm," and that he was sure he could make it to nightfall. Recalling his own experience, Simons told Hessberg it would be well past sunset before the capsule began to cool. Hessburg called McClure and insisted he descend.

The *Manhigh III* balloon had two vent valves. McClure opened both valves for four and a half minutes. He waited to see what effect releasing helium had on his altitude. McClure spent the next hour alternately venting helium and waiting to see its effect. After an hour McClure had only descended a few thousand feet, and had not yet established a steady descent rate. His temperature was up to 104.1°. McClure continued carefully venting more helium. Another hour passed, by which time McClure had established a descent rate of 500 feet per minute, but he was still at 87,000 feet. The temperature in the cabin reached 97°, and his heartbeat had climbed to 180 beats per minute.

Radio reception inside the capsule steadily deteriorated. The C-47 had a relatively low-power transmitter, and McClure could barely hear it. He had to turn the volume on his headset up just to make them out. Then, an airliner inbound to Phoenix Sky Harbor airport broadcast on the same frequency. It was so loud through *Manhigh's* radio it left McClure's ears ringing for several minutes. His receiver began to drift due to the extreme heat, and McClure constantly had to retune it. The radio dial was so hot that a wet finger placed against it began to sizzle after a few seconds. Because of the commercial air traffic on the 122.8 frequency, they shifted to the backup frequency of 121.5.

His heartbeat, which he had been able to feel since about 2:30, now pounded against the top of McClure's head. Even a small task like turning to reach a dial increased the throbbing in his head and tired him. McClure began spending more and more time just trying to conserve energy and focus on critical tasks.

Hessberg considered cutting the capsule away from the balloon and bringing it down with the parachute, but there was a strong chance it would land in the rugged San Andres Mountains that border the Tularosa Basin. Landing among the jagged peaks would not only make recovery difficult, but could seriously injure or kill the pilot. McClure sensed that option was being considered, and argued against it. For the time being, Hessberg let McClure retain control of the descent. By this point McClure spent most of the time slumped over with his head on the parachute. Time seemed to slow down for him. At one point, he sat there for what felt like an hour. When he looked at the clock, he was surprised to discover only 20 minutes had gone by.

Concerned that McClure wouldn't remain conscious much longer, Hessberg ordered him to fasten his lap and shoulder belts. His temperature was 105.6°. Fastening the belts and holding him tight against the 2-clo suit that lined his seat further restricted airflow around his body, but Hessberg figured that was better than risking a parachute landing with the pilot free to bounce around in the cabin. He tightened the belts and immediately felt hotter.

Realizing he had not urinated at all during the flight, McClure decided to empty his bladder. He had heard stories how a full bladder could burst, with fatal results, in an impact. Since he feared he might suffer a hard landing, McClure decided he'd better minimize his risk. The effort left him totally exhausted, and he struggled to regain his strength. Just as he was finishing he lost contact with the C-47. The Holloman Balloon Branch recovery team finally answered his calls. Knowing he might pass out at any time, McClure dictated his plan for landing to Lieutenant Roger Winquist. Then, just as abruptly as it stopped, communications with the C-47 were restored.

McClure was directed to stow the spot photometer. He was so weak that he dropped the seven-pound instrument. It jammed the foot switch that controlled his voice communications. Unable to reach it, McClure could no longer transmit to the ground. After that, the command group couldn't know for sure if McClure was

even conscious, but the descent proceeded smoothly, and his pulse rate remained steady, so they refrained from cutting the capsule away from the balloon. He was at 59,000 feet with a descent rate of 400 feet per minute.

Looking around inside the cabin, McClure began seeing shimmering green splotches, even when his eyes were closed. It took an extreme effort to sit up, but slumping forward didn't help either. The bottom of the cabin had become cluttered with equipment and litter, and he could not put his feet flat on the floor. With his feet raised, trying to lean forward strained his legs. This also meant the seat did not adequately support his thighs, so his weight was concentrated on his buttocks, adding to his misery. The green splotches were so bright that closing his eyes didn't provide any relief, and they actually weren't as bad with his eyes open.

Unsure of what happened, the command group kept trying to raise *Manhigh III* on the radio. With each radio call, McClure wanted to reply but couldn't, which caused him a great deal of frustration. This went on for about twenty minutes, when McClure realized that if he tried to continue fighting the involuntary urge to respond to the radio, he would either pass out or die from the stress. McClure pulled out the communications plug. Abruptly everything was silent, and he could focus what little energy he had left on the landing.

At sunset McClure turned on the capsule beacon light. Seeing the light come on, Hessberg and Simons knew he was still conscious and in control of the balloon. Watching from the ground, Simons saw a dark object fall away from the capsule. When its parachute opened, Simons realized it was a battery. McClure was lucid enough to drop ballast to slow his descent. Two more batteries were dropped.

Unsure of his location, McClure worried he might land on the edge of a cliff or a mountain peak. If either of these happened, he could hurtle down into a deep ravine after cutting away the balloon. Therefore, McClure decided to descend at the minimum speed possible, and bounce after landing until he was sure he was on solid ground. Even if he landed on the edge of a cliff, such an approach would allow him to slowly work his way down the side of the slope until he reached the bottom.

Descending in the dark, McClure sat back as best he could and rested. Peering out of the number 2 porthole, he could see the silhouettes of the San Andres Mountains and lights from small desert communities. At 24,000 feet the lights vanished, as though a mountain blocked them. McClure momentarily panicked, fearing he was about to land in mountainous terrain. Then, he realized no mountains in the area were that tall, and he concluded it must be a passing cloud. He shortly dropped out of the cloud layer.

Between 24,000 feet and 15,000 feet he reviewed his planned landing procedure. McClure reached to open the manual decompression valve, and painful muscle cramps started in both thighs. The pains nearly doubled him up, but there was nothing McClure could do to relieve them. He concentrated on the tasks he needed to accomplish.

He closed the air regenerator valves and turned off the blower. His windows immediately fogged over. Unable to wipe them fast enough to keep them clear, McClure decided to ignore the view outside and simply concentrate on his landing plan. Throughout the descent, McClure kept up a running commentary for his portable tape recorder. This way, if something happened to him, there would be a record of his actions.

Watching his vertical speed and altitude, he dropped at 850 to 900 feet per minute. His vertical speed decreased to 750 feet per minute. McClure braced for ground impact. At 4,300 feet he felt a "light bump," like he passed through a wind shear, followed by a solid impact about 100 feet lower. The capsule rocked slightly, then stood upright. McClure fired the squibs that released the balloon. He was back on the ground.

Manhigh III landed on a level area of desert only a few miles from the takeoff point. McClure's timing of the balloon release was so good that the capsule remained upright, the only one of the three flights to do so. McClure released the upper dome, and began to climb out on his own. His first thoughts were that he might have to spend the night in the desert, so he prepared to build a fire, eat something, and construct a shelter from his parachute. Then he heard an approaching helicopter. His pulse rate was 180 beats per minute; his temperature an incredible 108.5°!

Lee Lewis landed alongside in the recovery helicopter, and ran over to assist McClure. Taking a pair of wire cutters, Lewis pro-

ceeded to cut the remaining wires that kept the upper dome from falling freely away. McClure tried to warn him the wires were for the camera strobe and still carried quite a charge from the capacitors that fired the light. Ignoring the warning Lewis cut the wires, and was promptly knocked to the ground by the electrical shock.

Captain Ruff, who had also been in the recovery helicopter, tried to help him climb out of the capsule, but McClure felt a "compulsion" to make the final six feet of his descent on his own—he jumped down from the capsule and stood there. Only then did he feel a need to lean on someone or something. He even insisted on walking to the helicopter unaided. However, before he agreed to board the helicopter for the return to the base, he insisted he be given a dictaphone to immediately begin recording his impressions. By the next morning, McClure was back to normal.

Manhigh III pushed McClure well beyond any stress levels that would have been deliberately introduced during a ground test. Granted, the flight did not achieve its primary purpose, but it provided important data on the capabilities of a highly motivated individual under extreme stress. Captain Beeding summarized it well in his post-flight report when he wrote: "although our extensive pilot selection program, which included reactions to stress, was not perfect, it did serve its function, in that our pilot, in spite of the physical state discussed, brought his cumbersome flying machine in after dark for a perfect landing."

10

Post *Manhigh* Projects

The spring of 1958 was a very busy time for Winzen Research. Otto Winzen and his staff at WRI prepared three different proposals for projects to follow *Manhigh III*. Within three months of receiving the contract for the third flight, WRI proposed *Manhigh IV*, a capsule that would sustain a pilot for up to five days. This would have required a larger capsule than the ones used for previous *Manhigh* flights. Such a capsule would have needed additional life-support capacity, including provisions for a toilet and a sleeping berth. The pilot would have needed additional room for food and water storage. Winzen also proposed the capsule have an airlock for disposal of waste materials.

All these features increased the weight of the capsule, so to reach the desired altitude of 100,000 feet, *Manhigh IV* required a 5-million cubic foot balloon. The entire *Manhigh IV* program included seven flights. In a plan reminiscent of *Stratolab*, Operation *Manhigh IV* included two *Sky-Car* flights to 40,000 feet to test cap-

sule instrumentation packages and train pilots. The second capsule built, which had been used for animal test flights prior to *Manhigh I*, would be used as a ground-based simulator. Winzen called for an ascent to evaluate temperature control and other capsule systems "prior to the actual manned flight." There were three flights of 12, 24, and 48 hours duration to test the 5-million cubic foot balloons, then finally the piloted 5-day mission.

Even the Army planned to make use of *Manhigh* experience. On April 17, 1958, the Army Ballistic Missile Agency at Redstone Arsenal in Alabama submitted a "Development Proposal for Project Adam." *Adam* would have used an Army *Redstone* missile to propel a modified *Manhigh* capsule 150 miles above the earth on a suborbital space flight. Winzen was to be the contractor for the capsule, and provided input in its design.

Officially, *Adam* was the first step of a program to develop a way to transport soldiers to trouble spots around the world via

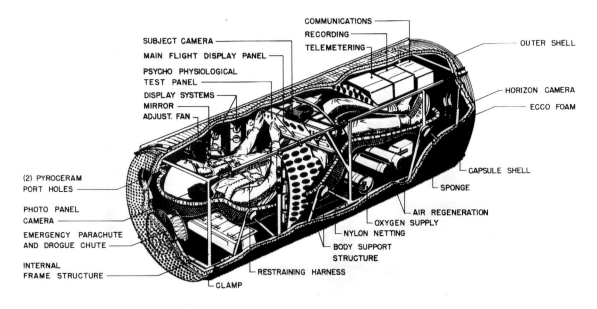

Project Adam proposed capsule.
Source: United States Army

PROJECT "ADAM"

CUTAWAY OF CAPSULE

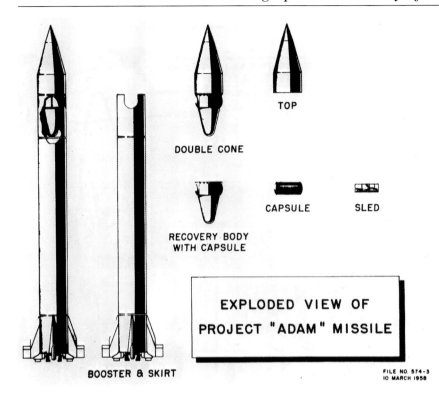

TOP

DOUBLE CONE

CAPSULE   SLED

RECOVERY BODY
WITH CAPSULE

EXPLODED VIEW OF
PROJECT "ADAM" MISSILE

FILE NO. 574-3
IO MARCH 1958

BOOSTER & SKIRT

Project Adam would have used a modified Redstone missile to launch a manned capsule on a sub-orbital space flight. *Source: United States Army*

rocket. However, Army plans went beyond transporting troops; they culminated in *Project Horizon*, a proposal for a lunar base. Sensing a lukewarm response to their plans, Army officials tried to elicit support from the Central Intelligence Agency for *Adam* as an important "political/psychological demonstration" to the world.

Planned biomedical measurements of the pilot included: electrocardiogram; breathing rate and depth; blood pressure; galvanic skin resistance; and body temperature. Capsule measurements were just as thorough: cabin air pressure; partial pressures of oxygen and carbon dioxide; humidity; spacecraft skin temperature; internal temperature; acceleration; noise levels; and vibration.

Simons traveled to Redstone Arsenal in Huntsville to discuss the project in late 1957. Representatives from the Air Force School of Aviation Medicine at Randolph Air Force Base and Pensacola Naval Air Station also participated in these talks. Everyone was enthusiastic about *Adam* and volunteered their services. Unfortunately, senior Air Force officials did not exhibit the same enthusiasm. Within a few months word came down from the ARDC to "get out and stay out." The Air Force officially decided not to support *Adam* because it feared the ballistic capsule project might take resources away from the service's X-15 rocket plane.

The Secretary of the Army forwarded *Adam* to the Director of the Advanced Research Projects Agency (ARPA), along with a request for $4.75 million, on May 19, 1958. *Adam* didn't survive very long after that: the Pentagon rejected the idea in July 1958. In testimony before the Congressional House Space Committee NACA Chairman Hugh Dryden compared "tossing a man up in the air and letting him come back...[to]...the circus stunt of shooting a young lady from a cannon."

The most ambitious balloon-borne project proposal from Winzen was *Satelorb*, a heavy capsule capable of carrying up to six people. Such a large crew would have allowed a "space surgeon" to conduct *in situ* observations of his crewmates. Overall, *Satelorb* resembled an enlarged *Manhigh* turned on its side. It would have been more than seven feet in diameter, so crewmembers could stand up and walk around inside it to reach various workstations. There was a platform on top of the capsule so that experiments could be conducted directly in the space equivalent environment. *Satelorb* would have had an airlock to permit crewmembers to climb outside the capsule while in flight. It even had bunks, and a separate control compartment.

The White House announcement in August 1958 that gave NASA responsibility for America's manned space flight program effectively ended Air Force aspirations for a manned space flight effort, and killed *Manhigh IV* and *Satelorb*.

NASA officially came into being on October 1, 1958. Within a week, NASA Administrator T. Keith Glennan announced the agency's plans for launching a person into orbit, which was named *Project Mercury*. In March 1958 a group of NACA engineers under the leadership of Robert R. Gilruth submitted a plan for a ballistic capsule launched by existing military missiles. This group, working at the Langley Aeronautical Laboratory, decided this was the fastest way to achieve manned orbital flight. Gilruth, who was deputy director of the Langley Laboratory, had formerly headed the NACA Pilotless Aircraft Research Division (PARD). PARD was the division that launched research rockets from Wallops Island, Virginia, and was the closest thing to a space organization that existed within the aviation-oriented NACA. With the creation of NASA, the Langley Aeronautical Laboratory became the Langley Research Center, and the group working on the manned satellite project became the Space Task Group (STG). Robert Gilruth headed the Space Task Group. As a graduate student at the University of Minnesota, Gilruth studied under Jean Piccard.

Otto Winzen proposed that the *Mercury* spacecraft recovery system be tested using a balloon. Winzen even championed this as a realistic simulation of an actual mission, and a good way to train NASA's astronauts. For a while *Project Mercury* plans called for a balloon test, but NASA managers soon realized that unmanned missions with *Redstone* and *Atlas* boosters eliminated the need for such flights.

Mercury did not mean the complete end of manned stratospheric balloon flights. The Navy continued with its *Stratolab* program (described in Appendix 2), and Joe Kittinger performed three stratospheric ascents during the Air Force's *Project Excelsior*, and one flight with *Project Stargazer*.

As airplane performance increased during the 1950s, so did the need to study high altitude escape techniques. At the time there only seemed two options, both of them deadly. An ejecting pilot

Captain Joseph W. Kittinger was project director and test subject for *Project Excelsior*. Source: *United States Air Force photograph*

could deploy his parachute right away and risk severe injury or death from opening shock, exhaust his oxygen supply under canopy, or freeze to death. Alternatively, he could delay opening and fall to a safer altitude. The problem with the latter option was that drop tests with dummies showed a tendency to go into a flat spin, with rates of up to 200 revolutions per minute. Under such conditions a human pilot would quickly lose consciousness and die. The Air Force began a series of high-altitude parachute tests using balloons in 1954. During the initial test program, named *Project High Dive*, dozens of anthropomorphic dummies were dropped from balloons high over the Tularosa Basin.

However, the dummies could not move their limbs or counteract any unwanted motion. To study the biophysics of high altitude bailout with a human test subject, the Air Force Aero Medical Laboratory at Wright-Patterson Air Force Base in Ohio devised *Project Excelsior*. At the time the project was created, Colonel John Paul Stapp commanded the Aero Medical Laboratory. *Manhigh* veteran Joe Kittinger was the project engineer and chief test subject. *Excelsior* is Latin for "ever upward." Kittinger planned to use a balloon to reach the stratosphere. He would then jump from the aerostat and delay opening his main parachute until reaching 18,000 feet.

Because of Kittinger's involvement in both *Manhigh* and *Excelsior* there has sometimes been confusion, and his parachute jumps have been reported as part of *Manhigh*. However, the two projects were totally different and distinct efforts.

One of the challenges facing Kittinger was to find a technique that could be used by pilots who were not trained skydivers. The solution came from Francis Beaupre of the Aerospace Medical Division of the Wright Air Development Center. Beaupre devised a three-stage parachute system. After leaving the gondola, Kittinger would fall for 16 seconds to build up speed. Then, a spring-loaded pilot chute would deploy. Building up adequate airspeed before deploying the pilot chute was critical because if it deployed too early, it would flop around due to insufficient dynamic pressure in the thin air. The pilot chute, in turn, deployed a six-foot diameter drogue chute that stabilized Kittinger in a feet-to-earth position. Along with the drogue chute, about one-third of the 28-foot diameter round main canopy was released from the parachute pack. Once he reached 18,000 feet, the rest of the main was released. Because a pilot ejecting from a crippled airplane could not be counted on to manually pull his ripcord, the entire activation sequence was automatic.

Wanting to prove operational pilots could use the system, Kittinger wore an Air Force MC-3 partial pressure suit covered by insulated winter flying coveralls. This was one of the most severe tests ever made of the pressure suit. If either the suit or helmet failed, unconsciousness would come in 10-12 seconds, followed by death in 2-3 minutes. In addition to the pressure suit and parachute system, Kittinger carried a box containing oxygen, instruments, and cameras. Wearing all his equipment, Kittinger tipped the scales at 320 pounds—more than twice his normal weight.

Following a series of 140 dummy tests with the Beaupre system at altitudes of up to 100,000 feet, and three live jumps from a C-130 at 28,000 feet, Kittinger was ready for his first stratospheric

Equipment worn by Kittinger for the *Excelsior* jumps.
Source: Photo courtesy of Dr. John Paul Stapp

Fully suited, Kittinger weighed 320 pounds, more than twice his normal weight. *Source: Photo courtesy of Dr. John Paul Stapp*

Kittinger prepares to enter the test chamber at WADC for an *Excelsior* flight simulation. *Source: Photo courtesy of Dr. John Paul Stapp*

rect the spin, but soon he could no longer compensate for it. He blacked out and didn't regain consciousness until he was floating beneath the reserve parachute. His main canopy tangled because of the spinning, and the reserve, which deployed at 10,000 feet, saved his life.

Excelsior II took place on December 11, 1959. The equipment problems had been corrected, and the Beaupre system worked perfectly as Kittinger jumped from 74,700 feet. Kittinger received approval for another test.

Early on the morning of August 16, 1960, Kittinger prepared to board the balloon for the third jump. For this flight, the gondola carried two placards. One was a license plate that his son had cut off of a cereal box. His son was in Ohio, the license plate was from Oregon, and the flight took place in New Mexico. Such details did not matter to the younger Kittinger—he felt the gondola needed a license plate. The other was a sign that read "This is the highest step in the world."

Excelsior III, launched from Tularosa, New Mexico, carried Kittinger to 102,800 feet. During the ascent the pressurization in his right glove failed, and his hand began to swell. It reached nearly twice its normal size, and was very painful. Afraid that he would be ordered to jump early because of the malfunction, Kittinger did not report the problem until he was at altitude. Seventy seconds before jumping, he cut away the radio antenna to prevent hitting it. For the first time in the flight, Captain Kittinger was truly alone.

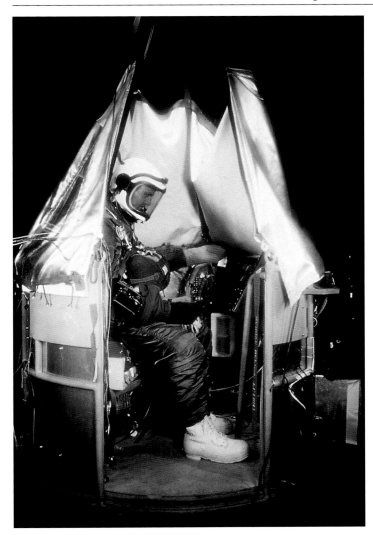

Seated in the gondola during a simulation in a test chamber. *Source: Photo courtesy of Dr. John Paul Stapp*

jump. Although the Aero Medical Laboratory in Ohio sponsored *Excelsior*, field operations took place at Holloman Air Force Base. The adjacent White Sands Missile Range provided a 40- by 100-mile landing area, but the target area was "only" 11 miles on a side.

Excelsior I took off from Truth or Consequences, New Mexico, on November 16, 1959. The balloon drifted east, arriving over White Sands Missile Range as Kittinger reached the intended jump altitude of 70,000 feet. Kittinger encountered some difficulties as he prepared to jump, and inadvertently climbed to 76,400 feet. Standing in the door of the gondola, he pulled the lanyard that activated the barometric release for the main canopy and the timer for the pilot chute. It took three tries to pull the lanyard clear. Unknown to Kittinger, the first pull started the timer, so the pilot chute deployed only two seconds after he left the balloon.

Without sufficient airspeed to create adequate dynamic pressure, the pilot chute flopped around in the thin air and wrapped around his neck. He began spinning. At first, Kittinger could cor-

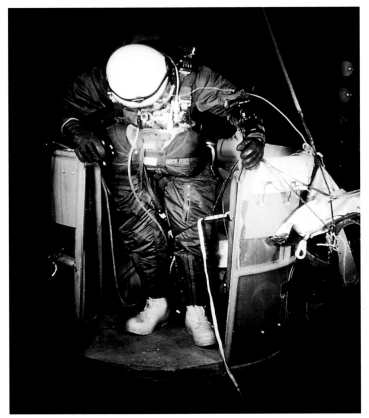

Practicing the exit in the test chamber. *Source: Photo courtesy of Dr. John Paul Stapp*

Kittinger standing in front of the *Project Excelsior* gondola prior to the third flight. *Excelsior* used an open gondola based on the Winzen *Sky-Car. Source: United States Air Force photograph*

Project *Stargazer* gondola. *Source: Photo courtesy of Dr. John Paul Stapp*

After stepping off "the highest step in the world," he fell on his right side for about eight seconds, then rolled over on his back to watch the silvery balloon against a black sky. Sixteen seconds after Kittinger left the gondola the pilot chute sprang out, followed by the drogue that stabilized him. His top speed, reached at 90,000 feet, was an incredible 625.2 miles per hour! While falling under the drogue chute he turned to face El Paso, Texas, then back to face New Mexico.

Suddenly, Kittinger felt as though he was being choked. This was a familiar problem. His helmet had a tendency to rise from his shoulders when the suit was pressurized. He had encountered this during ground tests, and on the previous two jumps. The support team tried several techniques to fix the problem, but none of them worked. Fortunately, as his descent continued, the sensation eased. At 21,000 feet Kittinger entered a solid layer of clouds. Instinctively, as though he were hitting a solid object, Kittinger drew his feet up. He had never fallen through clouds before. The main parachute deployed four and a half minutes after he left the balloon, after a fall of just over 16 miles. He emerged from the clouds at 15,000 feet. Two helicopters circled around him as he descended to the desert floor.

Prior to landing, Kittinger was supposed to release the instrument box beneath his parachute pack. Only one side released, so he landed with its additional weight. The landing was hard, and the seat kit inflicted a severe bruise on his leg. Otherwise, he was unhurt. The helicopters landed at almost the same instant as Kittinger, and medical technicians rushed to his aid. "I'm very glad to be back with you all," was how Kittinger greeted the recovery

team. The total time since leaving the balloon was 13 minutes, 45 seconds.

After *Excelsior*, Kittinger participated in an Air Force project called *Stargazer*. In 1959 the Air Force Office of Scientific Research began *Project Stargazer* at the Smithsonian Astrophysical Observatory to test the feasibility of doing astronomical research from a manned balloon. Responsibility for *Stargazer* was soon transferred to the Air Force Cambridge Research Laboratories. Dr. J. Allen Hynek from Northwestern University supervised the scientific aspects of the program.

Stargazer used a pressurized cylindrical gondola with a 12-inch Cassegrain-type reflecting telescope on its top. The telescope was mounted on a gyro-stabilized platform. The WADC provided the gondola. Joe Kittinger was project manager and chief pilot. General Mills built the 280-foot diameter Mylar balloon for the project. At launch, the aerostat towered 400 feet. One of the aspects that made *Stargazer* different from earlier Air Force stratospheric balloon projects was that the second crewmember was a

Opposite: The moment of truth—Kittinger jumps from 102,400 feet. *Source: United States Air Force photograph*

Kittinger and White take a break during a pre-flight simulation. *Source: Photo courtesy of Dr. John Paul Stapp*

Flight preparations—laying out the balloon. *Source: Photo courtesy of Dr. John Paul Stapp*

Bringing the capsule out of the hangar. *Source: Photo courtesy of Dr. John Paul Stapp*

Kittinger and White in the capsule prior to launch. *Source: Photo courtesy of Dr. John Paul Stapp*

trained astronomer (something that had already been done by the Navy during *Stratolab*.) Mr. William White, an astronomer at the Naval Ordnance Test Station at China Lake, California, accompanied Kittinger on the flight.

Stargazer lifted off from Holloman Air Force Base on December 13, 1962. Kittinger and White reached a peak altitude of 81,500 feet. They spent the night above 95% of the atmosphere. In addition to astronomical observations of Jupiter and the stars Capella, Aldebaran, Rigel, Betelgeuse, and Sirius, their experiments included observations of scintillation, and absorption of light by water vapor. The next morning Kittinger brought the balloon down to a soft landing in the desert. Original plans called for a series of four flights, but due to budgetary constraints this was the only *Stargazer* mission.

Otto Winzen continued to champion piloted stratospheric ballooning well into the mid-1960s. At a conference in 1965, Winzen delivered a paper titled "The Balloon as a Stepping-stone to Space Flight." He wrote:

"The plastic balloon vehicle, native to the United States, is a valuable, proven test platform which could serve to fill the gap between earth-bound simulators and final space flight. Balloons operate at an altitude where the environment, both physically and psychologically, resembles closely that of space flight. The balloon vehicle is uniquely capable as a manned space station analog with the capability of long flight duration, at low cost and immediate availability."

Winzen expanded on the role balloons might play in bridging what he described as the "wide gap" between simulators and space flight:

"In the effort to reduce the exorbitant cost and long lead-time of such test programs, we would be remiss not to explore and apply the unique capability of the balloon as a test bed operating in an environment which closely resembles that of orbital flight, within certain limits, of course." He pointed out that balloons oper-

The *Stargazer* emergency parachute. *Source: Photo courtesy of Dr. John Paul Stapp*

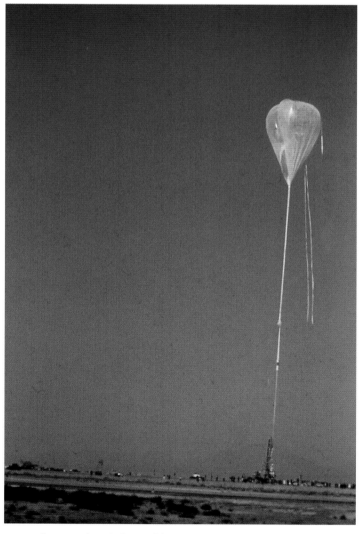

Stargazer launch. *Source: Photo courtesy of Dr. John Paul Stapp*

Stargazer in flight. Source: *Photo courtesy of Dr. John Paul Stapp*

White and Kittinger peer out of the capsule after landing. *Source: Photo courtesy of Dr. John Paul Stapp*

ate in an "environment more closely resembling that of space than achieved by any other simulator," and that they created what he felt was the "psychologically correct stress environment."

However, the age of piloted stratospheric balloon flights by the United States Air Force was over. *Manhigh* may have helped pave the way for *Mercury* and subsequent NASA programs, but the "glory days" of manned ballooning were finished. On March 23, 1965, NASA began launching the two-man *Gemini* spacecraft. By the end of the year, *Gemini 7* astronauts Frank Borman and James Lovell spent two weeks in space. Whatever knowledge gained by manned stratospheric balloon flights seemed minimal when compared to a 14-day space flight.

With the media focused on NASA's astronauts, the pilots who flew balloons to the edge of space faded into relative obscurity. After *Stargazer*, Joe Kittinger returned to flying fighters. In 1972 he was shot down over North Vietnam, and was imprisoned in the infamous "Hanoi Hilton" until his repatriation during "Operation Homecoming." Dave Simons became head of the Bioastronautics Branch of the Air Force School of Aviation Medicine. Cliff McClure left active duty, and became a fighter pilot in the South Carolina Air National Guard. The AMFL played a small, but very significant, role in Project *Mercury*. They provided the chimpanzees that flew aboard *Mercury* spacecraft before astronauts did.

Stratospheric balloons continue to be flown, but with automated payloads. Often instruments destined for satellites are first tested with balloons, and they have made many valuable scientific contributions. Except for the occasional unidentified flying object report, these flights go largely unnoticed by the public.

NASA's achievements during the 1960s were truly impressive, culminating with the first Americans on the moon in 1969, less than 11 years after the *Manhigh III* flight. However, during the time before NASA, the cutting edge in space biology could be found in a laboratory in southern New Mexico being conducted by a small band of Air Force scientists. In the era between World War II and the creation of NASA, the men who used balloons to venture to the edge of the atmosphere *were* the space program.

Capsule recovery in the New Mexico desert. *Source: Photo courtesy of Dr. John Paul Stapp*

Appendix 1:
Select Balloon Chronology

- June 4, 1783 – Jacques Étienne and Joesph Michel Montgolfier performed the first public demonstration of their hot air balloon near Annonay, France.
- August 27, 1783 – Professor Jacques Charles launched the first hydrogen-filled balloon, *The Globe*, from Paris. Jean and Noël Robert fabricated the balloon from rubberized silk. Like the Montgolfier's first hot air balloon, it was unmanned.
- September 19, 1783 – Montgolfiers launch hot air balloon from Versailles for King Louis XVI and his court. The balloon carried the first passengers, a lamb, a duck, and a rooster.
- November 21, 1783 – Pilatre de Rozier and Francois Laurent, the Marquis d'Arlandes, made history's first flight in a hot air balloon built by the Montgolfier brothers. They reached an altitude of 3,000 feet and traveled some 5 miles across Paris in a flight that lasted 25 minutes.
- December 2, 1783 – Professor Jacques Charles and Noël Robert made the first piloted flight in a hydrogen-filled balloon.
- November 30, 1784 – Jean Pierre Blanchard and Dr. John Jeffries performed a flight for the Prince of Wales and other dignitaries. Jeffries carried a thermometer, barometer, hygrometer, chronometer, and bottles to collect air samples for the Royal Society.
- January 7, 1785 – Blanchard and Jeffries made first aerial crossing of the English Channel in a hydrogen-filled balloon. Jeffries took a barometer and thermometer along.
- September 5, 1862 – Henry Coxwell and James Glaisher conducted an ascent to 26,400 feet to measure high altitude winds, temperatures and solar affects using a balloon they named *Mammoth*.
- April 15, 1875 – Joseph Crocce-Spinelli, Theodore Sivel, and Gaston Tissandier attempted a high altitude flight using a balloon they named *Le Zenith*. They reached 30,000 feet. Crocce-Spinelli and Sivel died of hypoxia.
- June 30, 1901 – Arthur Berson and Reinhard Süring reach 35,423 feet using a 300,000 cubic foot hydrogen-filled balloon they named *Preussen*.
- 1902 – Bort "discovers" the stratosphere
- August 20, 1905 – Spanish Army launched three balloons to study a total solar eclipse.
- 1911 – 1912 – Victor Franz Hess "discovers" cosmic radiation.
- March 9, 1927 – U.S. Army Captain Hawthorne C. Gray set an American altitude record of 28,510 feet while attempting to reach the stratosphere.
- May 4, 1927 -- Hawthorne C. Gray reached 42,470 feet in open basket balloon; had to bail out during descent so record was not official.
- November 4, 1927 – Hawthorne C. Gray attempted again to set an altitude record; reached 42,470 feet, but did not survive the flight.
- May 27, 1931 -- Auguste Piccard and Paul Kipfer make first balloon flight into the stratosphere using a sealed capsule from Augsburg, Germany; altitude 51,775 feet.
- August 18, 1932 -- Auguste Piccard and Max Cosyns set record altitude of 54,120 feet in balloon.
- September 30, 1933 -- Russian balloon *Stratostat USSR* reached 60,695 feet, but ascent never became an official record; crewed by Georgi Prokivief, Ernest Birnbaum, and Konstantine Godrenow.
- November 20 - 21, 1933 -- Lt. Commander Thomas G. W. Settle (USN) and Maj. Chester L. Fordney (USMC) established official world altitude record of 61,237 feet over Akron, Ohio in balloon *A Century of Progress*.
- January 30, 1934 -- Russian balloon *Osaviakhim* reached 73,000 feet, but crew died when gondola fell free; crewed by Paul F. Fedoseyenko, Andrei B. Wasienko (or, Vasenko), and Ilya Usyskin.
- July 28, 1934 -- *Explorer* balloon launched from *Stratobowl* near Rapid City, South Dakota; balloon failed at 60,613 feet; pilots Major William E. Kepner, Captain Orvil A. Anderson, and Captain Albert W. Stevens bailed out during descent.
- August 18, 1934 -- Max Cosyns and Nérée van der Elst piloted a balloon to an altitude of 52,952 feet following a take off from Hour-Havenne, Belgium; flight took them over Germany and Austria before they landed near Senaulje, Yugoslavia.
- October 23, 1934 -- Jeannette and Jean Piccard flew *A Century of Progress* balloon to 57,979 feet after launch from Dearborn, Michigan; Jeanette Piccard set an unofficial altitude record for women and became the first woman to reach the stratosphere.
- During 1935 – Jean Piccard and Thomas Johnson of the Bartol Research Laboratory of the Franklin Institute flew first plastic balloon from Swarthmore, PA. Balloon made from cellophane.
- July 26, 1935 -- Russian balloon *USSR* reached 52,000 feet; crewed by Warigo, Christofil, and Prilucki.
- November 11, 1935 -- Army Captains Orvil A. Anderson and Albert W. Stevens set new official altitude record of 72,395 feet aboard balloon *Explorer II* in ascent from *Stratobowl*.

- During Summer and Fall of 1936 – Jean Piccard and John Ackerman flew constant-level balloons made from cellophane from University of Minnesota.
- July 19, 1937 – Project Pleiades; Jean Piccard performed flight with cluster of rubber meteorological balloons.
- October 14, 1938 – Polish Captain Zbigniew Burzynski and Dr. Konstanty Jodko-Narkiewicz attempt flight in *Star of Poland*. Balloon caught fire when it was less than 100 feet above the ground.
- June 4, 1947 -- First balloon launch from Alamogordo Army Air Field (later renamed Holloman Air Force Base); cluster of rubber balloons launched by New York University team under contract to Air Materiel Command; part of Project Mogul.
- July 3, 1947 -- First polyethylene balloon launch at Alamogordo Army Air Field by New York University crew.
- September 25, 1947 -- Otto Winzen launched first polyethylene balloon to reach 100,000 feet from St. Cloud, Minnesota.
- November 3, 1949 – Charles B. Moore of General Mills made first manned flight with a polyethylene balloon over Minneapolis, Minnesota.
- September 8, 1950 -- First biological balloon flight from Holloman Air Force Base carried "14 or 16" white mice on a 7-hour flight which reached 47,000 feet; capsule's pressure relief valve leaked and the mice died.
- September 28, 1950 -- First live recovery of a biological balloon flight from Holloman Air Force Base; capsule carrying 8 white mice recovered after a 3-hour, 40-minute flight to 97,000 feet.
- July 18, 1955 – First biological flight with a two-million cubic foot capacity balloon; reached 120,000 feet.
- August 19, 1955 – Unmanned test flight of *Stratolab* system; emergency parachute test; reached 69,000 feet.
- September 11, 1955 – Unmanned test flight of *Stratolab* system; reached 55,500 feet.
- November 9, 1955 – Winzen Research received contract for *Project Manhigh*.
- February 9, 1956 – Unmanned *Manhigh* test flight; thermal insulation test with mockup capsule; reached 85,000 feet.
- April 20, 1956 – Unmanned test flight of *Manhigh* system; emergency parachute test; reached 86,000 feet.
- May 15, 1956 – Unmanned *Stratolab* flight test; balloon failed during launch.
- July 11, 1956 – Unmanned *Stratolab* flight test; reached 100,000 feet.
- July 23, 1956 – Unmanned *Stratolab* flight test; balloon reached 85,000 feet.
- August 6, 1956 – Unmanned *Stratolab* flight test; balloon reached 60,500 feet.
- August 10, 1956 -- Lt. Comdrs. Malcolm D. Ross and M. Lee Lewis make first piloted high-altitude flight with a polyethylene balloon, reaching 40,000 feet in an open basket as part of *Stratolab* program.
- August 20, 1956 – Unmanned *Stratolab* flight test; balloon reached 92,000 feet.
- September 25, 1956 – H. Froehlich and K. Lang reach 42,000 feet in an open basket as part of *Stratolab* program.
- November 8, 1956 -- Lt. Comdrs. Malcolm D. Ross and M. Lee Lewis established altitude record of 76,000 feet during *Stratolab High I* balloon flight.
- December 17, 1956 – Unmanned test flight of *Manhigh* capsule; reached 97,000 feet before balloon broke.
- March 17, 1957 – Unmanned test flight of WADC personnel parachute system for possible use with *Manhigh* with 180-pound anthropomorphic dummy; reached 90,000 feet.
- March 21, 1957 – Unmanned test flight of *Manhigh* capsule
- April 14, 1957 – Unmanned test flight of *Manhigh* capsule; reached 95,000 feet.
- April 27, 1957 – Unmanned test flight of *Manhigh* capsule; reached 111,800 feet.
- June 2, 1957 -- Captain Joseph W. Kittinger reached 97,000 feet during *Manhigh I* balloon flight.
- August 19, 1957 – H. Froehlich and K. Lang reach 38,000 feet in an open basket as part of *Stratolab* program.
- August 19 - 20, 1957 -- Major David G. Simons set official altitude record of 101,516 feet (AGL) aboard *Manhigh II* balloon flight; 102,400 feet above sea level.
- October 18, 1957 -- Lt. Comdrs. Malcolm D. Ross and M. Lee Lewis reached 85,700 feet in *Stratolab High II* balloon flight.
- May 6 - 7, 1958 -- Lt. Comdr. Malcolm D. Ross and Alfred H. Mikesell used open-gondola *Stratolab* to reach 40,000 feet; Mikesell was first astronomer to conduct observations from the upper stratosphere.
- July 26 - 27, 1958 -- *Stratolab High III* balloon reached 82,000 feet with crew of Lt. Comdrs. Malcolm D. Ross and M. Lee Lewis.
- October 8, 1958 -- Lieutenant Clifton McClure reached 99,700 feet in *Manhigh III* balloon flight.
- August 7, 1959 -- Commander Malcolm D. Ross and R. Cooper flew *Stratolab* balloon with an open gondola to 38,000 feet.
- November 16, 1959 -- Captain Joseph W. Kittinger reached 76,400 feet in *Excelsior I* balloon flight; high-altitude bailout test.
- November 28 - 29, 1959 -- Commander Malcolm D. Ross and Charles Moore reached 81,000 feet in *Stratolab High IV* balloon flight.
- December 16, 1959 -- Captain Joseph W. Kittinger flew *Excelsior II* balloon to 74,700 feet; high-altitude bailout test.
- August 16, 1960 -- Captain Joseph W. Kittinger reached 102,800 feet in *Excelsior III* balloon flight; high-altitude bailout test.
- May 4, 1961 -- Commander Malcolm D. Ross and Lt. Commander Victor G. Prather reached 113,740 feet in *Stratolab High V* balloon flight over Gulf of Mexico; Prather drowned during recovery.
- December 13 - 14, 1962 -- *Project Stargazer* balloon flight; Joseph Kittinger and William White reached 81,500 feet.

Appendix 2:
Project *Stratolab* Summary

Although it was conducted in parallel with *Manhigh*, the Navy's *Stratolab* program was very different than the Air Force effort. As described in Chapter 6, *Stratolab* can be traced to *Helios*, the piloted balloon project begun by Jean Piccard in the 1940s. Although *Helios* never reached the flight stage, General Mills fabricated the gondola shell under Navy contract N6 ONR-252. When the Office of Naval Research (ONR) canceled *Helios*, the shell went into storage at the Naval Air Station at Lakehurst, New Jersey. There it sat for seven years.

In 1954 Naval interest in manned stratospheric ballooning resumed, and Winzen began discussions with service officials about refurbishing the *Helios* shell and outfitting it for flight. On October 11, 1954, the shell was moved to the Winzen Research plant for safekeeping and storage. Five months later, Winzen Research received contract NONR 1460(03) to modify *Helios* for *Stratolab*. Because Piccard based *Helios* on gondolas built in the 1930s, in many respects *Stratolab* represented an evolutionary approach to sealed capsule design, rather than a revolutionary one like *Manhigh*.

The Navy conceived *Stratolab* as a program to conduct research in aerospace medicine; collect geophysical and astrophysical measurements; and evaluate military techniques and equipment for flight at extreme altitudes. One major difference between *Manhigh* and *Stratolab* was that the latter used two-man crews for all flights. *Stratolab* comprised a series of low, medium, and high altitude flights. Low altitude flights generally didn't go above 12,000 feet; the medium altitude ones went around 40,000 feet, which was in the stratosphere. Winzen's *SkyCar* was used for low- and medium-altitude flights. The pressurized gondola was used for high altitude missions. Navy Captain Normal Lee Barr, MD, was flight surgeon for *Stratolab*.

A conference was held in Washington on April 18, 1955, to map out *Stratolab* requirements. The Scientific Officer, Lieutenant Commander Malcom D. Ross, presented the project to interested members of the Armed Forces. This can be considered the real start of capsule design and construction, because this meeting was where specific requirements were established.

When he prepared *Helios* for *Stratolab*, Winzen made many modifications to the spherical gondola. The capsule was 7 feet, two inches in diameter, and was fabricated from 1/8-inch thick 3003-SO spun aluminum. It comprised eight segments joined together by a heliarc welding process. There were more than 100 feet of welded seams in the shell. Winzen X-rayed all the seams. Any defects were ground out, and the weld redone. Eliminating the internal load stanchions provided additional space inside the sphere.

The internal shelves were reworked to create more usable space inside the capsule. Two plastic seats were added; all critical flight controls were within reach of the seated aeronauts. Being able to sit during the majority of the flight reduced crew fatigue,

and added to the pilots' overall comfort. These seats had standard lap and shoulder belts.

Winzen re-engineered the gondola suspension system by welding eight attachment lugs to the top of the shell. To test the strength of the lugs Winzen filled the gondola with water, which brought its weight to 13,000 pounds. This was about nine times the normal flight weight. To test the cabin's ability to hold pressure, the water pressure was increased to 43 PSI. This was five times what the capsule had to contain during flight. After 30 minutes no leaks were detected. Despite positive results of the static load test, General Mills personnel expressed their lack of confidence in Winzen's attachment system.

All work on the gondola interior stopped while the issue of the suspension system was resolved. Two months after the first static load test Winzen conducted a second one. For this test, the cabin was filled with 6,633 pounds of water and suspended by two attachment points. This was the equivalent of 2 g's on each lug. Again, Winzen's attachment system proved more than adequate.

Stratolab had two inward opening hatches mounted in flat frames that Winzen welded into the shell. Having two hatches made normal entry and exit easier, and facilitated rapid exit in case of an emergency. Simple air pressure sealed the hatches. Within the cabin, a pressure equivalent to 17,000 feet was maintained. When the balloon ascended beyond that altitude, the pressure difference between the inside and outside atmospheres forced the hatches against their frames. A silicone O-ring around the outer diameter of each hatch created a pressure-tight seal. During descent, the hatches opened automatically.

Stratolab used a two-gas atmosphere supplied by a cryogenic system. The primary system comprised five liters of a mixture of 50% liquid oxygen and 50% liquid nitrogen. As a backup, *Stratolab* carried a second five-liter converter that contained only liquid oxygen. It provided an auxiliary supply for emergency cabin pressurization, and supplied oxygen to the pilots' pressure suits.

Lithium hydroxide and lithium chloride removed carbon dioxide and water vapor, respectively, from the cabin atmosphere. A fan forced cabin air through a cabinet that contained the chemicals. The Navy selected these chemicals based on their experience with submarines. This arrangement bore a strong resemblance to the cabinets of soda lime used on the *Explorer* flights. A pressure regulator built by the Firewel Company in Buffalo, New York, automatically maintained air pressure inside the cabin. As a backup to the cabin life support system, the pilots wore Air Force MC-3 partial pressure suits. The AMFL loaned the suits to the Navy.

The gondola had nine windows, sealed with 3/4-inch Plexiglas. A black and white paint scheme like that used on *Explorer II* provided passive thermal control for *Stratolab*. Fans inside the cabin blew air over either the warm lower half or cooler upper half, depending on the inside temperature. To insulate the cabin during the first flight, a shroud of clear polyethylene mounted on 2-inch standoffs covered the capsule. Designed by Dr. V. Suomi of the University of Wisconsin, the shroud prevented the capsule from becoming too cold during flight.

Piccard designed *Helios* for one flight; the Navy planned to use *Stratolab* multiple times. Basing his design on the cabins of the 1930s, Piccard suspended ballast bags and other equipment around the exterior of the gondola. To improve the system's durability and generally clean up the capsule, Winzen removed the exterior loads. He added a cylindrical undercarriage to the sphere that contained ballast, the radio beacon, batteries, a downward-looking camera, and other equipment that didn't need to be in the cabin. The undercarriage measured 53 inches in diameter and 24 inches high. Made from 1-1/2 inch diameter 6061-T6 aluminum tubing, the undercarriage supported the capsule before launch, and provided a crushable landing gear to absorb the impact of a hard landing. Aluminum pads welded to the bottom of the shell provided attachment points for the undercarriage, and let it be replaced quickly and easily.

WRI finished work on the gondola on November 10, 1955. Lieutenant Commander Ross inspected the finished craft and recommended some minor changes. These were made, and Winzen delivered the completed gondola to the Naval Air Station in Minneapolis on 30 November. Six months later, the Navy took the capsule to Naval Air Station Inyokern in California for testing at General Mills' direction. It was then returned to General Mills in Minneapolis.

On August 3, 1956, Winzen submitted a proposal, after invitation by the Navy, to recondition the capsule, and render it flight ready by the end of the month. While *Stratolab* was out of Winzen's control it sustained some damage. A circuit breaker installed in the floor had to be replaced because it was damaged by the flow of people in and out of the capsule. Wiring showed wear and had to be replaced. Some of the flight instruments had been damaged during testing at Inyokern.

There were several deep gashes in the gondola shell, most likely from dropped tools. These areas had to be rewelded and X-ray inspected. When WRI delivered the capsule, it had altimeters that were calibrated by the Bureau of Standards. They had been removed and sent to the Naval Air Station for calibration. Since they were part of the equipment necessary to establish a world altitude record, they had to be sent back to the Bureau of Standards for recalibration.

Just like *Manhigh* and the earlier biological capsule flights, *Stratolab* was suspended from the balloon via an open parachute. Due to the weight of the capsule, a 64-foot diameter nylon cargo parachute was used. If the crew were incapacitated, ground control could cut away the gondola. If both the balloon and cargo parachute failed, the pilots had personal parachutes that they wore throughout the flight.

Initially, Winzen proposed the company's 128 TT tapeless balloon be used. At the second *Stratolab* conference in June 1955, questions emerged regarding the safety of this type of balloon. The following month Winzen halted manufacture of the 128 TT balloon. Its design was considered too marginal for such a heavy payload. (A surplus 128 TT balloon was used for one of the *Manhigh* animal test flights with no problems. Winzen also used the 128 TT for two simulated *Stratolab* payloads with similar results.)

With the 128 TT removed from consideration, Winzen planned to use their natural shape FIST 2-million cubic foot balloons for *Stratolab*. At launch, this would make the aerostat about 300 feet tall. Otto Winzen looked to the *Stratobowl* as a potential launch site, but he did not feel it was deep enough to protect such a large craft. Winzen needed another launch site. He found an open-pit iron mine near Crosby, Minnesota, that fit their needs. The Portsmouth Iron Mine, which was also used for *Manhigh*, was 425 feet deep, and had piles of rocks around its rim that provided additional shielding from the wind.

To test launch techniques, flight characteristics, and the parachute recovery system, Winzen built a mockup of *Stratolab* from steel pipes covered with plastic sheeting. During the first flight attempt at Camp Ripley, Minnesota, the balloon failed. Two months later, the Winzen crew moved the flight to the Portsmouth Mine and tried again. This time the flight was a success. Three more flights were made with the mockup capsule, the last one on August 20, 1956.

By the time of the last mockup flight, Lieutenant Commanders Ross and M. Lee Lewis made the first manned flight of the *Stratolab* program. Riding in an open gondola, they ascended to 40,000 feet on August 10, 1956, to photograph condensation trails from jet aircraft. Secondary objectives were to make physiological measurements of the pilots and test their pressure suits. This was the first manned stratospheric balloon flight since *Explorer II* in 1935.

Ross and Lewis made the first flight in the *Stratolab* gondola on November 8, 1956. Winzen Research did not conduct the flight; their rival General Mills did. The ONR decided to use a 128 TT balloon made by General Mills. The company launched *Stratolab High I* from the *Stratobowl*. In an interesting twist of events,

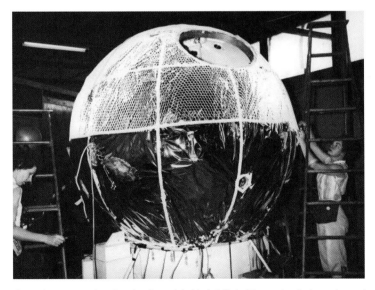

Capsule preparation for the *Stratolab High I* flight. The polyethylene shroud around the capsule kept it from getting too cold during the flight. *Source: Winzen Research, Inc. photograph*

the wooden frame that supported the *Explorer II* gondola before it took off was still there. *Stratolab High I* used the same frame before it took off. Charles Moore (who had left General Mills and was working for the Arthur D. Little Company) greeted Ross and Lewis when they prepared to board the capsule. Moore was the alternate pilot, and he was wearing an MC-3 pressure suit in case something happened to one of the primary crewmembers. He offered to take the place of either crewmember if they changed their mind at the last minute. After some additional good-natured banter between the three men, Ross and Lewis boarded *Stratolab*.

The 128-foot diameter balloon reached 76,000 feet. Ross and Lewis marveled at the view. Looking at the horizon, the sky formed a band of intense, bright white that faded to a "very delicate blue-white." Above that, the sky darkened to an eventual pitch black about 20° above the horizon. They began unpacking cameras to begin their observations when Ross observed the altimeter. It showed they were dropping.

At first, Ross and Lewis feared the balloon had torn. They returned to their seats, fastened their seat belts, and hooked the faceplates to their helmets. The descent rate quickened, and the pair felt like they were in a rapidly dropping elevator. They reported their situation to the ground. Once Lewis released the transmitter button, they heard Captain Barr congratulating them on their flight. Apparently, Barr began his transmission at the same time Lewis sent the distress report, and was unaware of any problems with the flight. Barr then asked for instrument readings. That was when Lewis advised him of the emergency.

The long plummet continued. Ross and Lewis considered cutting away from the balloon and descending via the emergency parachute, but they feared they might drift into the badlands, with its jagged mountain peaks and rough terrain. At least they weren't accelerating, so they decided to stay with the balloon. They dropped all their ballast, and after a few minutes the descent rate slowed. Then, as *Stratolab* passed through 37,000 feet, the descent rate increased again, reaching 1,400 feet per minute. Once they reached 17,000 feet they opened the hatches and began tossing equipment overboard. Ross and Lewis brought the descent down to 800 feet per minute by the time they landed in the capsule near Kennedy,

Stratolab High IV. This flight began from the *Stratobowl* near Rapid City, South Dakota. The capsule carried a telescope. *Source: United States Navy*

Nebraska. This was about twice the normal landing speed, but the styrofoam pad and crushable support under the capsule absorbed the impact. Ross and Lewis emerged from the capsule unscathed. No tear was found in the balloon; there had been a problem with the vent valve.

The second *Stratolab High* mission took place nearly a year later. Piloted once again by Malcolm D. Ross and M. Lee Lewis, *Stratolab High II* reached 85,700 feet on October 18, 1957. After taking off from the Portsmouth Mine in Crosby, the aeronauts landed in a heavily wooded swamp about three miles west of Hermanville, Michigan. An Air Force helicopter had to be used to lift the gondola out of the swamp. With so much attention focused on *Manhigh II* and the orbiting of the first artificial satellite, *Stratolab* received little attention in the press. Ross and Lewis spent several hours above 85,000 feet in a flight that lasted nine-and-a-half hours.

Stratolab High II was relatively routine, the only negative aspects of the flight being uncomfortably high temperatures and humidity in the capsule. When the crew began their descent a little past noon the temperature inside the capsule reached 80 degrees, and the relative humidity was around 60 percent. Wearing Navy thermal garments over the MC-3 pressure suits, Ross and Lewis were extremely uncomfortable. This seriously affected their ability to complete scientific observations. The flight journal contained the following remarks written after they conducted an instrument reading: "About stood on my head to do this. After several readings gave up. Strato-Lab of the future (as our manned satellites) must be far different if scientists are expected to work and do real research."

Ross again ascended into the stratosphere on May 6-7, 1958, this time accompanied by Alfred H. Mikesell, a Naval Observatory astronomer. They flew in the *Sky-Car*, and did not wear pressure suits. The aeronauts wore oxygen masks and Navy cold weather gear. Reaching 40,000 feet, Mikesell became the first astronomer to conduct observations from the stratosphere. Throughout the night, he used a Questar telescope with a quartz lens to measure changes in star brightness with time. Mikesell also made subjective observations of the effects of being in the upper fifth of the atmosphere on the appearance of the Moon, Jupiter, Venus, and Mercury.

Ross and Lewis ventured into the stratosphere together again for *Stratolab High III* on July 26-27, 1958. They reached 82,000 feet, and remained aloft for 34-1/2 hours. Not long after this flight, Lewis retired from the Navy and joined the staff of Winzen Research as chief of operations.

The Navy continued their stratospheric balloon program with the flight of *Stratolab High IV* on November 28-29, 1959. *Stratolab High IV* used the same capsule as the previous flights. This time, though, a 16-inch Schmidt infrared telescope was added to the capsule's top. Crewed by Malcolm Ross and Charles Moore, the flight lifted off from the Stratobowl and reached 81,000 feet. In 1949, Moore had been the first person to use a polyethylene balloon for a piloted ascent. Throughout the night Moore used the telescope to look for water in the atmosphere of Venus. They land-

Stratolab High IV liftoff from the *Stratobowl*. *Source: Winzen Research, Inc. photograph*

ed the following afternoon near Manhattan, Kansas. After *Stratolab High IV*, the spherical gondola was retired.

Stratolab High V, the last in the series, was different from previous high altitude flights. Instead of using a pressurized capsule, *Stratolab High V* used an open gondola. Commander Malcolm Ross, veteran of the previous *Stratolab High* missions, commanded this flight. Lt. Commander Victor G. Prather, a medical officer from the Naval Medical Research Institute in Bethesda, Maryland, accompanied him.

Stratolab High V carried emulsion plates to trap cosmic radiation particles and meteorological instruments, but the main objective of the flight was to test the Navy's Mark IV full pressure suit. Manufactured by B. F. Goodrich, the Mark IV was the basis for the Project *Mercury* space suits. Goodrich engineer Russel Colley, who built the first pressure suit ever flown by aviator Wiley Post, helped develop the Mark IV and Mercury suits. *Stratolab High V* was the most severe test of the suits ever conducted.

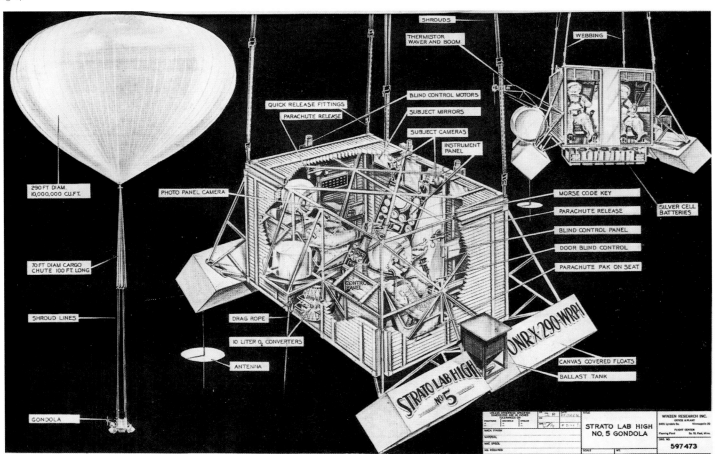

73 ARTIST DRAWING OF ONR-WINZEN RESEARCH PROJECT STRATO-LAB HIGH V, MANNED OPEN-GONDOLA BALLOON SYSTEM. This balloon system, carrying a crew of two, set a new official altitude record of 113,733 feet when flown on 4 May 1961 from the U.S.S. Antietam in the Gulf of Mexico. Gondola made a successful water landing at the end of the 9-hour flight. This system designed for evaluation of space suits and the psycho-physiological reactions of the crew in actual space environment. Temperature control of pilots, successfully accomplished by electrical orientation of venetian blinds with aluminum and black surfaces, with each blind individually controlled, keeps pilots comfortable and achieves adjustment of surface temperatures

Stratolab High V gondola schematic. *Source: Winzen Research, Inc. photograph*

Before the *Stratolab High V* mission, Ross and Prather conducted a practice flight to 6,000 feet in a mock-up of the gondola. *Source: Winzen Research, Inc. photograph*

The Mark IV comprised two layers: a neoprene rubber impregnated nylon pressure bladder, and a nylon cover that protected the bladder and kept it from overinflating. For space use, the outer layer was aluminized, giving it a silver look. Operational Mark IV suits were green in color. The *Stratolab High V* pilots wore an aluminized insulation layer over the standard Mark IV, giving their suits the same appearance as the Mercury garments.

The *Stratolab High V* gondola was an open box-shaped frame equipped with two seats. Venetian blinds attached to the frame controlled the temperatures inside the gondola. One side of the blinds was painted white, the other, black. By turning the blinds, Ross and Prather could control how much sunlight was either reflected or absorbed to control the temperature inside the gondola.

Ross and Prather took off from the deck of the aircraft carrier *USS Antietam* on the morning of May 4, 1961. The balloon envelope was the largest launched up to that time—10 million cubic feet! It was made from seven acres of polyethylene and weighed a ton. Fully inflated, it was 300 feet in diameter. The carrier was in the Gulf of Mexico, steaming with the wind, so the air speed on the deck was zero.

Ross and Prather endured bitterly cold temperatures, condensation on the visors of their helmets, and communications problems during their ascent. Despite these difficulties, they reached 113,740 feet. As later reported by Ross: "In silent awe, we contemplated the supernal loveliness of the atmosphere." It was 9:47 AM, a little more than two and a half hours after launch.

Ross decided to begin descending almost right away. He encountered the familiar problem of starting a steady descent. By 11:15 they were still floating at 110,000 feet. Ross mentally plotted their descent rate versus time versus oxygen supply, and realized they could very well run out of oxygen if they didn't descend soon. He continued valving helium, finally achieving a descent rate of 500 feet per minute at 90,000 feet. They "won the race with oxygen," but faced another all too familiar problem—the descent rate was too high as they passed through the tropopause. They quickly began jettisoning ballast.

Even after dropping all the ballast *Stratolab* continued to descend too fast, so they began throwing everything they could overboard, including the radio. By reducing the weight of the gondola the aeronauts brought the descent under control. They even relaxed enough once they were below 7,000 feet to open the visors on their helmets and smoke cigarettes. Preparing to land, Prather cut off the drag rope while Ross threw out the venetian blinds that had been used to control the temperature in the gondola. When the gondola splashed down in the Gulf Ross released the balloon.

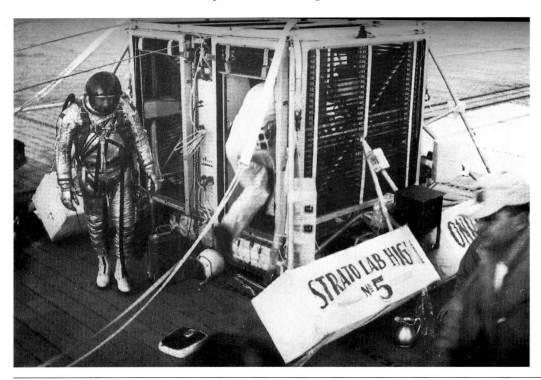

Ross and Prather wore space suits like those used by the *Project Mercury* astronauts. *Source: Winzen Research, Inc. photograph*

They sat there, floating comfortably, surrounded by the debris they jettisoned during the descent.

The *Antietam* was just a mile and a half away. With rescue helicopters overhead and the aircraft carrier approaching, Ross and Prather were in a jubilant mood, knowing they had completed all the objectives of the flight. As the helicopter moved into position it lowered a line to the pilots. Ross went first. Stepping on the hook at the end of the line, he slipped and fell into the water, but held onto the line, and was hauled aboard the helicopter. When it was Prather's turn, he also slipped and fell into the water, but was unable to keep hold of the line. Seawater poured into his suit through the open face plate. Rescue divers were quickly in the water, but they were too late—Prather drowned. Prather's tragic death devastated Ross, and marred what was otherwise a brilliant flight.

The next day, an American crossed the threshold from "space equivalence" to outer space for the first time. On May 5, 1961, Navy Commander Alan B. Shepard, Jr., reached an altitude of 115 miles in a *Mercury* spacecraft he named *Freedom-7*. His space suit was nearly identical to the ones worn by Ross and Prather.

Bibliography

Air Force Missile Development Center. *Manhigh III Manned Balloon Flight Into the Stratosphere*. Holloman Air Force Base, New Mexico: Aeromedical Field Laboratory Report AFMDC-TR-60-16, April, 1961.

"Airships and Balloons," *The Aircraft Year Book For 1935*. Aeronautical Chamber of Commerce of America, Inc., 1935.

"Airships and Balloons," *The Aircraft Year Book For 1936*. Aeronautical Chamber of Commerce of America, Inc., 1936.

Army Ballistic Missile Agency. "Development Proposal for Project Adam." Redstone Arsenal, Huntsville, Alabama: Report D-TR-1-58, April 17, 1958.

Baker, Norman L. "Air Force Won't Support Project Adam," *Missiles and Rockets*. June 1958.

Benford, Robert J. *The Heritage of Aviation Medicine*. Washington, D. C.: Aerospace Medical Association, 1979.

Bland, William M., Jr. "Project Mercury," *The History of Rocket Technology*. Detroit: Wayne State University Press, 1964.

Bower, K. E.. *Post Flight Report – Flight 752 Project Manhigh Parachute Test Flight From Fleming Field, South St. Paul On 27 April 1957*. Minneapolis: Winzen Research, Inc., Report No. 1210-R, May 1, 1957.

Clark, Evert. "Navy Balloon Flight Aids Space Research," *Aviation Week*. May 12, 1958.

Cross, W. F. *Project Skyhook – Office of Naval Research Balloon Project*. Washington, D. C.: Office of Naval Research, October 1976.

DeVorkin, David H. *Race to the Stratosphere*. New York: Springer-Verlag, 1989.

Emme, Eugene M. *Aeronautics and Astronautics, 1915 – 1960*. Washington, D. C.: U. S. Government Printing Office, 1961.

Fisher, Allan C., Jr., and Marden, Luis. "Aviation Medicine on the Threshold of Space," *The National Geographic Magazine*. Volume CVIII, Number 2, August, 1955.

"Gordon Bennett Race," *The Aircraft Year Book For 1928*, Aeronautical Chamber of Commerce of America, Inc., 1928.

Grimwood, James M. *Project Mercury: A Chronology*. Washington, D. C.: NASA SP-4001, U. S. Government Printing Office, NASA SP-4001, 1963.

Grosvenor, Gilbert. "The Society Announces New Flight Into the Stratosphere," *The National Geographic Magazine*. Volume LXVII, Number 2, February 1935.

Haig, T. O. "Plastic Balloons for High Altitude Research," *The Journal of Aviation Medicine*. Volume 25, Number 4, August 1954.

Hanrahan, James S., and Bushnell, David. *Space Biology*. New York: Basic Books, 1960.

Haymaker, Webb. "Operation Stratomouse," *Military Medicine*. Volume 119, Number 3, September 1956.

Headquarters, Department of the Army. *Aeromedical Training for Flight Person- nel*, Washington, D. C.: U. S. Government Printing Office, 18 January 1979.

Headquarters, United States Air Force. *The Roswell Report*. Washington, D.C.: U.S. Government Printing Office, 1995.

Henry, James P., et. al.. "Animal Studies of the Subgravity State During Rocket Flight," *Journal of Aviation Medicine*. V. 23, No. 10, October 1952.

Herrera, Emilio. *Flying: The Memoirs of a Spanish Aeronaut*. Albuquerque: University of New Mexico Press, 1984.

Historical Division, Air Force Missile Development Center. *Contributions of Bal- loon Operations to Research and Development at the Air Force Missile Devel- opment Test Center, 1947 – 1958*. Holloman Air Force Base, New Mexico, 1959.

Historical Division, Air Force Missile Development Center. *History of Research in Space Biology and Biodynamics at the Air Force Missile Development Center, Holloman Air Force Base, New Mexico, 1946 – 1958*. Holloman Air Force Base, New Mexico, 1958.

Honour, Alan. *Ten Miles High, Two Miles Deep*. New York: Whittlesey House, McGraw-Hill Book Company, 1957.

Huenke, Caroline. "To the Edge of Space and Back," *Covington News*. Covington, Georgia, September 10, 2006.

Jackson, Donald D.. *The Aeronauts*. Alexandria, Virginia: Time-Life Books, 1981.

Kennedy, Gregory P. *Germany's V-2 Rocket*. Atglen, Pennsylvania: Schiffer Publishing, Ltd., 2006.

Kittinger, Joseph W., Jr., with Caidin, Martin. *The Long, Lonely Leap*. New York: E. P. Dutton & Company,, 1961.

Ley, Willy. *Rockets, Missiles, and Men in Space*. New York: Viking Press, 1968.

Link, Mae Mills. *Space Medicine in Project Mercury*, Washington, D. C.: National Aeronautics and Space Administration SP-4003, 1965.

Mallan, Lloyd. *Men, Rockets and Space Rats*. New York: Julian Messner, Inc., 1955.

Mikesh, Robert C. *Japan's World War II Balloon Bomb Attacks on North America*. Washington, D.C.: Smithsonian Institution Press, 1973.

National Geographic Society. *The National Geographic Society – U.S. Army Air Corps Stratosphere Flight of 1934 in the Balloon "Explorer"*. Washington, D.C.: National Geographic Society, 1935.

National Geographic Society. *The National Geographic Society – U.S. Army Air Corps Stratosphere Flight of 1935 in the Balloon "Explorer II"*, Washington, D.C.: National Geographic Society, 1937.

New York University Purchase Order Number 42736, dated January 5, 1949, to Winzen Research, Inc., for 20 polyethylene balloons.

Peyton, Green. *50 Years of Aerospace Medicine*. Brooks Air Force Base, Texas: Aerospace Medical Division, Air Force Systems Command, 1968.

Peebles, Curtis. *The Moby Dick Project*. Washington, D. C.: Smithsonian Institution Press, 1991.

Piccard, Auguste. "Ballooning in the Stratosphere," *The National Geographic Magazine*. Volume LXIII, Number 3, March 1933.

Piccard, Auguste. *Earth, Sky and Sea*. New York: Oxford University Press, 1956.

Piccard, Jean. "The Pleiades II." Rosendahl Collection, University of Texas Dallas History of Aviation Collection, Box 263, Folder 5, undated.

Ross, Malcolm D. *Flight Prospectus Strato-Lab Open Gondola*. Washington, D.C.: Office of Naval Research, ONR:461:MDR:eew; July 1, 1959.

Ross, Malcolm D. *Flight Prospectus (Second Revision) Strato-Lab High #4*. Washington, D. C.: Office of Naval Research, ONR:461: MDR:ala, August 18, 1959.

Ross, Malcolm D.. *(Preliminary) Flight Prospectus Strato-Lab High #5*. Washing- ton, D.C.: Office of Naval Research, ONR:461: MDR:cs; January 24, 1961.

Ross, Malcolm D.. "Reactions of a Balloon Crew in a Controlled Environment," *The Journal of Aviation Medicine*. Volume 30, Number 3, May 1959.

Ross, Malcolm D. "We Saw the World From the Edge of Space," *The National Geographic Magazine*. November 1961.

Ross, Malcolm D., and Lewis, M. Lee. "The Strato-Lab Balloon System for High Altitude Research," *The Journal of Aviation Medicine*. Volume 29, Number 4, May 1958.

Ross, Malcolm D., and Lewis, M. Lee. "To 76,000 Feet by *Strato-Lab* Balloon," *The National Geographic Magazine*. Volume CXI, Number 2, February 1957.

Ross, Malcolm D., and Lewis, M. Lee, "The Role of Manned Balloons in the Exploration of Space." New York: Preprint No. 834, Institute of the Aeronautical Sciences, 1958.

Ryan, Craig. *The Pre-Astronauts*. Annapolis, Maryland: Naval Institute Press, 1995.

Scamehorn, Howard L. *Balloons to Jets*. Chicago: Henry Regnery Company, 1957.

Settle, T. C. W. "Stratosphere balloon flight, report on." 27 November 1933.

Sharpe, Mitchell R., and Burkhalter, Bettye B. "Mercury Redstone: The First American Man-Rated Space Launch Vehicle." 40th Congress of the International Astronautical Federation, Paper IAA 89-740, 1989.

Simons, David G. *Use of V-2 Rockets to Convey Primates to Upper Atmosphere*. Dayton, Ohio: United States Air Force Materiel Command, Air Force Technical Report 5821, May 1959.

Simons, David G. *Stratosphere Balloon Techniques for Exposing Living Speci- mens to Primary Cosmic Ray Particles*. Holloman Air Force Base, New Mexico: Holloman Air Development Center, HADC TR-54-16, November 1954.

Simons, David G. "A Journey No Man Had Taken," *Life*. vol. 43, no. 10, September 2, 1957.

Simons, David G. *Manhigh II*. Holloman Air Force Base, New Mexico: Air Force Missile Development Center, AFMDC-TR-59-28, June 1959.

Simons, David G. "Manhigh Balloon Flights in Perspective." Conference on the Peaceful Uses of Outer Space, May 1962.

Simons, David G. "Methods and Results of One Year of Balloon Flights With Biological Specimens," *The Journal of Aviation Medicine*. Volume 25, Number 4, August 1954.

Simons, David G. "Pilot Reaction During Manhigh II Balloon Flight," *Journal of Aviation Medicine*. Volume 29, Number 1, January 1958.

Simons, David G. "The 'Manhigh' Sealed Cabin Atmosphere," *Journal of Aviation Medicine*. Volume 30, Number 5, May 1959.

Simons, David G., and Cook, James E. "Primary Cosmic Radiation: Its Effects Upon Living Tissue." August 6, 1958.

Simons, David G., and Schanche, Don A.. *Man High*. Garden City, New York: Doubleday and Company, 1960.

Simons, David G., and Steinmetz, C. H. "The 1954 Aeromedical Field Laboratory Balloon Flights," *The Journal of Aviation Medicine*. Volume 27, Number 2, April 1956.

Smith, James R., and Murray, William D., *Constant Level Balloons, Section 1, General*. New York: College of Engineering, New York University, Technical Report No. 93.02, November 15, 1949.

Stearns, Charles R. *Final Report On A. F. Project Man-High Capsule Insulation Tests WRI Flight No. 550*. Minneapolis: Winzen Research, Inc., Report Number 1170-R, May 1, 1958.

Stearns, Charles R. *Progress Report On A. F. Project Man-High Capsule Sepa- ration Test WRI Flight No. 554*. Minneapolis: Winzen Research, Inc., Report Number 1169-R, May 1, 1956.

Stearns, Charles R. *Progress Report Project Man-High*. Minneapolis: Winzen Research, Inc., Report No. 1202-R, December 30, 1956.

Steinmetz, C. H., *Experimental Material Flown on Aero Medical Field Laboratory Balloon Flights 46 Through 71*. Holloman Air Force Base, New Mexico: Holloman Air Development Center Technical Note TN 56-2, AD No. 113031, 1956.

Stevens, Albert W. "Exploring the Stratosphere," *The National Geographic Magazine*. Volume LXVI, Number 4, October 1934.

Stevens, Albert W. "Man's Farthest Aloft," *The National Geographic Magazine*. January 1936.

Stevens, Albert W. "Scientific Results of the Stratospheric Flight," *The National Geographic Magazine*. May 1936.

Strughold, Hubertus. "The U. S. Air Force Experimental Sealed Cabin," *The Journal of Aviation Medicine*. Volume 27, Number 1, February 1956.

Taylor, James R. "Request for Proposal on PR 273489," Wright-Patterson Air Force Base, Ohio: Wright Air Development Center, August 14, 1952.

"The Fastest Man on Earth," *Time*. Vol. LXVI, No. 11, September 12, 1955.

"The Stratosphere Flight," *The Aircraft Year Book For 1934*,.Aeronautical Chamber of Commerce of America, Inc., 1934.

Thomas, Shirley. *Men of Space, Volume 1*. Philadelphia: Chilton Book Company, 1960.

Welinski, B. *Strato-Lab High #1 Post Flight Report of System Development*. Minneapolis: Winzen Research, Inc., February 1, 1959.

Letter, Otto C. Winzen to Commanding General, Wright Air Development Center. "Study and Design of a High Altitude Research Vehicle." October 13, 1952 (with attached Technical Proposal).

Technical Proposal, Otto C. Winzen to Commander George W. Hoover, Office of Naval Research. "Technical Proposal for the Design and Construction of a High Altitude Research Vehicle and Research Flights Therewith." December 31, 1952.

Winzen, Otto C. *Section I (Volume I) Final Report Contract No. AF 33(616)- 2427*. South Saint Paul, Minnesota: Winzen Research, Inc., 1 December 1954.

Winzen, Otto C. "10 Years of Plastic Balloons." Minneapolis: Winzen Research Technical Publication No. 7B, October 24, 1957.

Winzen, Otto C. "The 3 Manned Stratosphere Balloon Ascents of 1957." New York: Institute of the Aeronautical Sciences Preprint No. 833, 1958.

Winzen, Otto C. *Operation Manhigh II*. Minneapolis: Winzen Research, Inc., ca. 1958.

Winzen, Otto C. *Pre-Flight Report Air Force Project Man-High Winzen Research Project AF-383 First Manned Fligh.*, Minneapolis: Winzen Research, Inc., Report No. 1213-R, May 23, 1957.

Winzen, Otto C. *Progress Report Project Man-High*. Minneapolis: Winzen Research, Inc., Report No. 1205-R, March 1, 1957.

Winzen, Otto C. *Report on WRI 20 Ft. Dia. Operational Plastic Balloons*. South Saint Paul, Minnesota: Winzen Research, Inc., February 25, 1949.

Winzen Research, Inc. *Claustrophobia Tests Man-High Capsule*. Minneapolis: Winzen Research, Inc., Report No. 1196-R, 1956.

Winzen Research, Inc. *Documentation of Winzen Research Inc's Role in Project Stratolab* Minneapolis: Winzen Research, Inc., September 11, 1956.

Winzen Research, Inc. *Final Report Stratolab High No. 5*. Minneapolis: Winzen Research, Inc., August 17, 1961.

Winzen Research, Inc. *Final Report Volume I Contract No. AF 29(600)-632*. Minneapolis: Winzen Research, Inc., Report No. 1163-R, 31 October 1955.

Winzen Research, Inc. *Final Report Volume II Contract No. AF 29(600)-63*. Minneapolis: Winzen Research, Inc, Report No. 1163-R, 31 October 1955.

Winzen Research, Inc. *Manhigh* I. Holloman Air Force Base, New Mexico: Air Force Missile Development Center, Report AFMDC-TR-24, June 1959.

Winzen Research, Inc. *Pre-Flight Report Project AF-383, First 3 Million Cubic Foot Animal Flight From Open Pit Mine in Crosby*. Minneapolis: Winzen Research, Inc., Report No. 1193-R, October 22, 1956.

Winzen Research, Inc. *Pre-Test Report -- Project AF-383, Second Animal Flight on Project Man-High 3 Million Cubic Foot Balloon Launching Site Fleming Field*. Minneapolis: Winzen Research, Inc., Report No. 1206-R, March 1, 1957.

Winzen Research, Inc. Technical Staff. *Progress Report Air Regeneration Development Project Manhigh III*. Minneapolis: Winzen Research, Inc., Report No. 1227-R, April 29, 1957.

Winzen, Otto C., and Winzen Research, Inc. Technical Staff. *Man-High Parachute Recovery Data, Contract No. AF 29(600)-808*. Minneapolis: Winzen Research, Inc., 1 May 1957.

Winzen Research, Inc. *Sky-Car Low Level Manned Balloon System*. Minneapolis: Winzen Research, Inc., October, 1956.

Wells, Helen T., Whiteley, Susan H., and Karegeannes, Carrie E. *Origins of NASA Names*. Washington, D. C.: U. S. Government Printing Office, NASA SP-4402., 1976.

"World's Largest Free Balloon to Explore the Stratosphere," *The National Geographic Magazine*. Volume LXVI, Number 1, July 1934.

"Your Society Sponsors an Expedition to Explore the Stratosphere," *The National Geographic Magazine*. Volume LXV, Number 4, April 1934.

Index

Germany's V-2 Rocket

Gregory P. Kennedy

Germany's V-2 looks at one of the major technological advances of the Second World War, the V-2 ballistic missile. Although dwarfed by today's giant rockets, the V-2 represented a quantum leap beyond anything previously built. During the last six months of the war in Europe, Germany launched thousands of these missiles against the Allies. This book traces the origins and development of the V-2, from groups of individual experimenters in the 1930s to its use as a weapon system. Particular emphasis is paid to such topics as the structure and components of the missile, its ground support equipment, and field procedures. After the war, the V-2 formed the foundation for the space programs of the Soviet Union and United States. Information is included on previously ignored V-2 launches in the United States.

ISBN: 0764324527 Size: 8 1/2 x 11" Illustrations: over 130 b/w photographs Pages: 160 Hard Cover